THE

MYSTICAL PRESENCE

A VINDICATION OF THE REFORMED OR CALVINISTIC
DOCTRINE OF THE HOLY EUCHARIST

by

John Williamson Nevin

Edited by
Augustine Thompson, O.P.

Wipf and Stock Publishers
150 West Broadway • Eugene OR 97401
2000

Originally published:

   John W. Nevin, *The Mystical Presence: A Vindication of the Re-formed or Calvinist Doctrine of the Holy Eucharist.* (New York: Lip-pencott, 1846).

This text is that of the original edition;
typographical errors are silently corrected,
as are defective diacritical marks and punctuation.

The Mystical Presence

By Nevin, John Williamson

ISBN: 1-57910-348-0

Reprinted by *Wipf and Stock Publishers*
150 West Broadway • Eugene OR 97401

Previously published by Lippencott Publishers, 1846.

THE

MYSTICAL PRESENCE.

A VINDICATION OF THE

REFORMED OR CALVINISTIC DOCTRINE

OF THE

HOLY EUCHARIST.

BY THE

REV. JOHN W. NEVIN, D. D.

PROF. OF THEO. IN THE SEMINARY OF THE GER REF. CHURCH.

———————

PHILADELPHIA:
J. B. LIPPINCOTT & CO.
1846.

PHILADELPHIA:
KING AND BAIRD, PRINTERS,
No. 9 George Street.

PREFACE.

THE following work has grown directly out of some controversy which has had place, during the past year, in the German Reformed Church, on the subject to which it relates. This stands related to it, however, only as an external occasion, and has not been permitted to come into view, in any way, in the work itself. It is not felt that any apology is needed for the publication.—This is found in the importance of its subject, which must be left of course to speak for itself.

As the Eucharist forms the very heart of the whole Christian worship, so it is clear that the entire question of the Church, which all are compelled to acknowledge, the great life-problem of the age, centres ultimately in the sacramental question as its inmost heart and core. Our view of the Lord's Supper must ever condition and rule in the end our view of Christ's person and the conception we form of the Church. It must influence at the same time, very materially, our whole system of theology, as well as all our ideas of ecclesiastical history.

Is it true that the modern Protestant Church in this country has, in large part at least, fallen away from the sacramental doctrine of the sixteenth century? All must at least allow, that there is some room for asking the question. If so, it is equally plain that it is a question which is entitled to a serious answer. For in the nature of the case, such a falling away, if it exist at all, must be connected with a still more general removal from the original platform of the Church. The eucharistic doctrine of the sixteenth century was interwoven with the whole church system of the time; to give it up, then, must involve in the end a renunciation in principle, if not in profession, of this system itself in its radical, distinctive constitution. If it can be shown that no material change has taken place, it is due to an interest of such high consequence that this should be

satisfactorily done. Or if the change should be allowed, and still vindicated as a legitimate advance on the original Protestant faith, let this
ground be openly and consciously taken. Let us know, at least, where we
are and what we actually do believe, in the case of this central question,
as compared with the theological stand-point of our Catechisms and
Confessions of Faith.

The relations of this inquiry to the question concerning the true idea
of the Church, will easily be felt by every well-informed and reflecting
mind. If the fact of the incarnation be indeed the principle and source of
a new supernatural order of life for humanity itself, the Church, of course,
is no abstraction. It must be a true, living, divine-human constitution in

the world; strictly organic in its nature—not a *device* or contrivance in-
geniously fitted to serve certain purposes beyond itself—but the necessary, essential form of Christianity, in whose presence only it is possible
to conceive intelligently of piety in its individual manifestations. The life
of the single Christian can be real and healthful only as it is born from the
general life of the Church, and carried by it onward to the end. We are
Christians singly, by partaking (having *part*) in the general life-revelation,
which is already at hand organically in the Church, the living and life-
giving body of Jesus Christ. As thus real and organic, moreover,
Christianity *must* be historical. No higher wrong can be done to it than to
call in question its true historical character; for this is, in fact, to turn it
into a phantasm, and to overthrow the solid fact-basis on which its
foundations eternally rest. It must be historical, too, under the form of the
Church; for the *realness* of Christianity demands indispensably the
presence of the general life of Christ, flowing with unbroken continuity
from the beginning as the medium of all particular union with him from
age to age. Then, again, the historical Church must be *visible,* or in other
words, not merely ideal, but actual. The actual may indeed fall short
immeasurably of the idea it represents; the visible Church may be imperfect, corrupt, false to its own conception and calling; but still an actual,
continuously visible Church there must always be in the world, if
Christianity is to have either truth or reality in the form of a new creation.

A purely invisible Church has been well denominated a *contradictio in*

Spiritual Ecorporeal

adjecto; since the very idea of a Church implies the manifestation of the religious life, as something social and common.

The whole conception that the externalization of the Christian life is something accidental only to the constitution of this life itself—a sort of mechanical machinery, to help it forward in an outward way—is exceedingly derogatory to the Church, and injurious in its bearings on religion. An outward Church is the necessary form of the new creation in Christ Jesus, in its very nature; and must continue to be so, not only through all time, but through all eternity likewise. Outward social worship, which implies, of course, forms for the purpose, is to be regarded as something essential to piety itself. A religion without externals, must ever be fantastic and false. The simple utterance of religious feeling, by which the spirit takes outward form, is needed, not for something beyond itself, but for the perfection of the feeling itself. Forms, in this sense, not as sundered from inward life, of course, but as embracing it, enter as a constituent element into the very life of Christianity. As a real, human, historical constitution in the world, the outward and inward in the Church can never be divorced, without peril to all that is most precious in the Christian faith. We have no right to set the inward in opposition to the outward, the spiritual in opposition to the corporeal, in religion. The incarnation of the Son of God, as it is the principle, forms also the true measure and test, of all sound Christianity, in this view. To be *real,* the human, as such, and of course the divine in human form, must ever externalize its inward life. All thought, all feeling, every spiritual state, must take body, (in the way of word, or outward form of some sort,) in order to come at all to any true perfection in itself. This is the proper, deep sense of all liturgical services in religion. The necessity here affirmed is universal. The more intensely *spiritual* any state may be, the more irresistibly urgent will ever be found its tendency to clothe itself, and make itself complete, in a suitable external form. Away with the imagination, then, that externals in Christianity, (including the conception of the visible Church itself,) are something accidental only to its true constitution, a cunningly framed device merely for advancing some interest foreign from themselves. To think of the Church, and of Christian worship, as *means* simply to something else, is to dishonour religion itself in the most serious manner.

If the present work may serve to fix attention on the momentous point with which it is concerned, and thus contribute indirectly even to a clearer understanding, of Protestant truth, I shall feel that it has not been written in vain. May God accept it, and crown it with his blessing.

J. W. N.

Mercersburg, April, 1846.

CONTENTS.

CHAPTER I.

REFORMED OR CALVINISTIC DOCTRINE OF THE LORD'S SUPPER.

SECT. I—*Statement of the Doctrine.*

CHAPTER II.

MODERN PURITAN THEORY.

Sect. I.—*Historical Exhibition.*

Sect. II.—*Systems Contrasted.*

SECT. III.—*Faith of the Early Church.*

SECT. IV.—*Rationalism and the Sects.*

CHAPTER III.

SCIENTIFIC STATEMENT

SECT. I.—*Preliminary Positions.*

CONTENTS.

SECT. II.—*Theses on the Mystical Union.*

SECT. III.—*Theses on the Lord's Supper.*

SECT. IV.—*False Theories Exposed.*

CHAPTER IV.

BIBLICAL ARGUMENT

SECT. I.—*The Incarnation.*

SECT. II.—*The New Creation.*

SECT. III.—*The Second Adam.*

SECT. IV.—*Christianity a Life.*

SECT. V.—*The Mystical Union.*

CONTENTS.

12

Sect. VI.—*John* VI. 56–58

SECT. VII.—*The Lord's Supper.*

PRELIMINARY ESSAY.

IN the January number of the *Theologische Studien und Kritiken,* for 1845, there is an admirable article, from the pen of *Dr. C. Ullmann,** Professor in Heidelberg, on "THE DISTINCTIVE CHARACTER OF CHRISTIANITY," well worthy of being carefully studied by all who take an interest in the present state of the Church. It has occurred to me, that I cannot do better in the way of introducing the present work, than to furnish here a full abstract, or a free compressed translation rather of its valuable contents.

1.

Christianity, in its substantial contents, has been always the same. The form of its apprehension however, on the part of the Church, has varied with the onward progress of its history. At the start, it was the fresh life of childhood, without reflection. The first germs of a Christian theology, its great leading doctrines separately taken, were gradually produced during the first centuries, in the way of apologetic controversy with surrounding errors. From the *fourth century,* the entire intellectual strength of the Church appears devoted to the object of settling and establishing particular doctrines; still however only in their separate form. The *Scholastic* period of the middle ages, took up what was thus fixed in the way of faith, and laboured to reduce all to a general system.

---

*The distinguished author of the work *Reformatoren vor der Reformation*; for full historical knowledge, comprehensive views, clear, calm reflection, and masterly power of representation, one of the finest living writers certainly of Germany. The article here noticed has been published also as a separate pamphlet, and seems to have attracted more than usual attention. A new work, I may add, is recently announced from the same writer under the interesting title, *The Church of the Future,* in which no doubt the same views are more fully exhibited.

Throughout this whole progress of theological development, however, the distinctive constitution of Christianity itself, as compared with other forms of religion, can hardly be said to have come into view. Even the *Reformers* of the sixteenth century, thoroughly imbued as they were with its living spirit, were too fully occupied with the work of setting it free from church oppression, to bestow much reflection on this point. The question has been reserved for the *Modern Period;* which has felt itself urged moreover, by its philosophical and historical cultivation in particular, to direct towards it a large measure of its attention. During the last fifty years, numerous attempts have been made to determine the characteristic nature and genius of Christianity; of very different tendency of course, reflecting always the theological life under whose influence they were formed. Thus *Storr* made the distinction to consist mainly in the supernatural, the miraculous, the positive, as comprehended in the Christian religion; *Herder*, in its character of universal humanity; *Chateaubriand,* in its sublime and captivating beauty. But we owe it to the christological struggles of our own time in particular, that the specific nature of Christianity, and its inmost constitution, have begun to come more freely into the light, than ever before.

The theological position of the present time may be considered especially favourable, for a proper appreciation of the truth in the case of the important inquiry here brought into view. It has been too common heretofore, to proceed on some particular conception of Christianity, as Primitive, Catholic, Protestant, &c.; by which, as a matter of necessity, a single historical stadium, arbitrarily bounded according to the pleasure of the inquirer, has been made to stand for the idea of the whole; thus causing certain phases of the system, its divinity for instance, or its humanity, its doctrinal, or its ethical, or it may be its æsthetic character only, to represent the general life of which each could be said to form but a single side. Now however, as the result of our historical cultivation itself, we stand on higher ground. We are able to take a comprehensive survey of Christianity as an organic whole, under all the aspects in which it is presented to our view, in its origin, and throughout the entire stream of its development, down to the present time. In this way, it is made much more easy than before, to reach the true life centre of the whole, and to recognize the beating heart from which all has been formed, and that still continues to animate all perpetually in its several parts.

When we speak of the distinctive character of Christianity, it implies the idea of something general as well as particular in its constitution. As general it is *religion;* as particular the *Christian* religion. But these two conceptions, in this case, are bound inseparably together. We cannot so abstract from Christianity its particular specific character, as to leave the general idea of religion behind. It must exist under the specific form which belongs to it, or it is nothing, a mere abstraction, destitute of all reality. Christianity is not religion in the first place, with something added to it to make it Christianity; but as religion itself, it is at the same time in its inmost ground, this particular form of religion, exclusively complete in its own nature, and different in all its parts, by the spirit which pervades the whole, from every other religion. As thus individual and general at once, it claims to be the absolute truth itself; not *a* religion simply, as one among many, but the one, universal, all perfect religion of humanity in its widest sense. Essential and specific here flow together, and cannot be kept asunder.

2.

It belongs to the modern period, we have said, that it has come to exercise a conscious reflection on the nature of Christianity. This reflection has its history, its regular development from one stage still forward to another. This will be found to correspond strikingly, only with vast difference as to time, with the historical conformations under which the Christian life itself has appeared, from period to period, since its first revelation in the world. The spirit of Christianity has been carried first in a real way, by an evolution of many centuries, through the same phases, that have since been repeated, with more rapid succession, in the modern effort to determine theoretically in what this spirit consists.

It started, as before remarked, in the character of a new *life*. So it meets us, with full harmony and perfection, in the person of its Founder. So it is exhibited to us more inadequately in the apostles and the apostolical churches. The mere existence of this life however was not enough. It was necessary that the Church should come to a full and free apprehension of what it comprehended. This called for a separation of its elements, involving necessarily more or less confusion and conflict and one-sided action, as the only process by which it was possible, in the present state of the world, to advance from the simplicity of childhood to the consciousness of spiritual manhood. Hence the long course of development, revealed to us in Church History. In this process, the different constituent elements or forces included in Christianity could not, in the nature of the case, come in promiscuously at one time for such share of attention as they were entitled to claim. Some *one* interest must still take the lead of another, determined by the general character of the time; and thus for every grand period in history we have a particular side of Christianity standing forth prominently to view as its dominant characteristic form; till in the end, as the result of the whole process, all such single and separate manifestations may come to be united again in the full symmetrical perfection of that one glorious life to which they severally belong.

The process now mentioned began naturally with *Doctrine,* which it was attempted to settle first in a general way, and then in single articles. The dogma producing period extends in particular, from the fourth century on into the sixth. For this service the *Grecian* mind, which was then predominant in the Church, might be said to have a special vocation. With the fall of the old world, and the rise of a new life among the western nations, Christianity was required to exercise its power in a different way. It must form the manners, and regulate the life of the rude population with which it was called to deal. The main interest now accordingly was its moral authority. It became in the hands particularly of the *Roman* Church, a system of *Law,* a pedagogic institute for the government of the nations. In this character however, it only made room for itself to appear, with new life, as the *Gospel;* a change effected chiefly through the *German* spirit, which included in its very constitution an evangelical or free tendency, and was gradually prepared to assert its ecclesiastical independence in this way. With the Reformation, the mind of the Church, no longer in its minority, forced its way back to the proper fountain-head of Christianity, and laid hold of it in the form of *Redemp-*

tion; the justification of the sinner before God, and the principle of *freedom* for the consciousness of the justified subject himself in all his relations. Along with these three leading conceptions of Christianity, as doctrine, as a system of law, and as a source of redemption and spiritual freedom, we find still a fourth unfolding itself from an early period, with steadily increasing strength. It is the view, which makes religion to consist in the union of man with God, and of course finds in this the distinctive character of Christianity. It is regarded as the absolutely perfect religion, because it *unites the divine and human* fully as one life. This view may be traced to a remote antiquity, but comes forward more decidedly in the mysticism of the middle ages, and appears now most completely revealed in the philosophical and theological speculation of the modern time. From the first however, it has exhibited itself under two divergent tendencies, one pantheistic, and the other recognizing a personal God. Of these, the first has become widely prevalent at the present day; but the last must be regarded of course as the only legitimate form of thinking in the case, and may be expected in the end universally to prevail.

Such are the ground types, by which the conception of Christianity has been differently moulded under different circumstances. They are characteristically represented by as many several forms of *Church* life. The interest of doctrine finds its proper expression in the *Greek* Church, self-styled significantly the *Orthodox,* the Church of Christian *Antiquity.* As a disciplinary institute, the Christian system has its fit character in the *Roman* Church, with its claim of universal authority, challenging for itself the title *Catholic,* the Church of the *Middle Ages.* To the idea of redemption and freedom answers the Church which has sprung up among the nations of *German* extraction, rightly denominated *Evangelical,* the Church of the *Reformation.* The Church finally in which all these stages of development are to be carried forward together to their highest truth, under a form of Christianity that shall actualize the conception of a full life union with God, and to which it may be trusted the ecclesiastical agitations of our own time form the transition, may be characterized as the *Church of the Future,* whose attributes shall be spirituality, catholicity, and freedom, joined together in the most perfect combination.

Correspondent now we say with this historical progress through which the apprehension of Christianity has been carried in the actual life of the Church, appears the course of modern theology as concerned with the same subject in the way of *reflection*. It has been described successively as doctrine, as an ethical law, as a system of redemption, and ultimately, though not always in the same way, as a religion based on the idea of a real union with God. All this involves a regular *advance* undoubtedly from the outward to the more inward. It is most natural and obvious, to conceive of Christianity first as doctrine. Then in view of its practical ends, it seems to be essentially ethical, or as Schleiermacher terms it, teleological, in its character. Again, its highest morality is found to spring from the fact of redemption and atonement, and thus to centre upon the person of Christ. Finally it is felt that the person of the Redeemer can have such force, only as the divine and human, God and man are in the first place reconciled and united in its very constitution, as the ground of all redemption for the race.

As might be expected these different views of Christianity appear in close relation with the various forms in which the *idea of religion* itself has been held; for as it is taken to be the absolute truth of all religion, it must of course participate in its essential character, whatever this may be supposed to be. Viewed as doctrine accordingly, it finds support in the conception of religion as a mode of knowing God, its prevailing definition, especially among the orthodox, in the period preceding Kant. Its next character, that of law, corresponds with the theory by which, in conformity with the philosophy of Kant, all religion was resolved into a mere postulate of morality. In its evangelical form, as the power of a divine redemption, it rests on the idea of religion as a state of feeling or immediate consciousness. But the relation of man to God in religion does not spring either from his understanding, or will, or feeling, separately considered. It includes all at once in the totality of his personal life. On this view therefore is based lastly that apprehension of Christianity which makes it to be the union of God with humanity, and under this form only the source of all light and holiness and salvation.

The first three views which have been described have severally their measure of truth; but the full truth requires their comprehension, in a living way, under the last. Hence also this last, to be genuine and right, must incorporate in itself the other less perfect conceptions. Christianity can be properly regarded as the union of God and humanity, only where due account is made at the same time of its doctrinal, ethical, and soteriological character, and all is made to rest on its original, inalienable nature, according to which it is no matter of thought or logic merely in any form, but action, history, and life. No pantheistic view of course can be admitted, in the case. Christianity is a revelation of the living God, by which the divine and human are historically united in the person of Christ, and which continues to bring the race subsequently into union with God only by redeeming it at the same time from the power of sin. The proper expression to denote the fact is therefore, not "the unity of the divine and human," which is too general, and liable to be taken in a pantheistic sense; but what is far more definite and concrete, "the union of God and man."

3.

The modern theology, in its course of reflection upon the nature of Christianity, resolved it first, we have said, into the idea of *doctrine.*

This was done in two ways. Either all was taken in the form of a positive revelation, accredited as truth by God himself, and to be received on his authority alone; or without any regard to its historical character, the Christian system was considered to be simply the first manifestation of a theory of rational religion, which it was the business of theology to divest of its original temporary covering, that its proper everlasting verity might come fully into view. Thus we have *Supernaturalism* and *Naturalism.* With all their opposition to each other, they were agreed in making Christianity to be essentially doctrinal in its character. Here however an important difference had place. Along with other positive elements, Supernaturalism received of course also what is said in the Scriptures concerning the person of the Redeemer, though as a dogma simply among other dogmas, rather than in any other light. Naturalism on the other hand, with its aversion for all that is concrete and historical in religion, could not retain the idea of any significance whatever in the person of Christ. It went so far as to utter the wish even, that his name might have been wholly concealed from the Christian world, so that it could have enjoyed the full benefit of the truth be taught, without being led into a superstitious misuse of the teacher himself!

That the true nature of Christianity was not to be understood in this way, is now admitted on all hands. Naturalism is called to mind only as a spiritual curiosity, belonging to other days. But the other course also, though more conservative so far as the contents of the Gospel were concerned, was no better as to form in relation to the point now under consideration. It failed entirely to make known the distinctive character of Christianity. This consists not, under any view, exclusively or prevailingly in doctrine. The true idea of religion itself, as well as the whole history of the Christian revelation, contradicts such a supposition. Religion does indeed include knowledge as one of its elements; but to conceive of it as an intellectual apprehension only, is to mistake its true life entirely. Its inmost nature is love and reverence, a pervading sense of dependence on God and comminution with him, a full self-surrendry to the idea of his presence and will. If religion consisted in doctrine, it might be imparted fully, like logic or mathematics in the way of definition and demonstration. But this is impossible. Instruction is called for, it is true, in its service; but the proper creative impulse of its life is not found in the conceptions thus imparted; it must spring from the general life of religion itself, as something already at hand, acting on the religious susceptibility of the subject. So with the individual; so with the race. Parents and teachers, prophets and founders of religion, accomplish their commission best in the way of living representation. Compared with this, mere instruction is cold and dead. It is only life, in the sphere of religion, that can create and call forth life. The notion of doctrine falls immeasurably short of what we mean by *religion,* viewed in its living concrete character. To make the one synonymous with the other, is a sheer contradiction. Conceptions and thoughts with regard to divine things cannot even produce any true and sound piety; much less may they be taken for such piety itself.

So it is clear, that Christianity in particular appears among men under no such character. In one view it is indeed a doctrine. Not however in the modern sense, as a system of abstract propositions and proofs; in this form it might have founded, perhaps, a school, but never a Church, or world-religion. It is the proclamation primarily of something that has taken place, a testimony, or joyful message. Not in the way of thought, but in the way of actual occurrence and transaction, as the comprehension of a system of glorious religious facts, has Christianity extended and filled with new life the spiritual consciousness of the world. This is its proper original force; the doctrine follows afterwards, only as the representation of what God has done. But still the doctrine itself, even in this form , has no power as such to generate life. This springs only from the presence of a higher life, already derived in the teacher himself from Christ. His teaching is but the experimental expression, we may say, of his life. Thus the apostles and evangelists, as heralds of the Christian salvation, preceded in the beginning the proper teachers of Christian doctrine; and so in every age, the Church has always begun with testimony, and only afterwards proceeded to instruction and science; while the true power of her doctrine, at the same time, has ever resulted from the life which belongs originally to her Founder, and continues itself from him in his people. True, the actual in the case of Christianity has its significance not merely as something that has taken place, but as the realization of the highest religious ideas. These ideas may be abstracted from the facts, and formed into a system, either popular or scientific. Hence for theologians in particular, who are most occupied with this work, Christianity has the semblance of being itself a sum of doctrinal propositions. Only however as the idea of apprehension or science, in the case, is confounded with that of the object they embrace. Christianity must indeed be formed into doctrine for the purposes of popular and scientific instruction; but in its own nature, it still remains life, living power, a revelation of the Spirit in the form of facts.

Even if Christianity be regarded as doctrine mainly, we must still ask, in what the specific distinction of this doctrine consists? But no such distinction, it is plain, can be found in any particular religious or moral proposition, such as Christianity may have in common with other religions. It consists in what Christ speaks of himself and his relation to God, as also of the new posture towards God into which he has brought the human family; and again in the testimony of the Apostles concerning his person and work. This however carries us at once beyond the sphere of doctrine, to that which constitutes its ground and object, the creative force of the religious life itself as revealed under its highest character in Christ. That which is most essential in the mission of Christ, is his *self-exhibition*. This runs through his whole life. It includes, of course, his testimony concerning himself, and the account of the impression which was made by him upon others. Words and doctrines consequently belong to the representation. But what is thus partial only and independent, must not be taken for the original whole, by which alone the distinctive character of Christianity is determined. This is not the Christian doctrine, but the general life-revelation from which it springs. Only as life, is Christianity the light of men; as the Saviour himself clearly signifies, when he says, not that his doctrine is the truth, but, *I am the truth,* which is immediately referred again to this, that he is also the *life*.

4.

The next view places the distinctive character of Christianity mainly in its ethical force, its power as a *Rule of life*. This stands closely connected with *Kant* and *Rationalism,* as it proceeded from his school. It went along with the conviction, that the human mind can attain to no sure knowledge of the supernatural and divine in a theoretic way, but only as it may be necessary to assume it in obedience to the demands of our moral nature. What morality requires as a postulate for its own support, may be counted certainly true, though in other respects wholly unknown. The moral law became here the absolute measure of truth. Morality in man occupied the first and highest place. Religion was something secondary and subordinate, necessary only as required by the other for its own service. Christianity then was an *ethical law;* starting in the form of positive divine precepts, but identical at last, in its true and proper substance, with the demands of the practical reason itself, by which accordingly it is to be tried and interpreted. Christ was the great lawgiver for humanity; the Church a platform, for the grand contest of good and evil in the history of the race. Faith in God and the retributions of a future life, resolved itself into a firm persuasion that virtue must at last prevail. It was faith in the moral order of the world.

We freely allow the great importance of this ethical conception of Christianity. It surpasses the doctrinal in this, that it brings into view more fully its proper dynamic nature, its teleological character, the relation of the whole to a supreme moral end. It turns attention also more towards the author of the religion, as being himself, though indeed only in an idealistic way, the centre of the whole system. It served powerfully moreover, one may say to its credit, to hold the age to which it belonged on good terms with Christianity, by presenting towards it that side of the system, which alone it was prepared to appreciate and approve. Still the view is by no means sufficient. It proceeds again on a false idea of religion, and misses what is truly specific in Christianity. Piety is more than a mere support to morality, means for an end beyond itself. Christianity is not simply legislative, but creative. Its chief elements are presented to us in the words, redemption, atonement, grace, and are overlooked by this theory altogether. Christianity is not, like the moral law, a *shall* or *must,* but a fulfilment and satisfaction, a *yea* and *amen;* not a requisition in God's name, but a divine gift that of itself, when planted in the heart, impels it without commandment to the most free morality. Duty, which with Kant is all in all, becomes in the Christian sphere nothing; since love is every thing, and fulfils of itself the whole law. The categoric imperative is struck dumb before that great word: *We love him, because he hath first loved us!*

Viewed either as doctrine or law, the universal difference of Christianity from other religions, whether Pagan or Jewish, is not suffered to appear. As a doctrinal system merely, though it might be more perfect in its kind, it would not differ specifically from the schools of the heathen world; as a law, though with higher and more excellent requisitions, it would be still specifically of one class with Judaism and the religion of Mohammed; an exalted, purified Judaism only, not a new order of religion, with a principle altogether its own. In both cases we should be at a loss to explain, how it would become the ground of a complete regeneration of the human life, the source of a new order of world-history altogether; how it could give birth to characters and forms of thinking, such as we meet with in Paul and John; how in one word it could produce the Christian Church with all that it includes, not simply in the form of thought and precept, but in the way also of actual power and effect.

5.

To reach the distinctive character of Christianity then in this view, as something new, original, and different from all other religions, not merely in quantity but in quality, and for the purpose of doing fuller justice also to those cardinal elements of the system that are comprehended in the term Gospel, *Schleiermacher,* more historical than the Rationalists, sought to refer all back to its last ground or living root, the *person of Christ himself.* In doing so, he was viewed not as a teacher or lawgiver primarily, but with far more depth and comprehension as a *Redeemer;* and thus Christianity was made to be, in its ground character, the world historical *Religion of Redemption.* He did not deny that it was doctrinal, much less that it was ethical, in which view precisely he styled it teleological. But he felt that a thorough and full distinction of Christianity from all other monotheistic religions made it necessary, to single out that which has constituted it a peculiar religion from the beginning, and which may be said to form the interior unity that holds it together in the whole course of its development. This he found in the idea of redemption, and especially in the manner of its realization in the person of Jesus of Nazareth. This idea indeed is not wanting in other religions also, and in their way, by purifications, penances, and offerings, they endeavour to make it actual. But there is this essential difference in the case of Christianity. Christ does not simply order and prescribe the process of redemption, but accomplishes the whole work in himself; so that it is not merely *by* him, but *in* him, that it is made to reach the world, under the most perfect and all sufficient form; since he stood in full union with God and was free from all sin. Thus the person of its founder, in the case of this religion, becomes identified with its whole constitution, as in no case besides. Moses was the medium simply, *through* which a particular institute was established, for himself as much as for others. Not so Christ. The religion which he brought into the world, was not merely given by him; it was *in* him, and remains *in* him still, as its living fountain; he is *himself* its grand constituent, as being the perfect, everlasting Redeemer, and as such the One without a fellow, over against whom all others stand as subjects for redemption. That which constitutes Christianity, as distinguished from all other forms of religion, is the reference, according to Schleiermacher, which all that belongs to it is found to include, to the consciousness of redemption through the person of Jesus of Nazareth.

A most important advance certainly, in the process of reflection on this subject. Doctrine regards knowledge simply; law regards only the will; but redemption reaches out from feeling as its centre over the whole inner man. By this view accordingly, we are brought to a more full and deep conception of religion, than before. Christianity acquires a more concrete historical character. Its dynamic nature is placed in far clearer light, as not only revealing itself in the form of imperative authority, but as imparting also freedom and spiritual power in the way of a new creation. All this goes far beyond the previous definitions, in determining the universal peculiarity of the Christian religion. The epoch formed by the theology of Schleiermacher has at least carried us irrevocably beyond the conception of Christianity, as being either merely doctrinal or merely ethical. Every one, who is not in a state of absolute theological stagnation, understands now that the faith of Christ has respect not only to his doctrine but to his person; and that Christianity is a divine life, the principle of a new creation, which unfolds itself continually with free inward necessity by its own force and according to its own law. Every one knows too, that this new creation proceeds from Christ, in the character of a Redeemer, and that no other religion before or since has ever exhibited any thing of the same sort. But still the last point required for a complete definition of the subject is not yet reached. The general defeat of Schleiermacher's theology, meets us also in his conception of the specific nature of Christianity.

The principle of redemption does by all means give character to Christianity. But to this idea, which itself with Schleiermacher is found deficient through the want of a proper appreciation of the nature of sin, another of at least equal importance is always joined, the idea of *atonement*. Redemption supposes atonement. No one can feel himself to be redeemed who is not reconciled with God. This of itself implies that the idea of atonement is something higher and more original than the idea of redemption, which ought not therefore to be overlooked in settling the inquiry, what is Christianity? Again, redemption is internal, the deliverance of its subject from the power of sin; atonement carries in itself, for the subject, an outward reference, establishing a right relation between the sinner and a holy God. The first is essentially a matter of feeling, a state thus or condition of the individual man; the other looks beyond the individual to God, and includes in this way something objective, (forgiveness of sin, justification,) into which must enter necessarily also some knowledge of the divine nature. Schleiermacher, in full conformity with the prevailingly subjective character of his theological views, and his conception of religion as a form of feeling, has here also confined himself exclusively to what is matter of inward experience, the Christian salvation as carried forward in the life of the subject. But it is an inadequate view of religion to place it in feeling, to the exclusion of knowledge and action. A full, sound piety embodies the understanding and will also as original elements in its constitution. So especially, in the case of Christianity. It is a revelation indeed only as it is a system of redemption; but it is a system of redemption also, only as it reveals the character of God in a new and perfect light, making him known as a merciful and loving Father, the source of all grace and salvation through Jesus Christ. This goes beyond the mere state of the subject himself, and calls for a conception more suitable to the objective side of the case than that of redemption. Such is the conception of atonement. And then once more; both redemption and atonement, as accomplished by Christ, are a work. But all spiritual activity is based on some particular form of existence or being. So eminently, in the case of Christ. All that he did, took its character from what he was. As then the work of redemption rests on that of atonement, so do both together again rest on that of the proper being of Christ, as distinguished from all others. To this therefore, Christ's peculiar personality, which is of force apart from all that he does, but necessarily reveals itself also in this way, we are directed as to that which is last and highest. Here we must expect to find the true fountain of Christianity, and its most fundamental characteristic distinction at the same time.

6.

What now is that in the personality of Christ, by which he is constituted a perfect Saviour, in the way of atonement and redemption? We reply generally, his own substantial nature, at once human and divine; his life filled with all the attributes of God, and representing at the same time the highest conception of nature and man; complete and self-sufficient in its own fulness, and yet by this fulness itself the free principle of a new corresponding life-process, in the way of self-communication, for the human world. This life itself however has again its central heart, to which especially we must look for the peculiar being of Christ. Here the whole theology of the present time, in all its different tendencies, may be said to have but one voice. That which constitutes the special *being* of Christ, makes him to be what be is and gives him thus his highest significance for the world, is the absolute *unity of the divine and human in his person.* Deity and manhood in him come fully together and are made one. This is the last ground of Christianity. Here above all we are to look for its distinctive character.

All theological tendencies, we have said, are agreed on this point, so far as the general proposition is concerned. But when it comes to the particular sense and application of it, we find again a wide difference, amounting in part to full opposition. The main contradiction lies between the pantheistic speculation, which resolves the idea in question into a general fact belonging to the phenomenology of spirit, and the proper Christian view, by which all is made to rest on the acknowledgment of a personal God and a positive revelation, as something historically real and individual. This difference is complete. Under either view indeed, whether the union of the divine and human be taken in an idealistic or realistic sense, the idea, where it is received at all, must always be allowed to rule and characterize the entire conception of Christianity, as the last principle of its significance and power; for no higher idea can have place in the sphere of religion, and where this elevation is reached, either by God's becoming man or by man's coming to the consciousness of his own eternal divinity as the pantheists talk, all else must take its form accordingly, and the religion thus constituted will be essentially different from every other in which this ground principle may be wanting. Still for the whole apprehension of Christianity, we may say, not only that much, but that all depends on the question, which of these views shall be adopted; whether this central fact shall be regarded as a general "unity of the divine and human" realizing itself in the consciousness of the race as such, or be conceived of as a concrete "union of God and man," that actualizes itself from a definite point and only under certain moral conditions.

7.

Hegel acknowledged Christianity as the absolute truth of religion. He did so, because it has its essential nature in the incarnation, exhibiting thus the *unity of the divine and human.* On this ground mainly, he undertook to reconcile Christianity with philosophy, and to show their full identity in their last results. For both this unity is the highest idea; only, what Christianity holds in the concrete form of the individual, historical God-man, is raised by philosophy into the sphere of speculative thought as something general. It belongs to the nature of the absolute or divine spirit to actualize itself in humanity, and the human spirit accordingly, as it descends into the depths of its own being, recognizes itself to be divine. It is the nature of God to be human, and to be divine is the nature of man. The consciousness of this we owe to Christianity. It made known to man his inborn divinity, put an end to the opposition between eternity and time, brought heaven down upon the earth, overthrew the dualistic anta-gonism of finite and infinite, and laid the foundation in this way for that *Monismus des Gedankens,* as they call it, which forms the great triumph of modern speculation.

With this however the later *Hegelians,* of the so called left side, were by no means satisfied. The peace made between Christianity and philosophy by Hegel, appeared to them to be hollow. It was not allowed accordingly to stand. It was denied that Christianity includes such a unity of the finite and infinite as the truth requires. Either it was held to be in direct contradiction to the speculative principle of God's immanence in the world; or else it was said, that the unity which it allowed between God and man, as being restricted to a single individual, had no force for the general mass of humanity and nature, in the case of which accordingly the dualistic contradiction remained still unsurmounted. With this last view it was admitted indeed, that Christianity owes its world-historical power to such union of the divine and human as it exhibits, notwithstanding the isolated form in which it appears; the idea at least served to stimulate the human spirit to a new life, and places this religion high above all that had been known before. Still however the union in the case of Christ himself was not to be taken as real or historical; it was counted as mythical only, an idea made to take a concrete form in his person by the mere imagination of the Church. And then as it was but a transient fact for the Christian faith itself, which failed at the same time to acknowledge the universal oneness of God and humanity, Christianity, it was contended, still fell short of the truth. There was still no proper reconciliation, save for Christ only, between God and man, the infinite and the finite, heaven and earth; the unity allowed was not apprehended as a present divine fact, but only as something past in the Saviour himself, or as something still future in the heavenly world.

We find then three ways of looking at the subject in the same school. They agree in considering the absolute identification of God with the world, (pantheism and monism,) to be the highest truth. But the difference between them is very material. The first makes Christianity and specula-tion to be essentially the same; the second throws them absolutely asun-der; the third allows them to come together, but only in a single point, the isolated centre of Christianity, which the modern speculation has extended into a whole world of truth not acknowledged by Christianity itself.

Taking the school as a whole, it has the merit of having grasped with decision the main point in Christianity; it finds its grand distinction, its inmost nature, in the constitution of Christ's person, and places in full view thus its true specific character. But in doing so, it reduces this central point again to a mere *caput mortuum*, and sinks what in Christianity is the highest form of life, a divine act, most real and full of power, into an incomplete stage simply of speculation. For what is here styled unity of the divine and human, is not the union of God and man as different, accomplished in a real and perfect way in Christ, and taking effect also through him in the race; but an original and eternal oneness, in virtue of which divinity and humanity are held to be essentially the same, God only the truth of man, and man the reality of God; in such sort that man at a certain point of development, must necessarily come to the consciousness of his own truth, that is of his divine nature or unity with God. This point was reached in Christianity, whether in the consciousness of Christ himself, or only by means of him in the mind of the Church, would seem to be considered indifferent. In either case, the form in which the truth at first came into view, was very incomplete; since the unity which belongs properly to the race in general, was supposed to have place only in a single instance. It remained for modern philosophy to burst the bonds of this conception, and push the speculative germ contained in it to its proper perfection. But this was in fact to rob the conception itself of all its significance, whether retained as a symbol still or cast aside as of no farther use. Thus the system did indeed fix its eye on the centre, the very heart of Christianity; but it was only to aim its deadly arrow the more surely at this vital point.

Looking at the several views of the school separately, no attention whatever is due to that which regards Christianity as a religion which places God abstractly beyond the world. Every one who is at all acquainted with it must know, that while it distinguishes the one from the other, it teaches at the same time the existence of God in the world and of the world in God. It does not merge the being of God in the world, but allows him to fill it notwithstanding with his actual presence and power. The thought is in some sense correct, that Christianity has put an end to the opposition of the infinite and the finite, the divine and human. It is true at the same time however, that it acknowledges an absolute union of divinity and humanity only in Christ, and sees a hopeless dualism every where else. The unity in this case is not indeed restricted to Christ as a solitary, transient instance, in the way pretended by the objection; it proceeds from him over into the spiritual organism of which he is the head, and becomes thus a permanent constitution for the race; heaven and salvation belong not exclusively to the next world, but have place also in the present life. Still Christianity is not for this reason monistic, in the Hegelian sense. It allows by all means a dualism; a dualism that is not to be speculated or ignored simply out of the way, deeply seated as it is in the inmost consciousness of the whole human world; the dualism of *sin*. The existence of sin finds its evidence for every man in his own conscience. By it moreover, he feels himself to be involved in the most terrible self-contradiction, and what is still worse, in direct opposition to a holy God. This dualism can be denied, only by denying either sin or God, or else both together. That is, he who does so must sacrifice his moral or religious consciousness, or with the destruction of both at once, subvert his whole spiritual nature. In any case he must at least discard Christianity entirely, which without the acknowledgment of this dualism has no meaning whatever. Speculation sets the dualism aside in the way of logic, joining opposites that are held to have been originally one; but by such logical redemption no conscience is quieted, no duty turned into ability, no sinner born to a new life. Christianity makes full account of the opposition as it actually exists, shows holiness and sin, God and the world lying in wickedness, in sharp contradiction. But it overcomes all this in the way of historical fact, by bringing God and humanity to a true inward union, not in thought merely, but in an actual human life; establishing thus a real power of redemption, through which the race is made to participate in the same life, not by a single stroke of consciousness, but all the more surely by means of a severe moral process. Here accordingly the ethical and redemptional interests, of which Hegelian speculation makes so little account, are allowed to stand in their full force; and Christianity altogether retains its true character as a theistic religion, in which God and the world though not sundered are clearly distinguished, a religion that acknowledges the absolute holiness of God, and leads to union with him only in the way of deliverance from the power of sin.

8.

That *Christ* himself possessed the consciousness of entire *unity with God,* and that others were made to feel the presence of a divine life in his person, admits of no doubt. In one form or another this idea lay at the ground of the whole Christian faith. It wrought such world movement and world change, as no pious fiction, but a real life power only, could ever have produced. Equally clear is it, that Christ's will was to impart his spirit and life to his people, and thus to continue and extend his existence in them as the proper life of the world. Both thoughts are exhibited in the fourth Gospel particularly, under the most manifold representation, as the highest idea of Christianity. Christ, himself first glorified of the Father, will glorify himself again in his people; they shall eat his flesh and blood, that is, take into them his life; cast into the ground by death, like a grain of wheat, he shall rise again as a plentiful seed in the Church, and multiply and perpetuate himself in this way through all time. All concentrates however in this, that he will draw them, through himself, to the Father, and make them one with the Father: "that they all may be one, as thou, Father, art in me, and I in thee, that they also may he one in us"—and then again: "I in them, and thou in me, that they may be made perfect in one, and that the world may know that thou hast sent me, and hast loved them as thou hast loved me." All that belongs to God, belongs also to Christ, and with all this divine fulness he communicates himself to his people, makes his abode with them, and sanctifies them; or as the apostle Paul expresses it, only in reversed order: "All is yours, and ye are Christ's, and Christ is God's."

The ground of the Christian faith then, that to which it owes its origin and character, is the *unity of Christ with God;* but along with this it includes with equal necessity the assurance, that the fact thus constituted is not single, solitary and transient in its nature, but must with the spirit and life of Christ extend itself to those also who *believe* in him, and so by degrees to *humanity* as a whole. Christ is *alone,* as the unity in him was original and complete; but he is not *single,* since that which was in him, is to become, according to the measure of receptivity, the possession of the whole race. A living head is not to be thought of apart from the body. No redeemed Church without a Redeemer; but just as little a perfect Redeemer without a Church. Christ is made complete in his people.

There can be no deeper idea in the sphere of religion. Does it indeed reveal itself, not merely as the ground thought, but as the ground fact of Christianity, imparting to it its inmost constitution? If so, three things will necessarily follow. First, the religion which includes this revelation, will carry just here its most distinctive seal and criterion as compared with other religions. Secondly, it will hereby authenticate itself as the absolute religion, the faith of humanity. Thirdly, all that belongs to it will take its best form, and appear in its true light, from this centre. These several points then demand our attention.

9.

All religion stands essentially in the communion of man with God. The most perfect and intense form of communion between spiritual beings, where without the loss of individual, separate personality on either side, such a mutual interpenetration of spirit and nature has place, that the one may be said to live, without let or bar, freely and sweetly in the other, we call unity. The conception however will be different, as the relation to which it is applied may be that of creature to creature merely, or that of the creature to the Creator, which must ever involve infinite distance between, nature and nature, in the case even of the greatest affinity. As applied to this last relation, unity denotes that position of man towards God, in which God, meeting no obstruction in man, communicates himself to him in the entire fulness of his Spirit, his love, his holiness; whilst man acting purely and fully under the impulse of God's Spirit working in him, makes the divine will absolutely his own; so that between self-consciousness and God-consciousness there is no distinction or conflict, but the first is fully taken up into the second, and ruled by it, and filled with it at every point.

Such a union, though in unconscious form, belonged to that state of innocence, in which man was originally formed. But this has yielded to a state of sin, bringing with it separation from God. The object of religion now is to restore what has been lost. This can be accomplished only in the way of atonement; the last end however is always communion and perfect union with God, no longer in the form of unconscious innocence indeed, but with such ripe consciousness as springs from surmounted spiritual discord and conflict.

The religions which *preceded Christianity* aimed also at this end. Judaism, as actuated by the idea of the Holy One and its strong sense of sin, in the way of atonement; Heathenism, with its want of moral earnestness, in the way of more outward services. But it came not to a true communion, to say nothing of unity, between God and humanity, in either direction. The constitution of both systems rendered this impossible.

Heathenism never rose, as a religion, to the full conception of the divine, as something above nature, spiritual, holy, and in itself one. The divinity was pantheistically merged in nature, which itself came in this way to an apotheosis, and was honoured as divine. The two ideas were confounded, made to flow together. With such want of clear distinction, there was no room of course to speak of a real union. True, in its higher stages, Heathenism exhibits the divinity under the form of humanity, and seems in this way to join them together. But after all it is no true conjunction; since we have neither a true God in such case nor a true man; the God being subject to all sorts of human imperfection, and the man having an unearthly fantastic nature that overthrows his reality. The idea of a full union of God and man, by an act of condescending love on the one side and under the condition of holiness on the other, lay utterly beyond the whole sphere of thinking, which characterized the heathen world.

Such an idea could have place only on the ground of a constitutional-ly ethical, monotheistic religion, in which a full distinction was made between God and the world. *Judaism* had this character. But it was wanting on another side. What Heathenism confounded, Judaism not only distinguished but sundered. It was not indeed wholly without the concep-tion of God's being in the world (Inweltlichkeit); but this was most im-perfectly applied. According to the Jewish view, God works in the sphere of nature and humanity; but it is outwardly *upon* both, rather than inwardly *in* them both. He works in an extraordinary, miraculous way, rather than in the quiet, orderly course of things. Hence his interpositions have the character of isolated, abrupt, transient occasions, leaving nature and man to themselves, as before; whereas, the idea of a true and perfect union must imply always a constant communication of the divine Spirit, a permanent indwelling of the divine nature, a fellowship on the part of man in the divine life that shall cover the whole tract of his existence. Here then we have God in his truth and man in his proper reality; but the relation between them involves no true, full, unobstructed union.

This is conceivable only on the basis of a religion, in which God and the world may be distinguished without being sundered, with a full recognition of God's grace as well as holiness on the one hand, as also of the capacity of man, according to his original human constitution, to participate in the divine nature on the other. All this now we find in *Christianity*, and in Christianity alone. God, in the Christian faith, is the self-existent Creator and Preserver of all things; but all live, move and have their being also in him, and bear witness to his presence. He is the infinitely exalted, and yet the infinitely near; communicating himself in boundless love and condescension; in such sort, that where the condition of a sinless holiness is given, as in Christ, we find humanity admitted not merely to extraordinary illapses of the Spirit in the way of trance or vision or sudden inspiration, but to the privilege of a clear, full, unbroken consciousness of union with the divine life, as the natural and proper order of its own existence. Here we have the true God, holy and boundless in his love; in the most perfect form; and a true union, as holding in the undivided and indivisible oneness of a single living personality. Thus is the point reached, which all previous religions struggled to reach in vain. Here is the great seal and criterion of Christianity, not merely distinguishing it from Heathenism and Judaism, but setting it high above them, and showing it to be the end in which their very nature requires them to pass away.

10.

By this very fact, Christianity is shown to be the *absolute religion,* the faith of humanity, that form of piety in which the consciousness of an imperishable nature may take for its motto the words: "Jesus Christ, the same yesterday, to-day, and forever."

Religion in its very nature is Love. It starts in this character from God as love to man, and returns again in the form of human love to its source; a circling stream from God to God. Its highest manifestation on both sides, must constitute the utmost summit of the religious life. This we find in Christ. His mission, by which he was given up to suffering and death, proceeds from an everlasting love, which spares not even that which it held dearest, in order to restore and save lost man. He himself enters into the will of this love, with the most perfect freedom. In every part of his life he shows a power of love, which for its sublimity and touching simplicity, its purity and invincibleness, cannot be counted in its origin and nature other than divine. And as he offers himself, through the force of this love, unreservedly to God, so he offers himself also, through the force of the same love, to his brethren of mankind also, in life, suffering and death, for the purpose of drawing them to God, and uniting them among themselves and with God. He is at once accordingly the most perfect expression of love in both directions, from God to man and from man to God, as well as of love to the brethren. He is a centre of love, divine and human intensely interwoven, with power to embrace the whole circle of humanity; a fountain of love, from which all generations may draw without exhausting its fulness. No other religion exhibits any parallel, or resemblance even, to this. Hence it is only in Christianity that God is known as *Love;* that the love of man to God is derived from his love as first exercised towards them; that love to brethren is made identical with love to God; and that such a deep view of the first is taken as to make even the want of it seem the sin of murder itself. Nor has the world ever gone beyond this exhibition since. Christ stands still, and must ever stand, in this view, without a parallel in history. The fairest and greatest that history has to show besides, is itself only what has sprung from the kindling power of his love. There is no room in fact to think of anything higher than this. It includes all. Nor can the work of atonement and redemption ever be repeated, in the same form. Christianity then, even in this view, as comprehended in the person of its Founder, is the utmost of religion. It cannot be transcended.

But on this full fellowship of love rests also that moral and spiritual union between God and man, which forms the general criterion of what is highest in the religious sphere. In Christ, the Spirit of God worked without limitation or restraint; his will was fully pervaded by the divine will; he and the Father are one; the unity between God and man is shown to be complete, opening for the race a sure way to new life. The speculative philosophy tells us that the consciousness of this unity is to be considered merely a new point reached in the process of world-thought, either in the mind of Christ himself or by the Church in its zeal to glorify his person. Very well. One cannot see indeed how the Church could come to this, without finding some sufficient ground for its idea in Christ himself. But be it so. The conception still remains one that is peculiar to Christianity, and as a conception even it cannot be surpassed by anything higher in religion. If religion consisted in thought merely, we should have here, under such view also, its crowning height. Only one thing would be more, immeasurably more indeed, than this thought—its full actualization. This the Christian faith, in pointed contradiction to the modern speculative philosophy, exhibits as a fact in Christ. Speculation too indeed pretends reality for its idea. But here it is found to halt. It has no right conception, in the first place, of unity, but substitutes for it identity; if man is the manifestation of God by his very nature, there is no room to speak of his becoming one with God. And then, it comes to no true reality in the case. The reality is claimed for the race; but this is made up of individuals, or as they prefer to term it *copies,* in every one of which the unity in question is troubled at best and incomplete; yea, it is against the nature of the idea, we are told, to exhaust itself in *one* individual. How then shall it come in this way to a full, clear manifestation? Thus speculation seeks to extinguish the sun, that is actually shining pure and bright in the moral firmament, and offers in its room earthly tapers, which multiplied to any extent must ever fall immeasurably short of the same glory. We say on the contrary, if this idea of union between the divine and human be true, and the actualization of it necessary to satisfy the deepest want of the human spirit; and if every idea that is to be acknowledged as true and divine, requires to become actual; then what the race fails to furnish here, we must seek in an individual. All that the case demands, has been clearly reached in Christ. In his person then the absolute consummation of the religious life is brought to view, not in thought merely, but also in reality. All that remains, is that the theanthropic life thus constituted in the Redeemer himself, should be unfolded and carried out more and more in the human world. On this ground Christianity is the absolute religion in which all other religions may be said to culminate and become complete. Religion and Humanity here are one, equally universal and equally permanent.

11.

Finally, it is from this point that all which is comprised in Christianity may be *best arranged and understood.* It serves to set each part in its true light and proper position.

So in the case of *Doctrine.* This, as we have seen, is not an original or principal interest in Christianity, existing for itself or by itself. Its office is simply to represent and exhibit life. Like the statue of Mercury with which the Alcibiades of Plato compares Socrates, it is only as it were the hull, in which the real image of the deity, the person of the God-man, is enshrined. Self-representation and self-testimony, as before said, formed the main object in Christ's work. This included doctrine, it is true; but always only in the one great relation now affirmed. Only as significant of the very life and being of Christ himself, could it have any value or force. Doctrine *gives* us Christianity in an outward way; but the life of Christ *is* Christianity.

Here also the idea of *Revelation,* which is more full than that of doctrine though closely connected with it, comes to stand in its true light. Revelation is not simply an extension of the knowledge of God theoretically considered; as it can have place, for a sinful world, only hand in hand with the removal of sin or redemption, it must unfold an actual economy of grace and power for this purpose, a real manifestation of God, as actively employed in the work of educating, enlightening, redeeming and sanctifying the human race. In this case again, the bare word is not enough. Revelation in this form stands higher indeed than the dumb, unclear revelation of mere nature; but it falls itself again far short of revelation in the form of an act. Only in this last form by a sum of salvation *acts,* unfolding his mind and will, can the *living* God become fully revealed. In the Old Testament we find a preparatory, shadowy approximation towards this end. But the case required at last the personal manifestation of grace and truth, as they have been made to dwell among us by Jesus Christ. In this sense alone is Christianity a revelation, as the whole person of Christ, including his words and works, his life and death, his resurrection and exaltation, serves to bring into actual view the will of God as concerned in the salvation of men. This required on the part of the

Redeemer a full identification of mind and nature with God. But for this very reason, he himself, his person and not his doctrine, constitutes the revelation presented in Christianity; and so, as being *in* him rather than *through* him, it must be regarded as holding, not in any separate function of his life, but in the undivided whole of his personality and history, his being and working, doctrine, life, death, resurrection and glorification at the right hand of God, all that he was and is, as well as all that he has done and is doing still, as Head over all things to the Church to the end of time.

Christianity is also *Moral Law.* If however it were law only or law essentially even, it would not have transcended the order of the Jewish religion; it would be at best a reformed, generalized Judaism only, bringing with it no freedom or life, but leaving men still under the curse of sin and guilt. Law, however refined, always remains law, something over against the man, an outward *shall,* whose nature it is to exact, accuse, condemn, and kill. Spirit only and love can animate, and both spring only from personal life. By the all prevailing principle of love the law was fulfilled in Christ's life; and now with the communication of Christ's spirit, the spirit and power of the same active obedience are received at the same time. Thus the law comes to be written in the heart, and loses its character of mere outward authority in that of a spontaneous impulse belonging to the inmost life of its subject. Christianity has by fulfilling it taken it out of the way. To look upon Christianity itself then as being of the same nature, is not indeed wholly wrong, since it has its legal, judicial side, as related to the impenitent sinner; but it is to come short of the true depth of what is comprehended in the gospel. Freedom, redemption from the law, is the main thing.

Again, Christianity is *Redemption* and *Atonement;* but in this view also, it has its last and deepest root in the unity of Christ with God. Judaism had no power to set men free in this way. Its salvation stood mainly in symbolical provisions, that could not take away sin itself or reach to the creation of a new spiritual life. This required the medium of an actual *personality,* entering freely into a communion of life with the subjects of redemption; and could be reached, in an absolute perfect way, only where all that was to be abolished by this redemption on the one hand, and all that was to be produced from it positively on the other, might be found originally and completely abolished and actualized in this personality itself. Only one who is himself morally free can impart freedom to others; and he that is to set all free, must necessarily be sinlessly perfect and fully united with God. Such a life however, overflowing with blessedness and love, would include in its very nature, by its relation to humanity, the power of a universal redemption; for it must communicate itself with necessity to others, whose sense of want would at the same time urge them to lay hold of it as their own, while its divine constitution rendered it impossible that its fulness could ever be in this way exhausted or impaired. But redemption, to be complete, demands atonement, pardon of sin and peace with God. Such reconciliation again can be effected only by one, in whose soul the love and grace of God are identical with the consciousness of life itself, and whose life appears in such palpable unity of blessedness with God, as to exert a sort of moral violence on men in drawing them into the same communion. The original unity of Christ with the Father then, the being of God in his person, is the basis on which rests the atonement or restoration of union between man and God; and it is with good heed to the order of his words no doubt that the great apostle says: "God was in Christ, reconciling the world unto himself," plainly intimating that the existence of God in Christ was and still is that which holds the first place as a cause, while the atonement flows from it as an effect.

And so all *besides* in Christianity receives from this ground thought, or ground fact rather, its proper light and position. Here the Christian Theology and Anthropology come to their true termination and living conjunction; they are not left to devour each other, but find their completion in Christology. God appears in the fulness of his condescension and self-communicating love; man in his highest form of dignity and grandeur. On both sides the revelation satisfies the deepest religious want of our nature, restores to the spiritual world its inward harmony, and solves the riddle of the universe. The miraculous also, with which the manifestation of the God-man is attended, becomes natural and intelligible; since such an actual entrance of the divine into the life of the world, must necessarily involve the presence of higher powers and laws. The resurrection of Christ in particular, which has been from the first the grand prop of Christianity in its historical aspect, appears but as the natural and necessary consequence of the divine life which filled the constitution of his person; while it forms besides, in virtue of the life bond that unites him with his people, the ground of the whole Christian Eschatology, as connected with the resurrection of believers.

12.

In the way of brief recapitulation, our view of the whole subject may be expressed as follows.

That which forms the specific, distinctive character of Christianity is not its doctrine nor its morality, nor even its power of redemption; but the peculiar constitution and religious significance of its Founder, as uniting divinity and humanity, truly and perfectly, in his person. Doctrine, law and redemption rest on this as their basis.

As doctrine Christianity addresses itself to the understanding of man, as law to his will; in both cases, as something outward and mechanical, rather than as having power to produce a living piety. In the character of redemption, it reaches to the heart, and unfolds in much higher degree its true life-giving, dynamic nature; but viewed only in this light it is still but imperfectly apprehended, as an inward state or mere matter of feeling. Its complete sense and full objective value are reached, only when all is referred to the person of Christ, in which God appears united with human-ity, and which by its very constitution accordingly carries in it a reconcil-ing, redeeming, quickening and enlightening efficacy. Thus apprehended, Christianity is in the fullest sense organic, in its nature. It reveals itself as a peculiar order of life in Christ, and from him as a personal centre it reaches forth towards man as a whole, in the way of true historical self-evolution, seeking to form the entire race into a glorious kingdom of God. From this centre all takes its full significance; doctrine becomes power; law is turned into life; redemption and reconciliation find a solid objective basis, on which to rest. The natural and the human, sanctified by union with the divine in Christ, are sanctified also for all who partake of his spirit and life. Christianity thus neither deifies the natural as such, nor yet opposes it as evil; but purifies and transfigures it, and restores it to its true divine destination. It is the religion of Humanity, in which the *life of man* as man is advanced to its *full perfection and glory.*

In any case, the two highest conceptions of Christianity are those, by which it is made to be either the religion of redemption or the religion of the unity of God and humanity. These condition and complete each other. Redemption was possible only through this unity; and the unity connects to its full significance only as it works redemption. The unity is inward, the redemption goes abroad; this last the heart of Christianity, the other its head and mind. The apprehension of Christianity as redemption rests more on Paul's way of thinking, the apprehension of it as union with God on that rather which we find in John; the first regards chiefly the hindrances to be overcome and is more practical, the last looks chiefly to the crowning end and is more mystical and speculative; the first has to do most with faith and hope, the last with love. Inasmuch now however as redemption starts from the unity of Christ with God and leads to the union of mankind generally with him as its ultimate scope; inasmuch as redemption must cease when there is no more sin, while the unity it restores, like the love on which it rests, can never fail; inasmuch accordingly as redemption belongs more to time and the present state of the world, whilst union with God is something absolutely eternal, the end thus as it is the beginning, the alpha and omega of the whole process; we must hold this last to be the high all ruling constituent in the nature of Christianity. And so we say, putting all together, Christianity is that religion which in the person of its author has actualized in fact, what all other religious have struggled in vain to reach, the unity of man with God; and which as the power of a new creation organically working from this centre, by doctrine and moral energy, by redemption and reconciliation, conducts men as individuals and as a race to their true destination, to full communion and union with God, whereby all life is sanctified and exalted into a higher order of existence.

This view of Christianity is not absolutely new. We meet with it under a different form, in the older Mysticism, as exhibited in Germany during the middle ages. For this school also the union of God and man through the incarnation of the first and the deification of the second, forms the cardinal idea in the religion of Christ. In this, as well as in its whole treatment of Christianity, it shows a striking affinity with the modern speculative philosophy; except that what is the result in this last case of thought, reflection, criticism even, springs in the other from the force of deep, inward religious fervor, and of course carries on this account a different meaning. The general point of coincidence is found in this, that Mysticism also transfers the objective forces of religion into the spirit, and allows them thus to lose their proper reality. The historical transforms itself into the inward; Christ is not so much the outward Saviour who once lived in Palestine, as he is the Redeemer that still lives, with new birth, in every pious man; his history is accommodated to the spiritual life of the believer himself, and this, the Christ within us, becomes the main thing, from which the outward also first receives its true significance. Here again however we must distinguish carefully between two tendencies; the properly pantheistic Mysticism, whose chief representative is *Master Eckart*, so highly lauded by the modern speculation, and the prevailingly theistic. In the view of the first, union with the divine nature is taken to be the product of thought, a point in the development of consciousness; Christ in the end is but the type of humanity, and his history only figure and allegory; be was the first who came to the sense of his sonship in the relation to God; by him we learn that we also partake of the same nature, and are in like manner sons of God. In the other case, the unity of Christ with God is regarded as the result of a free act of self-communication on the part of God, conditioned by the moral character of Christ, who accordingly carries with him more weight as a historical prototype; and so also the union with God which is effected for men through Christ is of a far more decidedly moral nature. The first view resolves it mainly into the exercise of thinking; here it is reached by an essentially ethical or even ascetic process. There it is a matter of nature; here, a matter of grace, made possible through the redeeming influence of Christ, by mortification and a new inward life. The pantheistic Mysticism is the pattern and precursor of the modern speculation; the theistic, on the other band, by the inwardness and warmth of its religious life, prepared the way on one side for the Reformation. In the Reformation however, a new element came forward. The Mystics had more or less overlooked one thing, the dark point in human life, sin and the need of redemption and atonement. The consciousness of this was powerfully awakened in Luther, and wrought with vast effect in the work of the sixteenth century. Deliverance from the power of sin, and reconciliation with God, were now felt to be the main thing in Christianity; and as redemption in this form could not be accomplished by an ideal image, but only by a real person, the historical personality of Christ was clothed again with new authority and prominence. Thus was found once more the historico-ideal centre of Christianity. Still however, on the part of the Reformers, principally under one view; Christ as a real Redeemer and Mediator; but not with proper regard to that quality of his nature, by which alone he has this character, his perfect unity with God, constituting him at the same time a historical prototype and pattern for humanity. This refers us back again to the fundamental idea of the Mystics; but while we appropriate this in a more ripe and better digested sense we cannot consent to lose the true and genuine acquisition which was made by the Reformation. We have endeavoured accordingly to place the subject in such a form as may serve to combine what is right in both views, the more practical of the Reformation and the more speculative of the better Mystics. Christianity, we say, is by all means, essentially and primarily, the religion of unity with God in its Founder and union with God in believers; but all this in its right sense, only when the conception is found to rest on the inalienable Christian idea of a personal God, and along with this the elements of redemption and reconciliation, repentance and faith, knowledge and sanctification, are allowed to maintain their authority full and unimpaired, as dependent but still indispensable constituents of the new creation in Christ Jesus.

THE MYSTICAL PRESENCE

Ἐν ἀρχῇ ἦν ὁ λόγος. — Ἐν αὐτῷ ζωὴ ἦν. —Καὶ ὁ λόγος σὰρξ ἐγένετο. —Καὶ ἡ ζωὴ ἐφανερώθη. — Ὁ ἔχων τὸν, ἔχει τὴν ζωήν. —JOHN.

Θανατωθεὶς μὲν σαρκὶ ζωοποιηθεὶς δὲ πνεύματι. —PETER.

Ἐγένετο ὁ ἔσχατος Ἀδὰμ εἰς πνεῦμα ζῳοποιοῦν. — Ὁ δὲ κολλώμενος τῷ κυρίῳ, ἕν πνεῦμά ἐστι. — Ἔστι σῶμα πνευματικόν. — Ὅτι μέλη ἐσμὲν τοῦ σώματος αὐτοῦ, ἐκ τῆς σαρκὸς αὐτοῦ, καὶ ἐκ τῶν ὀστέων αὐτοῦ. —Τὸ μυστήριον τοῦτο μέγα ἐστίν. —PAUL.

Τὸ γεγεννημένον ἐκ τοῦ πνεύματος, πνεῦμά ἐστι. — Ἐγώ εἰμι ἡ ἀνάστασις καὶ ἡ ζωή. — Ὁ τρώγων μου τὴν σάρκα, καὶ πίνων μου τὸ αἷμα, ἔχει ζωὴν αἰώνιον· καὶ ἐγώ ἀναστήσω αὐτὸν τῇ ἐσχάτῃ ἡμέρα. — Ὅτι ἐγώ ζῶ, καὶ ὑμεῖς ζήσεσθε.—JESUS CHRIST.

CHAPTER I.

THE REFORMED OR CALVINISTIC DOCTRINE OF THE LORD'S SUPPER.

INTRODUCTORY REMARKS.

THE *Question of the Eucharist* is one of the most important belonging to the history of religion. It may be regarded indeed as in some sense central to the whole Christian system. For Christianity is grounded in the living union of the believer with the person of Christ; and this great fact is emphatically concentrated in the mystery of the Lord's Supper; which has always been clothed on this very account, to the consciousness of the Church, with a character of sanctity and solemnity, surpassing that of any other Christian institution.

The sacramental controversy of the sixteenth century then was no mere war of words; much less the offspring of mere prejudice, passion or blind self-will, as many in their fanatical superiority to the vast problem involved in it are ready to imagine. It belonged to the inmost sanctuary of theology, and was intertwined particularly with all the arteries of the Christian life. This was *felt* by the spiritual heroes of the Reformation. They had no right to overlook the question which was here thrown in their way, or to treat it as a question of small importance, whose claims might safely be postponed in favour of other interests, that might appear to be brought into jeopardy by its agitation. That this should seem so easy to much of our modern Protestantism, serves only to show, what is shown also by many other facts, that much of our modern Protestantism has fallen away sadly from the theological earnestness and depth of the period to which we now refer. With the revival of a deeper theology, there cannot fail to be a revival of interest also, on the part of the Church, in the sacramental question; as on the other hand there can be no surer sign than the want of such interest, in the case of any section of the Church at any given time, that its theology is without power and its piety infected with disease.

On this question, it is well known, the Protestant world split, from the very beginning, into two great divisions, which have never come since to a true and full inward reconciliation. Strangely enough however both sections of the Church have seriously receded, to no inconsiderable extent, from the ground on which they stood in the sixteenth century. This fact is most broadly and palpably apparent in the modern posture of the *Lutheran* Church, especially as known on this side of the Atlantic. All who have any knowledge whatever of history, are aware that the American Lutheran Church, in its reigning character, has entirely forsaken at this point the position originally occupied by the same communion in the old world. Not only indeed has the proper Lutheran position been surrendered in favour of the Reformed doctrine; but even this doctrine itself, as it stood in the beginning, has come to be looked upon as altogether too high toned in the same direction; so that the very view which was denounced in the days of *Joachim Westphal* and *Tilemann Hesshuss*, as foul sacramentarian heresy, by which cities and nations were exposed to the fierce judgments of heaven, is now counted an extreme on precisely the opposite side, little better than the popish error of transubstantiation itself. But this falling away from the orthodoxy of the sixteenth century is not confined to the Lutheran Church. The view of the Eucharist now generally predominant in the *Reformed* Church also, involves a similar departure, not so broad indeed but equally material, from its proper original creed, as exhibited in its symbolical books. An unchurchly, rationalistic tendency, has been allowed to carry the Church gradually more and more off from the ground it occupied in the beginning, till its position is found to be at length, to a large extent, a new one altogether.

In the nature of the case, this change must involve much more than the simple substitution of one theory of the Lord's Supper for another. The doctrine of the eucharist is intimately connected with all that is most deep and central in the Christian system as a whole; and it is not possible for it to undergo any material modification in any direction, without a corresponding modification at the same time of the theory and life of religion at other points. If it be true then, that such a falling away from the eucharistic view of the sixteenth century, as is now asserted, has taken place in the Reformed Church, it is very certain that the revolution is not confined to this point. It must affect necessarily the whole view, that is entertained of Christ's person, the idea of the Church, and the doctrine of salvation throughout. Not that the change in the theory of the Lord's Supper may be considered the origin and cause, properly speaking, or any such general theological revolution; but because it could not occur, except as accompanied by this general revolution, of which it may be taken as the most significant exponent and measure.

Under this view, the subject presents itself to us, as one of great interest and importance. The question involved in it, is not one of historical curiosity simply, the bearings of which in a religious view may be regarded as indifferent or of only slight account. It is a question of the utmost moment for theology and religion, which at this time particularly no friend of our evangelical Protestant faith should consider himself at liberty to overlook.*

To see and feel the truth of the assertion, that the modern popular view of the Lord's Supper is chargeable with a serious defection from the original Protestant orthodoxy at this point, it is only necessary to have some correct apprehension of what was actually believed and taught on the subject, by the Reformed Church as well as by the Lutheran, in the age of the Reformation. This cannot fail of itself to reveal, in the way of contrast, the true posture of the Church at the present time.

It is of course with the doctrine of the *Reformed* Church only, in the view now mentioned, as distinguished from the Lutheran, that the present inquiry is concerned. Our object is, to bring into view the theory of the Lord's Supper, as it stood in the general creed of this section of the Church in the sixteenth century. This requires, in the first place, a clear statement of the theory itself; in the second place, proper evidence that it was in fact of such established authority in the period just named.

---

*"The eighteenth century came, and the same processes which were used for shutting out the invisible in every other direction were applied also in this. And yet tens of thousands of men and women in every part of Europe, would in that day have rather parted with their lives, or with any thing more dear to them, than with this feast. And now, in this nineteenth century, there are not a few persons meditating on these different experiments, have arrived at this deep and inward conviction, that the question whether Christianity shall be a practical principle and truth in the hearts of men, or shall be exchanged for a set of intellectual notions or generalizations, depends mainly on the question whether the Eucharist shall or shall not be acknowledged and received as the bond of a universal life, and the means whereby men become partakers of it." *Maurice's Kingdom of Christ.* (London, 1842.) *Vol.* II., p. 72.

SECTION I.

STATEMENT OF THE DOCTRINE.

To obtain a proper view of the original doctrine of the Reformed Church on the subject of the eucharist, we must have recourse particularly to Calvin. Not that he is to be considered the creator, properly speaking, of the doctrine. It grew evidently out of the general religious life of the church itself, in its antagonism to the Lutheran dogma on the one hand, and the low Socinian extreme on the other. Calvin however was the theological organ, by which it first came to that clear expression, under which it continued to be uttered subsequently in the symbolical books. His profound far-reaching and deeply penetrating mind drew forth the doctrine from the heart of the Church, exhibited it in its proper relations, proportions and distinctions, gave it form in this way for the understanding, and clothed it with authority as a settled article of faith in the general creed. He may be regarded then as the accredited interpreter and expounder of the article, for all later times. A better interpreter in the case, we could not possibly possess. Happily, too, his instructions and explanations here are very full and explicit. He comes upon the subject from all sides, and handles it under all forms, didactically and controversially; so that we are left in no uncertainty whatever, with regard to his meaning, at a single point.

Any theory of the eucharist will be found to accord closely with the view that is taken, at the same time of the nature of the union generally between Christ and his people. Whatever the life of the believer may be as a whole in this relation, it must determine the form of his communion with the Saviour in the sacrament of the Supper, as the central representation of its significance and power. Thus, the sacramental doctrine of the primitive Reformed Church stands inseparably connected with the idea of an inward living union between believers and Christ, in virtue of which they are incorporated into his very nature, and made to subsist with him by the power of a common life.* In full correspondence with this conception of the Christian salvation, as a process by which the believer is mystically inserted more and more into the person of Christ, till he

---

*Conjunctio igitur ilia capitis et membrorum, habitatio Christi in cordibus nostris, *mystica denique unio* a nobis in summo gradu statuitur; ut Christus *noster factus*, donorum, quibus præditus est, nos faciat consortes. Non ergo *extra nos* procul speculamur, ut nobis *imputetur* ejus justitia: sed quia *ipsum induimus, et insiti sumus in ejus corpus, unum denique nos secum efficere dignatus est*; ideo justitiæ societatem nobis cum eo esse gloriamur. *Calvin. Inst.* III. 11, 10.

becomes thus at last fully transformed into his image, it was held that nothing less than such a real participation of his living person is involved always in the right use of the Lord's Supper. The following distinctions may serve to define and explain more fully, the nature of the communion which holds between Christ and his people, in the whole view now mentioned, as taught by Calvin and the Reformed Church generally, in the sixteenth century.

1. The union of *believers* with Christ is not simply that of a common humanity, as derived from *Adam*. In this view, all men partake of one and the same nature, and each may be said to be in relation to his neighbour bone of his bone and flesh of his flesh. So Christ took not on him the nature of angels, but of men. He was born of a woman, and appeared among us in the likeness and fashion of our own life, only without sin. But plainly our relation to his nature, and through this to his mediatorial work, as christians, is something quite different from this general consanguinity of the human race. Where we are said to be of the same life with him, "members of his body, of his flesh and of his bones," it is not on the ground merely of a joint participation with him in the nature of Adam, but on the ground of our participation in his own nature as a higher order of life. Our relation to him is not circuitous and collateral only; it holds in a direct connection with his person.*

2. In this view, the relation is more again than a simply *moral* union. Such a union we have, where two or more persons are bound together by inward agreement, sympathy, and correspondence. Every common friendship is of this sort. It is the relation of the disciple to the master, whom he loves and reveres. It is the relation of the devout Jew to Moses, his venerated lawgiver and prophet. It holds also undoubtedly between the believer and Christ. The Saviour lives much in his thoughts and affections. He looks to him with an eye of faith, embraces him in his heart, commits himself to his guidance, walks in his steps, and endeavours to become clothed more and more with his very mind itself. In the end the correspondence will be found complete. We shall be like him in all respects, one with him morally, in the fullest sense. But Christianity includes more than such a moral union, separately considered. This union itself is only the result here of a relation more inward and deep. It has its ground in the force of a common life, in virtue of which Christ and his

---

*Carnis et sanguinis communicationem non tantum interpretor *de communi natura*, quod Cristus *homo factus* jure fraternæ societatis nos Dei filios secum fecerit: sed distincte affirmo, *quam a nobis sumpsit carnem, eam* nobis esse vivificam, ut nobis sit materia spiritualis vitæ. Illamque Augustini sententiam libenter amplector, Sicut ex costa Adæ creata fuit Eva, sic ex Christi latere fluxisse nobis vitæ originem et principium. *Calvin, De Vera Partic. Opp. Tom.* IX. (*Amst. Ed.*) p. 726.—Neque enim ossa sumus ex ossibus et caro ex carne, quia ipse nobiscum est homo; sed quia Spiritus sui virtute nos in corpus suum inserit, ut vitam ex eo hauriamus. *Id. Comm. on Eph.* V. 30.

people are one even before they become thus assimilated to his character.
So in the sacrament of the Lord's Supper; it is not simply a moral
approach that the true worshipper is permitted to make to the glorious
object of his worship. His communion with Christ does not consist merely
in the good exercises of his own mind, the actings of faith, and contrition,
and hope, and love, the solemn recollections, the devotional feelings, the
pious resolutions, of which he may be himself the subject, during the
sacramental service.* Nor is the sacrament a sign only, by which the
memory and heart may be assisted in calling up what is past or absent, for
the purposes of devotion; as the picture of a friend is suited to recall his
image and revive our interest in his person, when he is no longer in our
sight.† Nor is it a pledge simply of our own consecration to the service of
Christ, or of the faithfulness of God as engaged to make good to us in a
general way the grace of the new covenant; as the rainbow serves still to
ratify and confirm the promise given to Noah after the flood.‡ All this
would bring with it in the end nothing more than a moral communication
with Christ, so far as the sacrament itself might be concerned. It could
carry with it no virtue or force, more than might be put into it in every
case by the spirit of the worshipper himself. Such however is not the
nature of the ordinance. It is not simply an occasion, by which the soul of
the believer may be excited to pious feelings and desires; but it embodies
the actual presence of the grace it represents in its own constitution; and
this grace is not simply the promise of God on which we are encouraged
to rely, but the very life of the Lord Jesus Christ himself. We
communicate, in the Lord's supper, not with the divine promise merely,
not with the thought of Christ only, not with the recollection simply of
what he has done and suffered for us, not with the lively present sense

*Ubique resonant scripta mea, *differre* manducationem a fide, quia sit fidei effectus.
Non a triduo ita loqui incœpi, nos credendo manducare Christum, quia *vere participes ejus
facti in ejus corpus coalescimus*, ut nobis communis sit cum eo vita. . . . Quam turpe igitur
Westphalo fuit, quum diserte verba mea sonent, manducare *aliud* esse quam credere; quod
ego fortiter nego, quasi a me profectum impudenter obtrudere lectoribus! . . . Ejusdem
farinæ est quod mox attexit, edere corpus Christi tantundem valere, si verbis meis locus
datur, quam *promissionem fide recipere*. Sed quomodo tam flagitiose se prostituere audet?
Calvin. Adv. Westph. Opp. Tom. IX., p. 669.
   †Ita panis non inanis est *rei absentis pictura*, sed verum ac fidele nostræ cum Christo
unionis pignus. Dicet quispiam non aliter panis symbolo adumbrari corpus Christi, quam
mortua statua Herculem vel Mercurium repræsentat. Hoc certe commentum a doctrina
nostra non minus remotum est, quam profanum a sacro. *Calvin. Opp. T.* IX., p. 667.
—Christus neque pictor est, neque histrio, neque Archimides quispiam, qui inani tantum
objecta imagine oculos pascat, sed *vere et reipsa præstat quod externo symbolo promittit.*
Ib. p. 727.
   ‡Panis ita corpus significat, ut vere, efficaciter, ac reipsa nos ad Christi
communicationem invitet. Dicimus enim veritatem quam continet promissio, *illic exhiberi*,
et effectum externo signo annexum esse. Tropus ergo signum *minime evacuat*, sed potius
ostendit quomodo non sit vacuum. *Calv. Opp. T.* IX., p. 667.

alone of his all-sufficient, all-glorious Salvation; but with the living Saviour himself, in the fulness of his glorified person, made present to us for the purpose by the power of the Holy Ghost.

3. The relation of believers to Christ, then, is more again than that of a simply *legal* union. He is indeed the representative of his people, and what he has done and suffered on their behalf is counted to their benefit, as though it had been done by themselves. They have an interest in his merits, a title to all the advantages secured by his life and death. But this external imputation rests at last on an inward, real unity of life, without which it could have no reason or force. Our interest in Christ's merits and benefits can be based only upon a previous interest in his person; so in the Lord's Supper, we are made to participate, not merely in the advantages secured by his mediatorial work, the rewards of his obedience, the fruits of his bitter passion, the virtue of his atonement, and the power of his priestly intercession, but also in his true and proper life itself, We partake of his merits and benefits only so far as we partake of his substance.*

4. Of course, once more, the communion in question is not simply with Christ in his *divine nature* separately taken, or with the *Holy Ghost* as the representative of his presence in the world. It does not hold in the influences of the Spirit merely, enlightening the soul and moving it to holy affections and purposes. It is by the Spirit indeed we are united to Christ. Our new life is comprehended in the Spirit as its element and medium. But it is always bound in this element to the person of the Lord Jesus Christ himself. Our fellowship is with the Father and with his son Jesus Christ, *through* the Holy Ghost. As such it is a real communion with the Word made flesh; not simply with the divinity of Christ, but with his humanity also; since both are inseparably joined together in his person, and a living union with him in the one view, implies necessarily a living union with him in the other view likewise. In the Lord's Supper, accordingly, the believer communicates not only with the Spirit of Christ, or with his divine nature, but with Christ himself in his whole living person; so that he may be said to be fed and nourished by his very flesh

---

*Neque enim tantum dico applicari *merita*, sed ex ipso Christi corpore alimentum percipere animas, non secus ac terreno pane corpus vescitur. *Calv. Opp. T.* IX., p. 668. —Sane non video, quomodo in cruce Christi redemptionem ac justitiam, in ejus morte vitam habere se quis confidat, nisi vera Christi ipsius communione imprimis fretus. Non enim ad nos bona illa pervenirent, nisi se prius nostrum Christus faceret. *Inst.* IV. 17, 11. —Satis sit monuisse lectores, Christum ubique a me vocari Baptismi Cœnæque *substantiam. Opp. T.* IX., p. 671.—Plus centies occurrit in scriptis meis, adeo me non rejicere *substantiæ* nomen, ut libenter et ingenue profitear spiritualem vitam incomprehensibili Spiritus virtute *ex carnis Christi substantia in nos diffundi*. Ubique etiam admitto, *substantialiter* nos pasci Christi carne et sanguine; modo facessat crassum de locali permixtione commentum. *Ib. p.* 725. *Substantialis* communicatio ubique a me asscritur. *Ib. p.* 732.

and blood. The communion is truly and fully with the *Man* Christ Jesus, and not simply with Jesus as the Son of God.*

These distinctions may serve to bound and define the Reformed doctrine of the Eucharist on the side towards *Rationalism*. All pains were taken to guard it from the false tendency to which it stood exposed in this direction. The several conceptions of the believer's union and communion with Christ which have now been mentioned, were explicitly and earnestly rejected, as being too low and poor altogether for the majesty of this great mystery. In opposition to all such representations, it was constantly affirmed that Christ's people are inserted by faith into his very life; and that the Lord's Supper, forming as it does an epitome of the whole mystery, involves to the worthy communicant an actual participation in the substance of his person under this view. The participation is not simply in his Spirit, but in his flesh also and blood. It is not figurative merely and moral, but *real, substantial* and *essential.*†

But it is not enough to settle the boundaries of the doctrine on the side of Rationalism. To be understood properly, it must be limited and defined, in like manner, on the side of *Romanism*.

1. In the first place then it excludes entirely the figment of *transubstantiation*. According to the Church of Rome, the elements of bread and wine in the sacrament are literally transmuted into the actual flesh and blood of Christ. The accidents, outward properties, sensible qualities only, remain the same; while the original substance is converted supernaturally into the true body of the glorified Saviour, which is thus exhibited and received in an outward way in the sacramental mystery. This transmutation too is not limited to the actual solemnity of the sacramental act itself, but is held to be of permanent force; so that the elements continue afterwards to be the true body of Christ, and are proper objects of veneration and worship accordingly. This theory was rejected as a gross superstition,

---

*Neque illi præterea mihi satisfaciunt, qui nonnullam nobis esse cum Christo communionem agnoscentes, eam dum ostendere volunt, nos Spiritus modo participes faciunt; *præterita carnis et sanguinis mentione. Calvin. Inst.* IV. 17, 7.—Christum corpore absentem doceo nihilominus *non tantum Divina sua virtute*, quæ ubique diffusa est, nobis adesse, sed etiam facere ut nobis vivifica sit sua caro. . . . Neque *simpliciter Spiritu suo* Christum in nobis habitare trado, sed ita nos ad se attollere, ut vivificum carnis suæ vigorem in non transfundat. *Opp. T.* IX., p. 669.—Hanc unitatem *non ad essentiam divinam restringo*, sed pertinere affirmo *ad carnem* et *sanguinem*: quia non simpliciter dictum sit, "Spiritus meus vere est cibus," sed *caro*; nec simpliciter etiam dictum sit. "Divinitas mea vere est potus," sed *sanguis. Ib. p.* 726. Fatemur ergo corpus idem quod crucifixum est, nos in Cœna edere. *Ib. p.* 727. —Augustino assentior, in pane accipi quod pependit in cruce. *Ib. p.* 729.

†Convenit etaim Christum *re ipsa* et efficaciter implere quicquid analogia signi et rei signatæ postulat; ideoque vere nobis in Cœna offerri communicationem cum ejus corpore et sanguine, vel (quod idem valet,) nobis arrham sub pane et vino proponi, quæ nos faciat corporis at sanguinis Christi participes. *Calv. Opp. T.* IX., p. 743.

even by the Lutheran Church, and of course found still less favor in the other section of the Protestant communion. The Reformed doctrine admits no change whatever in the elements. Bread remains bread, and wine remains wine.

2. The doctrine excludes, in the second place, the proper Lutheran hypothesis of the sacrament, technically distinguished by the title *consubstantiation*. According to this view, the body and blood of Christ are not actually substituted supernaturally for the elements; the bread and wine remain unchanged, in their essence as well as in their properties. But still the body and blood of Christ are in their very substance *present*, where the supper is administered. The presence is not indeed bound to the elements, apart from their sacramental use. It holds only in the moment and form of this use as such; a mystery in this respect, transcending all the common laws of reason and nature. It is however a true, corporal presence of the blessed Saviour. Hence his body is received by the worshipper *orally*, though not in the form and under the quality of common food; and so not by believers simply, but by unbelievers also, to their own condemnation. The dogma was allowed in the end to involve also, by necessary consequence, the ubiquity of Christ's glorified body. Bread and wine retain their own nature, but Christ, who is in virtue of the *communicatio idiomatum* present in his human nature in all places where he may please to be, imparts his true flesh and blood, *in, with* and *under* the outward signs to all communicants, whether with or without faith, by the inherent power of the ordinance itself.*

In opposition to this view, the Reformed Church taught that the participation of Christ's flesh and blood in the Lord's Supper is *spiritual* only, and in no sense corporal. The idea of a local presence in the case, was utterly rejected. The elements cannot be said to comprehend or include the body of the Saviour in any sense. It is not *there*, but remains constantly in heaven, according to the scriptures. It is not handled by the minister and taken into the mouth of the communicant. The manducation of it is not oral, but only by faith. It is present in fruition accordingly to believers only in the exercise of faith; the impenitent and unbelieving receive only the naked symbols, bread and wine, without any spiritual advantage to their own souls.†

---

*Credimus, docemus at confitemur, quod in Cœna Domini corpus at sanguis Christi vere at substantialiter sint præsentia, et quod una cum pane et vino vere distribuantur atque sumantur.—Credimus, corpus et sanguinem Christi non tantum spiritualiter per fidem, *sed eliam ore*, non tamen Capernaitice, sed supernaturali et cœlesti modo, ratione sacramentalis unionis, cum pane et vino sumi.—Credimus, quod non tantum vere in Christum credentes, et qui digne ad Cœnam Domini accedunt, *verum etiam indigni et infideles* verum corpus et sanguinem Christi sumant. *Form. Conc. Art.* VII. *Hase, Lib. Symbol. p.* 599, 600.

†Ego Christum in cœlesti sua sede relinquens, arcana spiritus ejus influentia contentus sum, ut nos carne sua pascat.—Neque enim aliter Christum in Cœna statuo præsentem, nisi

Thus we have the doctrine defined and circumscribed on both sides; with proper distinction from all that may be considered a tendency to Rationalism in one direction, and from all that may be counted a tendency to Romanism in the other. It allows the *presence* of Christ's person in the sacrament, including even his flesh and blood, so far as the actual participation of the believer is concerned. Even the term *real presence*, Calvin tells us he was willing to employ, if it were to be understood as synonymous with *true* presence; by which he means a presence that brings Christ truly into communion with the believer in his human nature, as well as in his divine nature.* The word *real*, however, was understood ordinarily to denote a local, corporal presence, and on this account was not approved. To guard against this, it may be qualified by the word *spiritual*; and the expression will then be quite suitable to the nature of the doctrine, as it has been now explained. A *real* presence, in opposition to the notion that Christ's flesh and blood are not made present to the communicant in *any* way. A *spiritual* real presence, in opposition to the idea that Christ's body is in the elements in a local or corporal manner. Not real simply, and not spiritual simply; but real, and yet spiritual at the same time. The body of Christ is in heaven, the believer on earth; but by the power of the Holy Ghost, nevertheless, the obstacle of such vast local distance is fully overcome, so that in the sacramental act, while the outward symbols are received in an outward way, the very body and blood of Christ are at the same time inwardly and supernaturally communicated to the worthy receiver, for the real nourishment of his new life. Not that the material particles of Christ's body are supposed to be carried over, by this supernatural process, into the believer's person.† The

---

quia fidelium mentes, sicuti illa est cœlestis actio, fide supra mundum evehuntur, et Christus Spiritus sui virtute obstaculam, quod afferre poterat loci distantia, tollens, se membris suis conjungit.—Hæc nostra definitio est, spiritualiter a nobis manducari Christi carnem, quit non aliter animas vivificat, quam pane vegetatur corpus; tantum a nobis excluditur subtantiæ transfusio. Westphalo non aliter caro vivifica est, quam si ejus substantia *voretur*. Hoc crimen est nostrum, obviis ulnis tale monstrum non amplecti. *Calv. Opp. T.* IX. *p.* 668, 669.

*Communicari nobis Christi corpus et sanguinem, nullus nostrum negat. Qualis autem sit corporis et sanguinis Domini communicatio, quæritur. Carnalem isti palam et simpliciter asserere quomodo sudeant miror. Spiritualem cum dicimus, fremunt, quasi hac voce *realem*, ut vulgo loquuntur, tollamus. Nos vero, si reale pro vero accipiant, et fallaci vel imaginario opponant, barbare loqui mallemus, quam pugnis materiam præbere. . . . Placidis et moderatis hoc testatum volo, ita secundum nos spiritualem esse communicationis modum, ut *reipsa* Christo fruamur. Hac modo ratione contenti simus, ultra quam nemo nisi valde litigiosus insurget, vivificam nobis est Christi carnem, quid ex ea spiritualem in animas nostras vitam Christus instillat; eam quoque a nobis manducari, dum in corpus unum fide cum Christo coalescimus, ut noster factus nobiscum sua omnia communicet. *Calv. Opp. T.* IX. *p.* 657, 658.—Præsentiam carnis Christi in Cœna urget Westphalus: nos simpliciter non negamus, modo nobiscum fide sursum conscendat. *Ib. p.* 668.

†Ingenue interea confiteor, *mixturam* carnis Christi cum anima nostra, vel trans-

communion is spiritual, not material. It is a participation of the Saviour's life. Of his life, however, as human, subsisting in a true bodily form. The living energy, the vivific virtue, as Calvin styles it, of Christ's flesh, is made to flow over into the communicant, making him more and more one with Christ himself, and thus more and more an heir of the same immortality that is brought to light in his person.

Two points in particular, in the theory now exhibited, require to be held clearly in view.

The first is, that the sacrament is made to carry with it an *objective* force, so far as its principal design is concerned. It is not simply suggestive, commemorative, or representational. It is not a sign, a picture, deriving its significance from the mind of the beholder. The virtue which it possesses is not put into it by the faith of the worshipper in the first place, to be taken out of it again by the same faith, in the same form. It is not imagined of course in the case that the ordinance can have any virtue *without* faith, that it can confer grace in a purely mechanical way. All thought of the *opus operatum*, in this sense, is utterly repudiated. Still faith does not properly clothe the sacrament with its power. It is the condition of its efficacy for the communicant, but not the principle of the power itself. This belongs to the institution in its own nature. The signs are bound to what they represent, not subjectively simply in the thought of the worshipper, but objectively, by the force of a divine appointment. The union indeed is not natural but sacramental. The grace is not comprehended *in* the elements, as its depository and vehicle outwardly considered. But the union is none the less real and firm, on this account. The grace goes inseparably along with the signs, and is truly present for all who are prepared to make it their own. The signs in this view are also *seals*; not simply as they attest the truth and reality of the grace in a general way, but as they authenticate also its presence under the sacramental exhibition itself. This is what we mean by the objective force of the institution; and this, we say, is one point that must always be kept in view, in looking at the doctrine that is now the subject of our attention.*

fusionem, qualis ab ipsis docetur, me repudiare; quia nobis sufficit, Christum e carnis suæ substantia vitam in animas nostras spirare, imo *propriam* in nos *vitam* diffundere, quamvis in nos non ingrediatur ipse Christi caro. *Calv. Inst.* IV. 17, 32.—Manet tamen *integer homo* Christus in cœlo. *Id. Opp. T.* IX., *p.* 699.

*Obtendit (Westphalus) *verbo* fieri sacramentum, *non fide nostra.* Hoc ut *concedam,* nondum tamen obtinet promiscue Christum canibus et porcis ita prostitui, ut carne ejus vescantur. Neque enim desinit e cœlo pluere Deus, licet pluviæ liquorem saxa et rupes non concipiant. *Calv. Opp. T.* IX., *p.* 674.—Nos ita asserimus, *omnibus* offerri in sacramento Christi corpus et sauguinem, ut soli fideles inæstimabili hoc thesauro fruantur: etsi autem incredulitas januam Christo claudit, ut priventur ejus beneficio qui ad Cœnam impure accedunt, negamus tamen quicquam decedere ex sacramenti natura; quia panis semper verum est pignus carnis Christi, et vinum sanguinis, veraque utriusque exhibitio semper

The other point to be steadily kept in sight is, that the invisible grace of the sacrament, according to the doctrine, is the substantial life of the Saviour himself, particularly in his human nature. He became flesh for the life of the world, and our communion with him, involves a real participation in him as the principle of life *under this form.* Hence in the mystery of the Supper, his flesh and blood are really exhibited always in their essential force and power, and really received by every worthy communicant.

Such is the proper sacramental doctrine of the Reformed Church as it stood in the Sixteenth century. It is easy to show that it labours under serious difficulties. With these however at present, we have no concern. They can have no bearing one way or another, upon the simply historical inquiry in which we are now engaged. My object has been thus far only to describe and define the doctrine itself. It remains now to show, that it was in fact, as thus described and defined, the accredited established doctrine of the Reformed Church, in the period to which the inquiry refers.

---

constat ex parte Dei. Adversarii nostri corpus et sanguinem ita sub pane et vino includunt, ut sine ulla fide vorentur ab impiis. *Ib. p.* 699.

SECTION II.

HISTORICAL EVIDENCE.

The *Reformed* Church, as distinguished from the Lutheran, cannot be said to have taken its rise in the person of any single man, or in the religious life of any particular country, separately considered. The great Protestant movement revealed itself from the beginning, under this general form, in different countries, independently of all merely outward historical connection. At the same time, the characteristic differences of doctrine between the two confessions were not clearly and fully developed from the start, on either side. The difference was felt, and in a certain way also expressed. But time was needed to carry it out to its last, satisfactory, logical statement, for the understanding. Thus the Lutheran system, after years of controversy, appears fairly developed, under all its true and necessary distinctions, only in the *Form of Concord*, framed towards the close of the century. And thus also in the same way, the sacramental dogma of the Reformed Church can be understood fairly, not from the form in which it may be found exhibited at the outset of the controversy, but only from the terms in which we find it stated at a later period, after its true substance and contents had come to be properly apprehended and defined at every point, with proper antithesis to all the errors with which it was felt to be surrounded.

It is not necessary then that we should trouble ourselves much, in the present inquiry, about the opinions of *Zuingli*, or *Oecolampadius*, or of the Swiss Reformed Church generally in their day on the subject of the Lord's Supper. The Reformed Church, as a whole, is not historically derived from Switzerland, in any such sense that it could ever be said to be bound legitimately in its faith by the theological views of that country, in the precise form in which they were held and published at the birth of the Reformation. Much less may it be imagined that any such obligation has existed, as it regards the authority of the great Reformer of Zurich in a separate view. With all his merits, entitling him as they do to the respect of the Protestant world through all ages, the relation of Zuingli to the proper life of the Reformed Church, must be allowed to have been exceedingly external and accidental. This appears in the fact, that he has left behind him no work, which has ever been held to be of symbolical force for any portion of the Church. In such circumstances, we are not at liberty of course to appeal to his authority, if it had been ever so clearly

expressed, in the case before us, as carrying with it any decisive weight.*
And just as little can we consider any judgment conclusive, which it may
be attempted to derive from the Helvetic Church generally, in the first
years of its history. Its views, in the nature of the case, were more or less,
chaotic and contradictory. Theological investigation, and much exercise
in the way of controversy, were still required to give them proper shape
and form. This work was accomplished gradually with the onward course
of history, and became complete especially, about the middle of the
century, through the instrumentality of that vast mind, which for years
served the whole Reformed Church as its central organ, in the city of
Geneva.

To learn the true character, then, of the eucharistic doctrine of the
Reformed Church in the sixteenth century, we must have recourse to the
time when the doctrine had become properly defined and settled in the
Church itself. The representations of this period are not to be ruled and
interpreted by statements drawn from an earlier day, but on the contrary,
these earlier statements, springing as they do from a comparatively
rudimental state of Protestant theology, must be of right interpreted and
ruled by the form in which the doctrine is made to appear afterwards,
when the same theology had become more complete. This later form of

---

*The view of Zuingli, with regard to the Lord's Supper, is not always consistent with
itself. At times, he appears to take the proper ground, as afterwards more clearly established
in the Reformed Church; and it may well be doubted whether he could have been de-
liberately satisfied at all with the poor, bald conception, which is too often made to pass
under the authority of his name at the present time. Still it must be confessed, that his
theory of the sacraments, altogether, was quite too low, as compared with the doctrine of
Calvin for instance, or the Heidelberg Catechism; and in some cases he allows himself to
speak of them in a way that sounds perfectly rationalistic. He tells us indeed: "Verum
Christi corpus credimus in Cœna sacramentaliter et spiritualiter edi, a religiosa, fideli et
sancta mente;" but in the same connection resolves all into the most common moral
influence. For the sacraments have their value and efficacy, he says, in this; *that* they are
venerable institutions of Christ—*that* they are *testimony* to great facts—*that* they are made
to *stand for* the things they represent and to bear their *names*—*that* these things are of vast
worth, and *reflect* their own value on their signs, as a queen's wedding-ring, for instance,
is more than all her other rings, however precious besides—*that* there is an *analogy* or
resemblance between the signs and the things they signify—*that* they serve as *sensible
helps* to our faith—and *that* they have, finally, the force of an *oath*. See his *Clara Expos.
Fidei*, addressed to the King of France shortly before his death, and published'afterwards
in the year 1536: quoted by *Hospinian*, II., p. 239–241. "Credo, omnia sacramenta tam
abesse, ut gratiam conferant, ut *ne offerant* quidem aut dispensent." *Ad. Car. Imp. Fidei
Ratio.* "Sunt sacramenta signa vel ceremoniæ—quibus se homo *ecclesiæ probat* aut
candidatum aut militem esse Christi, redduntque ecclesiam totam potius certiorem de tua
fide, quam te." *De Vera et Falsa Rel.* This is low enough, certainly, and in full
contradiction to the true Reformed doctrine. Calvin went so far as to call it *profane*. See
quotation from a letter to *Viret*, in *Henry's Leben J. Calvin's*, vol. I., p. 271: Nunquam ejus
(Zuinglii) omnia legi. Fortassis sub finem vitæ retractavit et correxit, quæ primum invito
exciderant. Sed in scriptis prioribus memini, *quam profana* sit ejus de sacramentis
sententia.

the doctrine moreover, as developed and enforced especially by Calvin, is the same which it is found to carry in the symbolical books of the Church generally, and in this view again must be regarded of course as of paramount and exclusive authority in the present inquiry.

In what is now said, however, it is not intended to allow that the doctrine of the Reformed Church on the subject of the sacrament was essentially different at the start from what it came to be afterwards. The doctrine we suppose to have been substantially the same, in the consciousness of the Church, from the beginning. Calvin did not bring in a new faith at this point, to supplant that which had previously prevailed. He simply contributed to the right understanding, and full enunciation of the faith which was already at hand. It may be admitted that this had been held with some measure of confusion. It is difficult to say what Zuingli believed. Probably his view was by no means clear and fixed to his own mind. Uncertainty and contradiction too appear in the Helvetic creed, to some extent, after his death. But it is still sufficiently plain, that the creed itself was felt to include something more than the conception of a merely symbolical force in the sacrament. We see in it always an internal demand at least for a higher form of expression, such as the doctrine was brought subsequently to assume, through the influence mainly of Calvin.

Early Helvetic Church.

Thus with all their opposition to Luther's idea of a bodily presence, the old Helvetic divines teach clearly that the sacraments carry with them an *objective* force. The signs are held to *exhibit* in fact what they represent. And this. in the case of the Lord's Supper, is such a participation on the part of the soul in Christ, as involves a real connection with the power of his whole life, by which believers may be said to be nourished with his very body and blood. A view altogether, which is much higher certainly than that commonly entertained in our own time, by those who pretend to agree here with the faith of the original Swiss Church.

In illustration and proof of what is now said, I may refer even to what is styled the *First Confession of Basel*; published January, 1534, in compliance with Bucer's request; to show the world that the Swiss were not fairly liable to the reproach of "having the Supper without Christ." It is supposed to have been the production originally of *Oecolampadius*, revised and improved by his successor *Oswald Myconius*. On the subject of the Lord's Supper, Art. VI. (*Hospinian, Hist. Sacram. Pars Altera*, p. 221,) it uses the following language:

> "In the Lord's Supper, (in which with the bread and wine of the Lord are represented and offered to us by the minister of the church the true body and blood of Christ,) bread and wine remain unchanged. We

firmly believe, however, that Christ himself [ipsummet Christum] is the
food of believing souls unto eternal life; and that our souls, by true faith
upon Christ crucified, are made to eat and drink the flesh and blood of
Christ; so that we, members of his body as of our only head, live in
him, as he also lives in us; whereby we shall at the last day, by him and
in him, rise to everlasting joy and blessedness."

The strength of this language, it must be added, is in some measure
reduced by two or three brief qualifying explanations thrown into the
margin; by which we are reminded that it is the *soul* only that is thus fed
and nourished, in a *spiritual* way, by the apprehension of Christ, and that
the true, natural and substantial body of the Saviour is in no sense
included in the ordinance. The whole representation too is considerably
ambiguous, as compared with the statements of a later time. But still it
shows the sense of something deeper in the doctrine, than could well be
made intelligible by words. The elements are more than signs simply and
outward pledges. They *offer* what they signify; and this is, in some way,
a *real* communication with the *human* Christ.

More distinct and full, in this view, in some respects, is the Second
Confession of Basel, more commonly known as the *First Helvetic*. It was
framed by *Bullinger, Myconius, and Grynaeus*, A.D. 1536, under the appointment of an ecclesiastical convention, which had assembled in the
name of the different Protestant cantons at Basel for this purpose; by
whose authority also it was afterwards ratified and made public. On the
subject of the sacraments, it speaks thus:

"The signs called *sacraments* are two, namely baptism and the
Lord's Supper. These sacraments are expressive holy signs of high
secret things; not however naked and empty signs; but they consist of
signs and real things. For in baptism the water is the sign, but the thing
itself is regeneration and adoption into the family of God. In the Lord's
Supper or eucharist the bread and wine are the signs, but the spiritual
realities are the communion of the body and blood of Christ, the
salvation procured on the cross and the forgiveness of sins. These real
spiritual things are received by faith, as the signs are in a bodily way."
Art. 20.

Here we are taught expressly, that the sacraments are not simply
signs, nor yet pledges merely, of a grace in no way bound to their
particular constitution. But they consist of real things as well as signs.
There is an actual *exhibition* of these real things in the ordinances
themselves. They are there independently of all thought or feeling on the
part of the worshipper; although, of course, they can become his only by

faith. Thus baptism is described, in the next article, as the "laver of
regeneration, which the Lord extends, by a visible sign, to his elect,

through the ministry of the church." And then of the Lord's Supper, it is said again:

> "Concerning the mystical Supper we thus judge, that the Lord in it truly offers to his people his own body and blood, that is himself, to the end that he may live more and more in them, and they in him. Not that the body and blood of the Lord are naturally united with the bread and wine, or locally included in them, or are made carnally present in any way; but that the bread and wine are, by divine appointment, symbols under which, by the Lord himself, through the ministry of the church, the true communication of his body and blood is exhibited, not as perishable food for the belly, but as the aliment of eternal life." *Art.* 23. (*Niemeyer's Col. Conf.* p. 112.)

This Confession was afterwards submitted to the examination of Luther, by Bucer and Capito, on the occasion of the meeting held at Wittemberg the same year, through the agency of the Strasburg divines, for the purpose of effecting, if possible, a reconciliation between the two confessions; the result of which was the celebrated *Wittemberg Concord.* Strange to tell, Luther pronounced the Confession orthodox; although it contradicts palpably his own system, and falls short even of the full force of the Reformed doctrine, as afterwards more clearly and successfully stated.

Calvin.

To gain a full view of the doctrine, as already intimated, we must have recourse especially to Calvin. No authority in the case can be entitled to greater respect. He was emphatically the great theologian of his age. On this point, moreover, he is clearly the organ and interpreter of the mind of the church, in whose bosom he stood. It will not do to speak of his view of the Lord's supper as the private fancy only of a single man. If there be any point clear in the history of the time, it is that the doctrine exhibited by Calvin on this subject is to be regarded as the same, in all substantial points, that was recognized in the end as of general symbolical authority, throughout the whole Reformed Church, in the sixteenth century.

It is not necessary to bring forward quotations in detail, for the purpose of showing the true character of the view he held, or its correspondence with the doctrine which has been already described, as the true and proper doctrine of the Reformed Church in the beginning of its history. That description has been in fact taken mainly from Calvin himself, and is supported accordingly by references to his writings at every point already. The difficulty here is, not to find proofs and illustrations, but to make choice among the multitude that are presented. Calvin has written much on the Lord's Supper; and he is always clear, always consistent, always true to himself. Over and over again, in all forms of expression and explanation, he tells us, that Christ's body is indeed locally in heaven only, and in no sense included in the elements; that he can be apprehended by faith only, and not at all by the hands or lips; that nothing is to be imagined like a transfusion or intromission of the particles of his body, materially considered, into our persons. And yet that our communion with him, notwithstanding, by the power of the Holy Ghost, involves a real participation—not in his doctrine merely—not in his promises merely—not in the sensible in manifestations of his love merely—not in his righteousness and merit merely—not in the gifts and endowments of his Spirit merely; but in his own true substantial life itself; and this not as comprehended in his divine nature merely, but most immediately and peculiarly as embodied in his humanity itself, for us men and our salvation. The Word became flesh, according to this view, for the purpose not simply of effecting a salvation that might become available for men in an *outward* way, but to open a fountain of life *in* our nature itself, that might thenceforward continue to flow over to other men, as a vivific stream, to the end of time. The flesh of Christ, then, or his humanity, forms the medium, and the *only* medium, by which it is possible for us to be inserted into his life. To have part in him at all, we must be joined to him in the flesh; and this not by the bond of our common relationship to Adam, but by the force of a direct implantation through the Spirit, into the person of Christ himself.

"That Christ is the bread of life," he says in his Institutes IV. 17, 5, "by which believers are nourished to eternal salvation, there is no man, not entirely destitute of religion, who hesitates to acknowledge; though all are not equally agreed respecting the manner of partaking of him. For there are some who define in a word, that to eat the flesh of Christ and to drink his blood, is no other than to believe in Christ himself. But I conceive that in that remarkable discourse in which Christ recommends us to feed upon his body, he intended to teach us something more striking and sublime; namely that we are quickened by a real participation of him, which he designates by the terms of *eating* and *drinking*, that no person might suppose the life which we receive from him to consist in simple knowledge. For as it is not *seeing* bread, but *eating* it, that administers nourishment to the body, so it is necessary for the soul to have a true and complete participation of Christ, that by his power it may be quickened into spiritual life. At the same time, we confess that there is no other eating than by faith, as it is impossible to imagine any other; but the difference between me and those whose opinion I now oppose is this. They consider eating to be the same thing as believing; while I say, that in believing we eat the flesh of Christ, because he is made ours actually by faith, and that this eating is the fruit and effect of faith. Or to express it more plainly, they consider the eating to be faith itself; but I apprehend it to be rather a consequence of faith."

Again, (IV. 17. 8,) he tells us that Christ was from the beginning that life giving Word of the Father, from which all things have derived their existence. "In him was life," the source and fountain of all creaturely existence, even before he appeared in our nature. But this "life was manifested," when he assumed our flesh, to restore the ruin produced by the fall. "For though he diffused his influence over the whole creation before that period, yet because man was alienated from God by sin, had lost the participation of life, and saw on every side nothing but impending death, it was necessary to his recovery of any hope of immortality, that he should be received into the communion of that Word. For what confidence can it raise in any one, to hear only that the fulness of life is comprehended in the Word of God, a great way off, whilst in himself and all around nothing but death is presented to his eyes! Now, however, since that fountain of life has come to dwell in our flesh, it is no longer thus hidden from us by distance, but open to our reach and free use. The very flesh moreover in which he dwells is made to be vivific for us, that we may be nourished by it to immortality. 'I am the living bread,' he says, 'which came down from heaven; and the bread that I will give is my flesh, which I will give for the life of the world.' (John 6: 48, 51.) In these words he teaches, not simply that he is Life, as the everlasting Word descending to us from heaven, but that in thus descending he has infused this virtue also into the flesh with which he clothed himself, in order that life might flow over to us from it continually."

Again, sect. 10: "We conclude that our souls are fed by the flesh and blood of Christ, just as our corporeal life is preserved and sustained by bread and wine. For the analogy of the sign would not hold, if our souls did not find their aliment in Christ; which however cannot be the case, unless Christ truly coalesce into one with us, and support us through the use of his flesh and blood. It may seem incredible indeed that the flesh of Christ should reach us from such immense local distance, so as to become our food. But we must remember how far the secret power of the Holy Spirit transcends all our senses, and what folly it must ever be to think of reducing his immensity to our measure. Let faith embrace then what the understanding cannot grasp, namely that the Spirit unites things which are locally separated. Now this sacred communication of his flesh and blood, by which Christ transfuses his life into us, just as if he penetrated our bones and marrow, he testifies and seals also in the holy supper; not by the exhibition of a vain and empty sign, but by putting forth there such an energy of his Spirit as fulfils what he promises. What is thus attested he offers and exhibits to all who approach the spiritual banquet. It is however fruitfully received by believers only, who accept such vast grace with inward gratitude and trust."

The following passage, sect. 11, is entitled to particular attention, as bringing strongly into view some of the leading points of the doctrine, in a way not to be misunderstood or contradicted.

"I say then, (what has always been held in the church, and is still taught by all of sound feeling,) that the sacred mystery of the Supper consists of two parts; the corporeal *signs*, which being placed before our eyes represent to us invisible things according to the infirmity of our apprehension; and the *spiritual truth*, which these symbols typify and exhibit. This last I am accustomed to describe in a familiar way, as including three things; the *signification*, the matter answering to this, and the virtue or effect which follows from both. The *signification* holds in the promises, which are in some sense interwoven with the sign. What I call the *matter* or *substance*, is Christ, with his death and resurrection. By the *effect* I mean redemption, righteousness, sanctification, eternal life, and all the other benefits which Christ confers upon us. Moreover, though all these things have a relation to faith, I allow no room for the cavil, that, in representing Christ to be received by faith, I make him an object simply of the understanding or imagination. For the promises present him to us, not that we may rest in contemplation merely and naked notion, but that we may enjoy him in the way of real participation. And truly, I see not how any one can have confidence, that he has redemption and righteousness by the cross of Christ, and life by his death, if he have not in the first place a true communion with Christ himself. For those benefits could never reach us if Christ did not first make himself ours. I say, then, that in the mystery of the Supper, under the symbols of bread and wine, Christ is truly presented to us, and so his body and blood, in which he fulfilled all obedience to procure our justification; in order that we may first coalesce with him into one body, and then, being thus made partakers of his substance, may experience the virtue also which belongs to him, in the participation of all blessings."

The *Catechism of Geneva* was formed by Calvin in the year 1536, (enlarged and improved in 1541,) for the use of the Church whose name it bears. Take from it the following extract on the subject of the Lord's Supper:

> *Quest.* Why is the Lord's body figured by *bread* and his blood by *wine*?
>
> *Ans.* To teach us, that such virtue as bread has in nourishing our bodies for the support of the present life, the same is in the body of the Lord for the spiritual nourishment of our souls; and that as by wine the hearts of men are exhilarated, their strength refreshed, the whole man invigorated, so our souls receive like benefits from the Lord's blood.
>
> *Q.* Do we then eat the body and blood of the Lord?
>
> *A.* We do. For since the whole hope of our salvation consists in this, that his obedience, which he rendered to the Father, may be placed to our credit as though it were our own, it is necessary that he himself should be possessed by us. He does not communicate his benefits to us except as he makes himself ours.

CALVINISTIC DOCTRINE OF THE LORD'S SUPPER.

Q. But did he not give himself to be ours at that time, when be exposed himself to death, that he might reconcile us, being redeemed from the sentence of death, to the Father?

A. That is true. But it is not enough for us unless we receive him now, in order that the efficacy and fruit of his death may reach us.

Q. Is not the mode of receiving him, however, by faith?

A. This I allow; but add at the same time, that this takes place, not only as we believe that he died to redeem us from death, and rose again to acquire life for us, but as we acknowledge also that he dwells in us, and that we are joined to him with such union as holds between members and their proper head; in order that by the grace of this union, we may become partakers of all his benefits."—Sect. v. (*Niemeyer's Coll. p.* 164, 165.)

One more extract from the great Reformer must suffice. It is taken from a short appendix to his tract, *De vera participatione carnis et sanguinis Christi in sacra cœna,* written against the virulent *Hesshuss* in the year 1561, near the close of his life. The object of the appendix is to set forth distinctly the points of agreement and disagreement, in the case of the sacramental question, with a view to ultimate concord. After stating the points with regard to which both sides were agreed, touching the sacraments in general and the Lord's supper in particular; this among the rest, that Christ in the Supper really and efficaciously fulfils all that the analogy of the signs demands, so that there is offered to us a true communication with his body and blood; he goes on to say:

"It remains to notice the points with regard to which it is still unsettled, in what light they are to be viewed or represented.

All however, who are possessed of sound judgment, and approach the subject at the same time, without passion, must allow that the controversy is simply on the *mode* of eating; since we openly and ingenuously affirm, that Christ becomes ours, in order that he may afterwards impart to us the benefits he possesses; that his body also was not only once offered for our salvation, when he was slain upon the cross to expiate sin, but is daily extended to us for our nourishment; so that while he himself dwells in us, we may have an interest also in all his blessings. We teach finally, that he is vivific because he inspires his life into us, just as we derive strength from the nutriment of bread. It is in fixing the method of eating then, that contentions arise. Now our definition is, that the body of Christ is eaten, inasmuch as it forms the spiritual aliment of the soul. We call it aliment again in this sense, because by the incomprehensible power of his Spirit, he inspires into us his own life, so that it becomes common to us with himself, in the same way precisely as the vital sap from the root of a tree diffuses itself into the branches, or as vigor flows from the head of the body into its several members. In this definition, there is nothing captious, nothing obscure, nothing ambiguous or deceitful.

That some, not satisfied with this clear simplicity, require the body of Christ to be swallowed, is agreeable neither to the authority of Scripture nor the testimony of the ancient Church; and it is marvellous that men possessed of moderate judgment and learning, should contend so pertinaciously for the new comment. What the Scriptures teach is not at all called by us into question, namely, that the flesh of Christ is truly meat and his blood truly drink; since they are truly received by us, and avail to solid life. We profess also that this communication is exhibited in the Sacred Supper. Whoever insists on more, certainly exceeds proper limits."

Again: "It is a vain dispute moreover that is made about the twofold body. The character of Christ's flesh was indeed changed when it was received into celestial glory; whatever was terrene, mortal or perishable, it now put off. Still however it must be maintained, that no other body can be vivific for us, or may be counted meat indeed, save that which was crucified to atone for our sins; as the sound of the words also indicates. The same body then which the Son of God once offered in sacrifice to the Father, he offers to us daily in the Supper, that it may be our spiritual aliment. Only that must be held which has been already intimated as to the mode, that it is not necessary that the essence of the flesh should descend from heaven in order that we may be fed by it; but that the power of the Spirit is sufficient to penetrate through all impediments, and to surmount all local distance. At the same time we do not deny, that the mode here is incomprehensible to human thought; for flesh naturally could neither be the life of the soul, nor exert its power upon us from heaven, and not without reason is the communication, which makes us flesh of Christ's flesh and bone of his bones, denominated by Paul a great mystery. In the sacred Supper then we acknowledge it a miracle, transcending both nature an our own understanding, that Christ's life is made common to us with himself, and his flesh given to us as aliment. Only let all comments be kept at a distance that are repugnant to the definition already given, such as those concerning the ubiquity of the body, or its secret inclusion under the symbol of bread, or its substantial presence upon the earth.

These things being disposed of, a doubt still appears with respect to the word *substance*, which is readily allayed, if we put away the crass imagination of a manducation of the flesh, as though it were like corporal food, that being taken into the mouth is received by the belly. For if this absurdity be removed, there is no reason why we should deny that we are fed with Christ's flesh substantially; since we truly coalesce with him into one body by faith, and are thus made one with him. Whence it follows that we are joined with him by substantial connection, just as substantial vigor flows down from the head into the members. The definition must stand then, that we are made to partake of Christ's flesh substantially; not in the way of any carnal mixture, or as if the flesh of Christ drawn down from heaven entered into us, or were swallowed with the mouth; but because the flesh of Christ as to its power and efficacy vivifies our souls, not otherwise than the body is nourished by the substance of bread and wine.

Another subject of controversy is the word *spiritually*; to which many are averse, because they think that it implies something imaginary or empty. On the contrary however, the body of Christ is said to be given to us spiritually in the Supper, because the secret energy of the Holy Spirit causes things that are separated by local distance to be notwithstanding joined together; so that life is made to reach into us from heaven out of the flesh of Christ; which power and faculty of vivification may be said not unsuitably to be something abstracted from his substance, provided only it be taken in a sound sense, namely that Christ's body remains in heaven, while nevertheless life flows out from his substance and reaches to us who sojourn upon the earth."—*Calv. Opp. edit. Amstelod. Tom.* IX., *p.* 743, 744.

It seems strange in view of such quotations as have now been presented, that any should think of still calling in question Calvin's faith in the doctrine of a real communication with Christ's life in the Lord's Supper. It will not do to talk of figurative language in the case, and to remind us that all is resolved by him constantly into a *spiritual* manduca- tion as distinguished front one that is oral and physical. This is allowed on all hands; he was no Romanist nor Lutheran. But if there ever was a clear case we have one here, when we affirm that Calvin's *spiritual* manduca- tion was intended by himself to include full as much, in the case of believers, as was involved in the Lutheran hypothesis itself, that is a true participation of the substantial life of Christ's body and blood, according to the faith of the universal Church from the beginning. To guard against carnal misconstruction, he was accustomed indeed to speak of this as effected by the ascent of the soul to Christ in heaven, through the power of the Holy Ghost, rather than by a proper *descent* of Christ's nature in the sacrament to the earth. But this affects not at all the substance of his doctrine. In whatever way it might be supposed to occur, he held and taught the *fact* of a real presence of the Saviour's human life, for the soul of the believer, in the sacramental transaction. Of this presence and communication too, the sacrament as such was by the Spirit the true supernatural vehicle and bearer. The Lutherans have pretended indeed, that he acknowledged no inward connection between the institution and the grace it represented. But this is manifestly false. He does, to be sure, say of the *signs* that they have no virtue or force in themselves *as such*. Augustine says the same thing. But both Calvin and Augustine hold the *transaction* to be more than what falls upon the senses. In this view, it is held to be truly and properly the form, under which and by which, through the Spirit, Christ is made present. Thus on 1 Cor. X. 3, he says: "The Papists confound sign and thing; profane men, such as Schwenkfeld and others like him, rend them asunder; let *us* keep the middle; that is, let us hold the conjunction established by the Lord, but with proper distinction, so as not to transfer rashly to one what belongs to the other." So, still more clearly, on 1 Cor. XI. 24. "Why is the appellation *body* attributed to the bread? All will allow, I presume, for the same reason that John denominates a dove the Holy Ghost. Thus for it is agreed. But now the Holy Ghost was so called, because he had appeared under the form (*sub specie*) of a dove; whence the name is transferred to the visible sign. And why should we deny a similar metonymy here, by which the name of the body is attributed to the bread, because it is its sign and symbol." Next comes the meaning of the metonymy itself. It is more, he tells us, than a figure or a picture. "The dove is called the Spirit, as being the sure pledge (*tessera*) of the Spirit's invisible presence. So the bread is Christ's body, as it assures us certainly of the exhibition of what it represents, or because the Lord in extending to us that visible symbol, gives us in fact along with it his own body; for Christ is no juggler, to mock us with empty appearances. Hence it is to me beyond all controversy, that the reality is here joined with the sign, or in other words that, so far as spiritual virtue is concerned, we do as truly partake of Christ's body as we eat the bread."*

According to *Schleiermacher* (Der. chr. Glaube, § 140), the Calvinistic view of the Lord's Supper connects, not indeed with the elements as such, but with the act of eating and drinking, not simply such a spiritual enjoyment of Christ as was taught by Zuingli; but the real presence of his body and blood to be had no where else (die nirgend sonst zu habende wirkliche Gegenwart seines Leibes und Blutes). Both views, the Lutheran and Calvinistic, he tells us, acknowledge a real presence of Christ's body and blood. It will hardly be pretended, that such a theo-

---

*F. D. *Maurice*, of King's College, London, in his late work entitled *The Kingdom of Christ*, which has attracted some attention, falls grossly into the same error with regard to Calvin, which it is here attempted to expose. The Calvinist, he says, (vol. II., p. 105,) "requires that we should suppose there is no object present, unless there be something which perceives it; and having at into this contradiction, the next step is to suppose that faith is not a receptive, but a creative power; that it *makes* the thing which it believes." He admits, at the same time, "that there were characteristics in the creed of the Calvinist, which ought especially to have delivered him" from the general tendency of Protestantism to run into this false view. So far as Calvin himself is concerned, it must be perfectly plain from the testimony which has now been presented, that the charge quoted is utterly erroneous. He taught clearly an *objective* presence of Christ's life in the sacramental transaction as such, which could become available only through faith, but which faith could not be said, in any sense, to create; since the very guilt of the unworthy communicant proceeds mainly from this, that he treats the actually present grace as though it were a mere figment, *not discerning the Lord's body.* That the "Calvinist" of modern date has too often fallen into the contradiction of making faith creative, in the sacrament, rather than receptive, is indeed most painfully true. But in doing so he has fallen away entirely from the standpoint of the man whose name he professes to honour. Whether this stand. point is to be held itself responsible for the apostacy, is another question, perfectly legitimate and of immense practical importance; which it becomes the friends of the *Reformed* Church to look steadily in the face. If Calvinism—the system of Geneva—*necessarily* runs here into Zuinglianism, we may, indeed, well despair of the whole interest. For most assuredly no Church can stand, that is found to be constitutionally *unsacramental.*

logian as Schleiermacher has mistaken the sense of Calvin in this case. It deserves to be noted besides, that this great master of ratiocination, with all his cool and free spirit of theological inquiry, finds no absurdity or contradiction whatever in the Calvinistic theory itself. He prefers it on the whole to the view of Luther: although he thinks the truth may require still some higher middle theory, in which both at last shall be reconciled and made complete. The Zuinglian doctrine he says has the advantage of being very clear and easy to be understood; but it is quite too low for the subject.

Farel and Beza.

At the *Colloquy of Worms*, held A.D. 1557, certain delegates presented themselves from the Reformed Gallic Churches, namely, *William Farel*, pastor at the time in Neufchatel, *John Budaeus*, a citizen of Geneva, *Caspar Carmel*, minister of the Church in Paris, and *Theodore Beza*, then professor at Lausanne. They exhibited here a Confession of Faith, which is to be considered important, as embodying not simply their own views, but the views also of the wide religious communion which they represented. In the article of the Lord's Supper it employs the following language, which will be found at once closely coincident with the representation embraced in the extracts just furnished from Calvin:

> "We confess that in the Supper of the Lord not only the benefits of Christ, but the very substance itself of the Son Man; that is, the same true flesh which the Word assumed into perpetual personal union, in which he was born and suffered, rose again and ascended to heaven, and that true blood which he shed for us; are not only signified, or set forth symbolically, typically or in figure, like the memory of something absent, but are truly and really represented, exhibited, and offered for use; in connection with symbols that are by no means naked, but which, so far as God who promises and offers is concerned, always have the thing itself truly and certainly joined with them, whether proposed to believers or unbelievers."

This last clause deserves especially to he noted, as affirming in the strongest manner the *objective* force of the institution. The power which it carries, as the medium of a real communication with the flesh and blood of Christ, is in no sense the product of our piety and faith. It exists in the divine constitution of the ordinance itself; though it can be of no value of course, where no organ is at hand for its reception. The article proceeds:

> "As it regards the mode now in which the thing itself, that is, the true body and true blood of the Lord, is connected with the symbols, we say that it is symbolical or sacramental. We call a sacramental mode not such as is figurative merely, but such as truly and certainly represents,

under the form of visible things, what God along with the symbols exhibits and offers, namely, what we mentioned before, the true body and
blood of Christ; which may show that we retain and defend the presence
of the very body and blood of Christ in the Supper. So that if we have
any controversy with truly pious and learned brethren, it is not
concerning the thing itself, but only concerning the mode of the presence, which is known to God alone, and by us believed.

"Finally, as to the mode in which the thing itself, that is, the
natural and true substance of Christ, is truly and certainly communicated to us, we do not make it to be natural, nor imagine a local
copulation, or a diffusion of Christ's human nature, or that crass and
diabolical transubstantiation, or any gross mingling of the substance of
Christ with ours; but we say that it is a spiritual mode, that is, such as
rests on the incomprehensible energy of God's Spirit, as unfolded to us
in that word of his own, *This is my body.* And we now beg all brethren
dispassionately to consider, whether it is proper that those who thus
think and teach concerning the sacraments of Christ,' should be branded
as infidels and heretics."—*Hospinian, Hist. Sacram. Pars. Alt. p.* 433.

Beza and Peter Martyr.

In the year 1561 a conference was held on the subject of religion, at
Poissy, in France, in the presence of the king of Navarre, and many other
distinguished personages. *Beza*, who was now settled as a minister at
Geneva, and *Peter Martyr*, professor of divinity in Zurich, appeared here,
by special invitation, to represent the interest of the Reformed faith. Beza
on this occasion made a long speech, in exposition of the leading articles
of the new confession, which was characterized by great eloquence and
power, and filled the court and all present with the highest admiration. On
the subject of the Eucharist, he reiterates the view which we find exhibited
in the extract last given; namely, that the communion of the believer with
Christ in this ordinance involves a real participation in his flesh and blood.

"We do not say what some, through misapprehension of our language, have supposed us to teach: that there is in the holy Supper a
commemoration only of the death of our Lord Jesus Christ. Nor do we
say, that we are by it partakers only of the fruit of his death and passion;
but we join the ground also with the produce, (*fundum cum fructibus,*)
which it is found to yield; asserting with Paul, that the bread which we
break by divine appointment, is the *communion*, that is, the communication of Christ's body for us crucified, and the cup which we drink, the
communication of his true blood for us poured out; yea, in that same
substance, which he took in the womb of the virgin, and which he
carried up into heaven. And what is there then, I pray, which *you* can
find in this sacrament, that we too may not seek and find?"—*Hosp. II.
p.* 515.

After this strong statement, he goes on to exclude from the doctrine, in terms equally distinct, the idea of transubstantiation in the first place, and then of every thing like a local comprehension of Christ's body in, with or under the elements, as taught by Luther. In opposition to every such imagination he says: "We affirm that his body is as far removed from the bread and wine, as heaven is exalted high above the earth;" though he adds immediately, that the reality of the communion is in no respect impaired by this consideration; since by the power of faith, in a spiritual way, we still partake of his body and blood "as truly as we see the sacraments with our eyes, touch them with our hands, take them into our mouths, and are nourished and supported by their substance in our corporal life."

The remark that Christ's body and the elements locally considered, are as far apart as heaven and earth, caused a general murmur, we are told, in the assembly, and was made the occasion afterwards of no small reproach. Beza thought, it necessary in consequence to address a letter to the queen of Navarre, craving an opportunity to explain himself more fully on this point. In this he says:

"I was led to the remark which has given offence, in meeting the objection of some who, through misunderstanding, charge us with wishing to exclude Christ from the sacrament; which would be indeed manifestly impious. Whereas the fact is we hold it sure from the word of God, that this precious sacrament was instituted by the Son of God, for the purpose of making us more and more partakers of the substance of his true body and his true blood, in order that we may thus become more closely united to him, and coalesce with him unto eternal life. If this were not the case, it would not be the Supper of Jesus Christ. So far are we then from saying Jesus Christ is absent from the Supper, that we of all men abhor that blasphemy. But we say it makes a great difference here, whether we hold Jesus Christ to be present in the Supper, in so far as he gives us in it truly his own body and his own blood, or make his body and blood to be included in the bread. The first we affirm; the second we deny, as repugnant to the truth of Christ's nature, to the article on the ascension, and to the doctrine of the fathers."—*Hosp. II.* p. 516.

This colloquy of Poissy was continued from the first part of September till towards the close of November. It was thought best, however, in the progress of it, to give it a private form, in place of the public character under which it was commenced. For this purpose five delegates were appointed on the part of the Romanists, including two doctors of the Sorbonne, and five on the part of the Reformed, to confer together in a free way on the various subjects in debate. The representatives of the Re formed Church were Beza, Martyr, Gallasius, Marloratus, and Espinæus. A large share of their attention was given by these collocutors, of course, to the sacramental question. As the result of the discussion, they agreed finally in the following formula, as expressing their common belief.

> "We confess that Jesus Christ in the Supper offers, gives, and truly exhibits to us, the substance of his body and blood, by the operation of the Holy Ghost; and that we receive and eat, spiritually and by faith, that true body that was slain for us; that we may be bone of his bones and flesh of his flesh, and so be vivified by him and made to partake of all that is wanted for our salvation. And whereas faith, resting on the divine word, makes what it perceives to be present; and we by this faith receive truly and efficaciously the true and natural body and blood of Jesus Christ, by the power of the Holy Ghost; we acknowledge in this respect the presence of the body and blood themselves in the Supper."

To this formula the delegates on the Romanist side declared themselves willing to subscribe, as well as those on the side of the Reformed Church; and most of the prelates in attendance seemed also to be satisfied with it, when it was first submitted for their approval. But the authority of the Sorbonne led subsequently to its general rejection as treasonable to the Catholic faith; and the five Romanist collocutors fell under no small reproach in consequence, as having conspired with heretics to wrong the orthodox doctrine of the Church. *Hosp. II. p.* 519–521.

The way is now fairly open for bringing forward the testimony of the several *Confessions* which were formed about this time, for their own use, by the different national branches of the Reformed Church. We find among them all a truly remarkable correspondence throughout; but no where is it more striking, than in the case of this very article of the Lord's Supper. The language they employ is sufficiently distinct in itself, for the most part, to exclude all doubt as to their true meaning on the point with which we are now concerned. But if any room might seem to be left for hesitation, it must be altogether barred surely by the view now presented of the actual state of opinion, at the time when these symbolical books were framed. The more fully we become acquainted with the historical connections and relations under which they started into life, the more shall we feel it to be impossible that they should mean any thing less than the full strength of their language seems to mean. And it is hardly necessary to add, that their *historical* sense, as thus determined, must be admitted to be in the end their only true sense.

The Gallic Confession.

This was formed by an assembly of delegates from the Reformed Churches of France, who were called together for the purpose, in Paris, in the year 1559. It follows closely the doctrine of Calvin and Beza, as already presented. Some have supposed indeed that it proceeded from the pen of Calvin himself. But of this there is no historical evidence, and the supposition is in no respect necessary to account for the agreement just mentioned. The agreement serves only to show, that the doctrine of Calvin in this case, was the doctrine in fact of the Reformed Church, which came now to be incorporated into its symbolical books accordingly, in the most distinct terms. The Confession teaches that Christ "truly feeds and nourishes us with his flesh and blood, that being made one with him, we may have with him a common life."

"For although he is now in heaven, and will remain there also till he shall come to judge the world; we believe, notwithstanding, that through the secret and incomprehensible energy of his Spirit, apprehended by faith, he nourishes and vivifies us by the substance of his body and blood. We say, however, that this is done *spiritually*, not as substituting thus an imagination or thought for the power of the fact, but rather because this mystery of our coalition with Christ is so sublime, that it transcends all our senses, and so also the whole course of nature."—*Art.* 36.

"We believe, as before said, that in the Supper, as in Baptism, God in fact, that is, *truly* and *efficaciously*, grants unto us all that is there sacramentally represented; and so we join with the signs the true possession and fruition of what is thus offered to us. We affirm, therefore, that those who bring to the Lord's table the vessel of a pure faith, truly receive what the signs there testify; namely, that the body and blood of Jesus Christ are not less the meat and drink of the soul, than bread and wine are the food of the body."—*Art.* 37. (*Niemeyer Coll. Conf. p.* 338.)

Old Scotch Confession.

The overthrow of Popery took place in Scotland in the year 1560; at which time also this Confession was produced, under the auspices particularly of the distinguished Reformer, *John Knox.* On the point now in hand it utters itself in the following style:

"We do then utterly condemn the vanity of those who affirm that the sacraments are nothing else but mere naked signs. Rather, we surely believe, that by baptism we are inserted into Christ, and made partakers of his righteousness, by which all our sins are covered and remitted. And also, that in the Lord's Supper, rightly used, Christ is so united to us as to be the very nutriment and food of our souls. Not that we may imagine any transubstantiation of the bread into the natural body of Christ, and of the wine into his natural blood, as the papists have perniciously taught, and believe to their own damnation. But this union and conjunction which we have with the body and blood of Jesus Christ, in the right use of the sacrament, is effected by the operation of the Holy Ghost, who carries us by true faith above all that is seen, and all that is carnal and terrestrial, and causes us to feed upon the body and blood of Jesus Christ, once broken for us and poured out, but now in heaven, appearing for us in the presence of the Father. And though the distance be immense in space between his body now glorified in heaven and us mortals still upon the earth, we do notwithstanding firmly believe that the bread which we break is the communion of his body and the cup which we bless the communion of his blood; and so we confess that believers in the right use of the Lord's Supper thus eat the body and drink the blood of Jesus Christ, and we believe surely that he dwells in them and they in him, yea, that they become thus flesh of his flesh and bone of his bones; for as the eternal Deity has imparted life and immortality to the flesh of Jesus Christ, so likewise his flesh and blood, when eaten and drunk by us, confer upon us the same prerogatives.—*Art.* 21. (*Niemeyer, p.* 352, 353.)

Belgic Confession.

This dates from 1563; and is of great authority and force as a standard exhibition of the faith of the Reformed Dutch Church, both in Holland and in this country. It was solemnly approved besides by the Synod of Dort, and may be said to be clothed in this way with a sort of œcumenical character, as a true exposition of the faith of the entire Reformed Church, as it stood in the beginning of the seventeenth century. Its testimony on the subject before us is particularly strong.

"The sacraments are signs and visible symbols of invisible internal realities, through which as means God himself works in us by the power of the Holy Spirit. Those signs then are by no means vain or void; nor are they instituted to deceive or disappoint us. For the truth of them is Jesus Christ himself, without whom they would be of no force whatever."—*Art.* 33.

"He has instituted terrene and visible bread and wine to be the sacrament of his body and blood; by which we are assured, that as truly as we receive and hold in our hands this sacrament, and eat the same with our mouth, to the sustentation of our natural life, so truly also do we by faith, which is as it were the hand and mouth of our soul, receive the true body and true blood of Christ, our only Saviour, in our souls, to the promotion of our spiritual life. Moreover, it is most certain that Christ commends his sacrament to us so earnestly not without cause, as himself performing in us really all that he represents to us in those sacred signs; although the mode is such as to surpass the apprehension of our mind, and cannot be understood by any; since the operation of the Holy Spirit is always secret and incomprehensible. We may say, however, that what is eaten is the very natural body of Christ, and what is drunk, his true blood; only the instrument of medium by which we eat and drink these is not the corporeal mouth, but our own spirit itself, and this by faith."—*Art.* 35. (*Niemeyer, p.* 383, 365.)*

Second Helvetic Confession.

What is called the *Second* or *Later Helvetic* Confession, was drawn up by *Henry Bullinger*, in the year 1562; though it did not become of public authority before the year 1566. It became in the end the standing, universally acknowledged exposition of the faith of the whole Helvetic Church, and had great credit also in foreign countries. On the subject of the Lord's Supper it is particularly full. Take on the point immediately before us the following extract:

"Believers receive what is given by the minister of the Lord, and eat the Lord's bread and drink of the Lord's cup; inwardly, however, in the mean time, by the work of Christ through the Holy Spirit, they partake also of the Lord's flesh and blood, and are fed by these unto eternal life. For the flesh and blood of Christ are true meat and drink unto eternal life; and Christ himself, as delivered up for us and our salvation, is that which mainly makes the Supper, nor do we suffer any thing else to be put in his room."—*Art.* 21.

*I translate from the Latin; and there are frequent variations in the text of the Confession itself, as given in different editions. This may explain any deviations from the letter of the *English* version, as used by the Reformed Dutch Church in this country. For any one who is at all familiar with the view of Calvin, or with the true character of the sacramental question in the sixteenth century, the sense of the Confession is too clear to be mistaken. Christ, it is true, is held to "sit always at the right hand of his Father in the heavens;" but notwithstanding all this, he "doth not cease to make us partakers of *himself* by faith." And to guard against the idea of a mere moral communication in the case, it is added, that he conveys to us, at his table, not simply his benefits or merits, but these as inhering in his person; "*both* himself, *and* the merits or his sufferings and death." Christians have a twofold life; one natural, the other spiritual, beginning with their second birth "in the communion of the body of Christ." This last life is supported by a living bread, sent from heaven for the purpose, "namely Jesus Christ, who nourishes and strengthens the spiritual life of believers when they *eat him*, that is to say, when they apply and receive him by faith in the spirit." A spiritual reception of course, but still a *real* reception of Christ's true human and heavenly life; otherwise the article must be held guilty of the most egregious trifling, in the case of one of the most solemn and perilous points in theology. The Form for the administration of the Lord's Supper, in the Liturgy of the Reformed Dutch Church, corresponds fully with the doctrine of the Confession. "That we may now be fed with the true heavenly bread, Christ Jesus," the service exhorts, "let us not cleave with our hearts unto the external bread and wine, but lift them up on high in heaven, where Christ Jesus is our advocate at the right hand of his heavenly Father, whither all the articles of our faith lead us; not doubting but we shall *as certainly* be fed and refreshed in our souls, through the working of the Holy Ghost, *with his body and blood*, as we receive the holy bread and wine in remembrance of hm."

The article then goes on, in explanation of this statement, to describe different forms of manducation. There is first a *corporal* manducation, such as the Capernaites had in their mind, when they strove among themselves saying, How can this man give us his flesh to eat? Then there is a *spiritual* manducation, by which Christ is so appropriated in the way of ordinary faith, that he lives in us and we in him. "By this is not meant a merely imaginary, undefinable food, but the body of the Lord itself delivered up for us, which however is received by believers, not corporally, but spiritually by faith." Still different from this lastly is the *sacramental* manducation, "by which the believer not only participates in the true body and blood of the Lord spiritually and internally, but outwardly also by coming to the Lord's table receives the visible sacrament of the Lord's body and blood." The sacrament adds something of its own to the ordinary life of faith. "He that partakes of the sacrament outwardly with true faith, partakes not of the sign only, but enjoys also, as already said, the thing itself which this represents." (*Niemeyer,* p. 519, 520.)

The occasion by which this confession became public, was as follows. A spirit of the most violent intolerance had come to prevail on the part of the rigid Lutherans, excited by such men as Westphal, Timann, and Hesshuss, against all who professed the Reformed doctrine; but in no direction was it more active than towards the elector of the Palatinate, Frederick the Third. Fears were entertained even, that he would be excluded from the peace between the Catholics and Protestants. In these circumstances, it became an object of great importance, to bring all the Reformed Churches into as close a connection as possible. Frederick especially had his heart set upon this point. Towards the close of the year 1565, he wrote to Bullinger on the subject, and begged him in particular to send him as soon as possible a confession of faith, that might serve to repress the cavils of the Lutherans, with a view to the imperial diet which was then close at hand. Bullinger forwarded him the confession which he had prepared three years before; which so pleased the elector, that he proposed at once to have it translated and published in the German tongue. It was now felt important, to make it if possible of still more general authority; for which purpose it was submitted to the other Helvetic Churches; and in this way, being generally approved it became known in time following as the proper Swiss Confession. The historical relation now mentioned, in the case of this confession is important, as it serves to show the substantial harmony of Switzerland and the Palatinate on the sacramental question, at the time it was published. A harmony too that rested on the basis of the Calvinistic doctrine, as it has been already explained; for that this doctrine formed the reigning view of the Reformed Church in the Palatinate, will soon be placed beyond all shadow of doubt.

The Heidelberg Catechism.

Next in order comes the venerable symbol of the German Reformed Church, the Catechism of the Palatinate; drawn up, in obedience to an appointment from the elector, Frederick III., by *Caspar Olevian*, a disciple of Calvin, and *Zacharias Ursinus*, a friend of Melancthon; approved and ratified by a general ecclesiastical synod called at Heidelberg for the purpose; and solemnly published as a confessional standard in the year 1563. It has been translated into all modern civilized tongues, honoured with countless commentaries, and exalted by general acknowledgment to a sort of symbolical authority for the whole Reformed Church.

To place its testimony in a proper light, it is necessary to notice a little more particularly than has yet been done, the actual posture of the sacramental controversy in Germany at the time it was formed. Only in this way, can we come to a clear view of the circumstances in which it had its origin, by which, in the nature of the case, its character and meaning are to be interpreted.

After the death of Luther, A.D. 1546, the controversy on the subject of the sacrament was allowed for some years to remain at rest. As it began to appear, however, before long. that the high ground occupied by the great Reformer was coming to be silently abandoned by many, who still considered themselves true to the Augsburg Confession, a violent movement was gradually created, antagonistically to this tendency, in the opposite direction. It commenced with an assault, in the first place, upon Calvin and Peter Martyr, who had both been led to declare themselves openly upon the subject, in a way that was necessarily offensive to such as were still disposed to insist rigidly on the extreme view; though no thought of giving offence, or provoking controversy, was entertained probably at the time; as it was supposed the mind of the church had come to be very generally inclined to the same moderate view, or that it was prepared at least to treat it with patient indulgence. But the case soon showed itself to be different. The war was opened, in the year 1552, by Joachim Westphal, preacher in Hamburg, with his *Farrago*; which was intended to be at once a battle challenge to the Swiss churches, with Calvin at their head and a call to arms upon all who could be made to feel with himself that the strong towers of Lutheran orthodoxy were in danger of being overthrown. This was followed by a second attack, the following year; and then again, the year after, by a third. Meanwhile other influences also were employed, but too successfully, to rouse the spirit of party hatred and party strife, in the same direction. Calvin found himself now compelled to take up the pen, in self-defence. Gradually the battle thickens. Other champions appear in the field. The Lutheran church is torn with dissension and distraction in her own bosom. The rigid party, "fierce for orthodoxy," have their hands full at last with the work of suppressing heresy at home. The horrible sacramentarian doctrine is found everywhere lifting up its head, or at least struggling to do so, under the very shadow of the Augsburg Confession itself. And what is worse still, the venerable author of the Confession, still living at Wittemberg, refuses to lift a finger in opposition to the mischief; nay, is more than suspected of being himself in league with it in his heart. No wonder that all Protestant Germany is mad with theological excitement and passion.

A full account of these agitations and conflicts, may be found in Planck's "*Geschichte der Protestantischen Theologie*," vol. V. *Second Part*. They form one of the most strange and interesting chapters, in the church history of the sixteenth century.

But what was the nature of the question, on which the parties showed themselves to be at issue in this case, with regard to the Lord's Supper? It related not at all to the reality of the sacramental presence, but only and wholly to its *mode*. The controversy was not at all between the high view of Luther and the low theory commonly attributed to Zuingli. The great point was conceded now on all hands, that the sacrament involves a real participation in the substance of Christ's flesh and blood, that is in his true human life itself, as the only ground of our salvation. With this confession however the rigid party were not satisfied. They insisted on certain definitions and admissions besides, which appeared to them necessary to carry out the doctrine in its true sense. They contended for the formula, "*In, with, and under*," as indispensable to a complete expression of the sacramental presence. The communication must be allowed to be by the *mouth*. It must be granted in the case of *all* who eat, whether with or without faith. Finally, the ubiquity of Christ's body, and the *communicatio idiomatum* in its full extent, must be accepted also, as the only basis on which the doctrine could find a solid foundation. It was for refusing to admit these extreme requisitions only, that the other party was branded with the title *Sacramentarian*, and held up to odium in every direction as the pest of society. It was not the Zuinglian view of the Lord's Supper, but the Calvinistic view, in all its length and breadth, as already described, which was now recognized as the proper doctrine of the Reformed Church, and as such pursued with unrelenting hate by the high toned orthodoxy of the day. It is important to bear this continually in mind.

The intestine war broke forth first in the city of Bremen; where it soon became very violent, and gradually involved the whole country in commotion. The immediate occasion of it was furnished by the distinguished preacher, *Albert Hardenberg*; a man who stood in the highest credit for learning and piety, and was considered in some respects the main ornament of the place to which he belonged; but who, unfortunately for himself, was suspected of being more Reformed than Lutheran in his view of the Lord's Supper. It was not the least consideration in his prejudice, that he was known to be in regular correspondence with Melancthon, as one of his most intimate and confidential friends. The movement against him was commenced in 1555, by *John Timann*, one of his colleagues in the ministry of Bremen, who now came forward with great zeal to the assistance of Westphal in his crusade against heresy. The other preachers were after some time fully engaged also in the process of persecution. Every effort was made to bring the man into discredit with the magistracy and the people, as an enemy of the true Lutheran faith. The pulpits, in the end, were made to ring with reproaches, hurled upon his head. Conspiracy and intrigue knew no rest for years. Timann died in the midst of the controversy; but his mantle fell upon others, who easily supplied his place. Other cities and states, Hamburg, Lubeck, Lunenburg, Saxony, Mecklinburg, Wirtemburg, Denmark, were secretly engaged to interpose their mediation. In the end, Hardenberg found it necessary to retire. The controversy, however, was still continued, and came to a more favourable result ultimately than might have been expected. It lasted altogether thirteen years, holding the city of Bremen in violent disturbance the whole time.

In close connection with the religious struggle of Bremen, so far as its interior history was concerned, stands the religious revolution of the Palatinate, which fell like a thunderbolt on the ears of Lutheran Germany, while that struggle was still in progress. It took place under the following circumstances.

One of the most violent, unsettled spirits of this turbulent period, was *Tilmann Hesshuss*; rendered memorable if by nothing else, at least by the merciless castigation inflicted upon him by Calvin, in his last tract on the Sacrament.* He was a man of inordinate ambition, fond of money, constitutionally intolerant and overbearing; and withal, whether by conviction or accident, a perfect zealot in the cause of Lutheran orthodoxy. In the year 1558, he was appointed first professor in the University of Heidelberg, and general superintendent of all the churches in the Palatinate. Six months, however, had not elapsed, before he had made himself here, as in all places where he had lived before, an object of very general dislike. In particular, he was drawn into strong collision with one *William Klebiz*, who occupied the situation of a deacon at the time in

---

Dilucida Explicatio Sanœ Doctrinœ de Vera Participatione Carnis et Sanguinis Christi, in Sacra Cœna. Ad discutiendas HESHUSII nebulas. Published 1561. In this tract, Hesshuss is handled, as we say, without gloves. *Inscitia cum imprudentia, stoliditas et protervia, delirium, &c.*, are charged upon him in full measure; and such epithets as *impurus scurra, epilepticus, noster Thraso, impura bestia, &c.*, appear plentifully sprinkled over the whole discussion. In conclusion, the writer excuses himself from further controversy with the man as being destitute of all modesty and reason, delivering him over at the same time to the discipline of Beza. "Si qua esset in bestia ingenuitas, vel docilitas, ab ejus calumniis me purgarem; sed quia taurus est indomitus, lasciviam in qua nimis exultat, Bezæ subigendam trado." *Opp.* IX., p. 723–742.

Heidelberg; a man also, it would seem, of most unclerical temper, and but little inclined to maintain friendly relations with the new superintendent. It soon came between them to an open, violent rupture; in which the sacramental question was made the prominent subject of quarrel. Hesshuss charged Klebiz with heresy, as favouring the Calvinistic view of Christ's presence in the Lord's Supper rather than the strict Lutheran. The point of his apostacy was found mainly in this, that he affirmed the participation of Christ's body in the Supper to be by faith and not by the mouth. Hesshuss grew savage in his denunciations; and poured forth his indignation every sabbath, from the pulpit, upon the new *Arius*, who had made his appearance in the Heidelberg Church; not sparing at the same time the university and the authorities of the city, for their supposed indifference to the portentous mischief with which they were threatened. Klebiz returned violence for violence. The whole city was thrown into commotion. In these circumstances, Frederick III. succeeded to the electorate. The moderate measures he employed in the first place, to allay the strife, proved unavailing. In the end, he found it necessary to resort to more vigorous means. Both Hesshuss and Klebiz were dismissed accordingly from office; and in this way the public quiet was restored.

Frederick was now made to feel the importance of having the subject of this controversy brought to some such settlement, in his dominions, as might preserve the peace of the country in time to come. He formed the plan accordingly of establishing a rule of faith for the Palatinate, to which all should be required to conform. To sustain himself in this object, he wrote to Melancthon, asking his counsel and advice. This drew forth the celebrated *response* of Melancthon, which became public after his death, and involved his memory in no small reproach, with the stiff party to whose views it was found to be opposed. It approved the elector's course, in silencing the sacramental controversy, and also his purpose of excluding strife by requiring all to submit to some common form of words; whilst it very decidedly condemned the use of any such terms for this purpose, as were pressed upon the Church by Hesshuss and men of the same stamp. The elector was already decided in his own mind, in favour of the moderate or Calvinistic view of the sacrament. He found the same disposition predominant also among his people. In these circumstances, his election was soon made. It was resolved that the Palatinate should become *Reformed*.

This event created, of course, a great sensation. Among others, the son-in-law of the elector, duke John Frederick of Saxony, was much disturbed and troubled at the tidings. He immediately took a journey to Heidelberg, carrying with him a pair of his most expert theologians, *Morlin* and *Stessel*, to rescue his relative, if possible, from the dangerous snare of Calvinism, into which he had so unhappily fallen. For this purpose a public disputation was proposed, to be held between the two theologians just mentioned, and any the elector might see fit to nominate for the defence of his own cause. The proposal was accepted; and a disputation followed, which was continued for five full days in the presence of the two princes. It was held in the month of June, 1560.

The Calvinistic cause was maintained by Peter Bocquin, one of the most distinguished theologians at the time in Heidelberg. The whole debate turned only upon the *mode* of the eucharistic presence. The divines of John Frederick contended for the high Lutheran doctrine of a true corporeal presence, *in, with* and *under* the bread; to be apprehended orally and not simply in a spiritual way; for unbelievers accordingly, as well as for believers. Bocquin, on the other hand, maintained the view, that Christ is present to the organ of faith only, by the power of the Holy Ghost. He allowed, however, not only "that the body is presented *with* the bread," but also "that the true substance of the true body is received by believers;" and showed convincingly, that this does not make it necessary to suppose an oral communication, or to hold that the body is either *in* the bread or *under* it. The result of the whole disputation was, that the elector found himself only more confirmed than before, in his resolution to establish the Reformed doctrine in the Palatinate.

In these circumstances, the *Heidelberg Catechism* was produced, and made the public formulary of faith, in the way already stated. We may easily understand, from the nature of the case, on what view its doctrine of the Lord's Supper must necessarily be constructed. It occupies the Calvinistic ground, as distinguished from the Lutheran on the one side and the Zuinglian on the other. It rejects explicitly the idea of an oral man-ducation; but, as Planck remarks, teaches also in the clearest terms, that the soul of the believer is truly fed, in this sacrament, by an actual participation of the body and blood of Christ. But let us now hear the Catechism itself.

> In answer to Question 75, it is said that Christ, "feeds and nourishes my soul to everlasting life, with his crucified body and shed blood, as assuredly as I receive from the hands of the minister, and taste with my mouth, the bread and cup of the Lord, as certain signs of the body and blood of Christ."
>
> "Quest. 76. *What is it then to eat the crucified body and drink the shed blood of Christ?*
>
> "Ans. It is *not only* to embrace with a believing heart all the suffer-ings and death of Christ, and thereby to obtain the pardon of sin and life eternal; but also, *besides that,* to become more and more united to his sacred body, by the Holy Ghost who dwells both in Christ and in us; so that we, though Christ is in heaven and we on earth, are not-withstanding, 'flesh of his flesh and bone of his bone;' and that we live and are governed forever by one spirit, as members of the same body are by one soul."

"Quest. 79. *Why then doth Christ call the bread his body, and the his blood, or the new covenant in his blood; and Paul the communion of the body and blood of Christ?*

"Ans. Christ speaks thus, not without great reason; namely *not only* thereby to teach us that as bread and wine support this temporal life, so his crucified body and shed blood are the true meat and drink whereby our souls are fed to eternal life; but *more especially,* by these visible signs and pledges to assure us, that we are as *really* partakers of his true body and blood, (by the operation of the Holy Ghost,) as we receive by the mouths of our bodies these holy signs in remembrance of him; and that all his sufferings and obedience are as certainly ours as if we had in our own persons suffered and made satisfaction for our sins to God."

Here we have all the characteristic positions and distinctions of Calvin's theory, plainly brought into view; and with the knowledge of this theory familiar to our minds, and the historical conditions under which the Catechism was created full in sight, we must do violence to all sound interpretation, if we can allow ourselves to understand it in any *other* sense. True to the general form in which the controversy stood at the time, it affirms a real communion with Christ's flesh and blood; allows the *fact*; but refuses to be bound by the Lutheran determination of the *mode*. The presence of Christ is not "*in, with and under*" the bread, but only *with* it; not for the *mouth*, but only for *faith*; and so of course, though this is not expressly mentioned, not for *unbelievers* but for *believers* only. It is however, in this way, a true presence. The believer partakes of Christ, not only in figure, but in fact; not of his benefits simply, but of his actual life; not of his life as divine merely, but of the substance of his human life, as denoted by his body and blood. The signs not only testify to us the general truth that Christ is our life, but seal this truth to us as a fact actualized along with their exhibition and use. To say that by the participation of Christ's body and blood the Catechism means only a moral union with him, by faith and an interest in the benefits of his death, is to charge it with the most wretched tautology, where with its "*besides that*" and its "*more especially*" it plainly intends a climax; since according to this view the second proposition, in each case, must be considered an unmeaning repetition simply of the sense of the first, in terms far more obscure and hard to understand. No such poor tautology can be allowed. The Catechism counts it not enough, that we embrace the offer of salvation, as something separate from Christ; we must be incorporated with his life, we must have part in the very substance of his flesh and blood, in order that we may have part truly at the same time in all the blessings he has procured, as though "we had in our own persons suffered and made satisfaction for our sins unto God."

We may be told indeed that the language of the Catechism, and of the other Confessions also which have been quoted, *must* be taken to some extent in a figurative sense; since it is admitted that the body and blood of Christ are not corporeally present in the sacrament, and they cannot therefore be taken literally into the believer's person. Allowing this however, in the sense of the objection itself, it by no means follows that the figure may be resolved into any such low meaning as would empty it of its force and spirit altogether. If by eating the flesh and blood of Christ the framers of these confessions meant only to express, by a strong figure, the act of believing upon him and appropriating his merits, they must be allowed to have uttered themselves in a most careless way; all the more marvellous, not to say absolutely senseless, that it was directly adapted to encourage that very superstition of a gross corporeal presence, based upon the letter of Christ's words, which with all their force they continually opposed. The thought is absurd. By flesh and blood, they mean the true body of Christ; the same that was born of Mary, and hung upon the cross, and is now enthroned in heaven. *This* the believer feeds upon, not carnally, but spiritually; so however that its true and proper substance, the reality which belongs to it as life, *human* life, is conveyed over into his person. In this way he "becomes united more and more to his sacred body, by the Holy Ghost," so as to be truly "flesh of his flesh and bone of his bone," even as limb and head are filled and ruled with the same life in the body physically considered.

But this "sacred body" of the Saviour, we hear it sometimes said, is the *Church*. Allow it to be so; it only follows that the totality of Christ's life, including his substantial humanity, is in the Church, by organic derivation from himself as its head. So that we come at last to the same result. To be incorporated with the Church, in this sense, is to be incorporated with Christ at the same time in his true human life, in the way already described. But the Catechism has no reference to the Church in this case; especially not to the Church in any such external view, as the interpretation now noticed is meant to imply. The "sacred body" to which his people are more and more united, is his own proper person in human form, once crucified for our sins and now gloriously exalted for our justification in heaven.* Such was the view of the Reformed Church at this time. Such is the sense of the Catechism.

Should any doubt however still linger, with regard to the sacramental doctrine of the Catechism, as now stated, it must be annihilated certainly by our next authority. This is the testimony of Ursinus himself.

---

*Calvin expressly rejects the idea, that by the body of Christ, to which we are united in the sacrament, is to be understood merely the Church. He repels as slanderous the attempt to fasten on his view this consequence; "quasi mysticum in Cœna corpus sumamus pro Ecclesia. Hoc certe, velint nolint, nobis principium cum ipsis commune est, designari Christi verbis *verum illud corpus*, cujus immolatio nos Deo reconciliavit." *Opp.* IX., p. 701.

Ursinus.

The works of this divine have been published in three folio volumes. Having unfortunately no access to these in their original form, I can only refer to them in an indirect way. They include a good deal on the subject of the sacraments. Hospinian (*Hist. Sacram. Pars Altera, p.* 659, 660) mentions particularly a tract from his pen, which was first published, A.D. 1546, in the name of the theological faculty of Heidelberg. It bore for its title, "The True Doctrine of the Holy Supper of our Lord Jesus Christ, faithfully expounded from the principles and sense of the divine Scriptures, the ancient and orthodox Church, and also of the Augsburg Confession." In the third chapter of this work, it is proposed to settle the true state of the question, which was the subject of controversy in the Protestant Church. This, it is declared, is *not* whether the flesh of Christ be eaten; for this none of us deny; but *how* it is eaten." Here the Lutherans answer, corporally and orally, by the godly and ungodly. We say, on the contrary, spiritually only by believers."

The earliest commentary we have upon the Heidelberg Catechism, is that of Ursinus himself, published from his divinity lectures, after his death, by *David Pareus.* This has been translated from the original Latin into English. Not having the Latin work at hand, I can only appeal to the translation, the "*Summe of Christian Religion by Zacharias Ursinus,*" as published, London, 1645. The subject of the sacraments is discussed in it, of course, at large. The following quotations will serve to give a fair view of the author's doctrine, with regard to the Lord's Supper.

> "These two, I mean the *sign* and the *thing signified,* are united in this sacrament, not by any *natural copulation,* or *corporal* and *local existence* one in the other; much less by transubstantiation, or changing one into the other; but by signifying, sealing, and exhibiting the one by the other; that is by a *sacramental union,* whose bond is the promise added to the bread, requiring the faith of the receivers. Whence it is clear, that these things in their lawful use, are always jointly exhibited and received, but not without faith of the promise, viewing and apprehending the thing promised, now present in the sacrament; yet not present or included in the sign as in a vessel containing it; but present in the *promise,* which is the better part, life, and soul of the sacrament. For they want judgment who affirm, that Christ's body cannot be present in the sacrament, except it be *in* or *under* the bread; as if, forsooth, the bread alone, without the promise, were either the sacrament, or the principal part of a sacrament." p. 434.
>
> "There is then in the Lord's Supper a double *meat* and drink. One *external,* visible and terrene, namely, bread and wine; and another *internal.* There is also a double *eating* and receiving; an *external* and *signifying,* which is the corporal receiving of the bread and wine; that is, which is performed by the hands, mouth, and senses of the body; and an *internal, invisible,* and *signified,* which is the fruition of Christ's

death, and a spiritual ingrafting into Christ's body; that is, which is not performed by the hands and mouth of the body, but by the spirit and faith. Lastly, there is a double *administrator* and dispenser of this meat and drink; an *external*, of the external, which is the minister of the church, delivering by his hand the bread and wine; and an *internal*, of the internal meat, which is Christ himself, feeding us by his body and blood." p. 470.

"As therefore the body of Christ signifieth both his proper and natural body, and his sacramental body, which is the bread of the eucharist; so the eating of Christ's body is of two sorts; one *sacramental*, of the sign to wit, the external and corporal receiving of the bread and wine; the other *real* or *spiritual*, which is the receiving of Christ's very body itself. And to believe in Christ dwelling in us by faith, is, by the virtue and operation of the Holy Ghost, to be ingrafted into his body, as members to the head and branches into the vine; and *so* to be made partakers of the fruit of the death and life of Christ. Whence it is apparent that they are falsely accused who thus teach, as if they made either the bare signs only to be in the Lord's Supper, or a participation of Christ's *death* only, or of his *benefits*, or of the *Holy Ghost*, excluding the true, real, and spiritual communion of the very body of Christ itself." p. 470, 471.

In an appendix to this part of the work, we find the following brief summary of the leading objections, made by the "Consubstantiaries," as they are styled, against the "sincere doctrine of the Lord's Supper" as held by those who were nicknamed "Sacramentaries," together with proper answers.

"1st Obj. *The errors the Sacramentaries are, that there are but bare signs and symbols only in the Supper.*

"Ans. We teach that the things signified are, together with the signs in the right use exhibited and communicated, albeit not corporally, but in such sort as is agreeable unto sacraments.

"2d Obj. *The Sacramentaries say that Christ is present only according to his power and efficacy.*

"Ans. We teach that he is present and united with us by the Holy Ghost, albeit his body be far absent from us; like as a whole Christ is present also with his ministry, though diversely according to the one nature.

"3d Obj. *The Sacramentaries affirm that an imaginary, figurative, or spiritual body is present, not his essential body.*

"Ans. We never spake of an imaginary body, but of the true flesh of Christ, which is present with us, although it remain in heaven. Moreover, we may that we receive the bread and body, but both after a manner proper to each.

"4th Obj. *The Sacramentaries affirm, that the true body of Christ which hung on the cross, and his very blood which was shed for us, is*

*distributed and is spiritually received of those only who are worthy
receivers; as for the unworthy, they receive nothing besides the bare
signs, to their own condemnation.*

"Ans. All this we grant, as being agreeable to the word of God, the
nature of sacraments, the analogy of faith, and the communion of the
faithful."—P. 472.

In conclusion, a statement is given of the general points "wherein the
churches which profess the gospel agree or disagree in the controversy
concerning the Lord's Supper." Among the points of agreement, the third
one mentioned is, "that in the Supper we are made partakers not only of
the Spirit of Christ, and his satisfaction, justice, virtue and operation, but
also of *the very essence and substance of his true body and blood,* which
was given for us to death on the cross, and which was shed for us; and are
truly fed with the self-same unto eternal life: and that this very thing
Christ should teach and make known unto us, by this visible receiving of
this bread and wine in his Supper." The disagreement is represented to
hold in the three following particulars.

"1. That one part contendeth that these words of Christ, *This is my
body,* must be understood as the words sound, which yet that part itself
doth not prove; but the other part, that those words must be understood
sacramentally, according to the declaration of Christ and Paul,
according to the most certain and infallible rule and level of the articles
of our Christian faith.

"2. That one part will have the body and blood of Christ to be
essentially *in* or *with* the bread and the wine, and so to be eaten that
together with the bread and wine, out of the hand of the minister, it
entereth by the mouth of the receivers into their bodies; but the other
part will have the body of Christ, which in the first Supper sat at the
table by the disciples, now to be and continue, not here on earth, but
above in the heavens, and without this visible world and heaven, until
he descend thence again to judgment, and yet that we notwithstanding
here on earth, as oft as we eat this bread with a true faith, are so fed
with his body, and made to drink of his blood, that not only through his
passion and blood shed, we are cleansed from our sins, but are also in
such sort coupled, knit, and incorporated into his true, essential human
body, by his Spirit dwelling both in him and us, that we are flesh of his
flesh, and bone of his bones; and are more nearly and firmly knit and
united with him than the members of our body are united with our head,
and so we draw and have in him and from him everlasting life.

"3. That one part will have all, whosoever come to the table of the
Lord's Supper, and eat and drink that bread and wine, whether they be
believers or unbelievers, to eat and drink, corporally and with their
bodily mouth, the flesh and blood of Christ, believers to life and
salvation, unbelievers to damnation and death; the other holdeth, that
unbelievers abuse indeed the outward signs, bread and wine, to their
damnation, but that the faithful only can eat and drink, by a true faith,

and the fore-alleged working of the Holy Ghost, the body and blood of Christ unto eternal life."—P. 480.

Calvin himself is hardly more explicit, in the statement of his own doctrine. We seem to hear, in these quotations, the very echo of the words to which we have already listened from his lips. It is the testimony, however, of Ursinus, the principal author of the Catechism of the Palatinate, speaking *ex cathedra* of the doctrine it was supposed to contain. Where shall we find an expositor of its sense more worthy to be trusted and believed?

Hospinian.

Omitting all other testimony that might still be brought forward from the sixteenth century as entirely superfluous, after what has been already exhibited, I present finally the authority of a single Helvetic divine, that may be said to cover at once the entire period. I refer to *Rodolph Hospinian*, the distinguished author of the great work on the History of the Sacrament. His theological life was passed in Zurich, and reached from the year 1563 some distance over into the following century. His sympathies are all, of course, with the Helvetic Church. His whole work, however, in the case of the sixteenth century, proceeds from beginning to end on the assumption that the Reformed doctrine of the eucharist was always, from the very first, what we have found it to be in the authorities already quoted; and as such not only conformable to the view of Calvin, but in harmony even with the proper sense of the Augsburg Confession itself, at least as understood by Melancthon and a large part of the Lutheran Church. He refers to Calvin's statements always with approbation, as a true representation of what was held and taught in the Reformed communion; and will have it, that Zuingli himself inculcated, in all substantial respects, the very same doctrine. Altogether, it must be admitted that Hospinian is wrong, in the general theory on which his work is constructed. But this does not affect, of course, the weight of his testimony, as it regards the fact with which we are now concerned. Nay, it serves only to render it the more worthy of attention. His work has the form of an apology for the sacramental orthodoxy of the Helvetic church, while the standard by which it is measured is always the Calvinistic, as distinguished from the Ubiquitarian view. He takes it for granted, that this, and nothing lower than this, was, and had been all along, the true and proper doctrine of the Reformed Church; and it is exhibited accordingly always under this view. The controversy between the two confessions is with him one that relates, not to the question of *fact*, as it regards the power of the sacraments, but only to the question of *mode*. Thus, in speaking of the Augsburg Confession, he gives the article on the eucharistic presence, as presented in the Wittemberg German text of the year

1531; in which it is said, "that the body and blood of Christ are truly present, and *with* the bread and wine distributed to them that eat, in the Lord Supper;" and immediately adds, "These words contain nothing contrary to *our* view." Afterwards he tells us, still more explicitly: "Ours do not reject the tenth article of the Augsburg Confession, in its sound, true, right, pious, and catholic sense, as held by the fathers, and all the true Christian saints always in the Church; namely, that in the Lord's Supper, along with the bread and wine, that is, while the sacrament of the Lord's body and blood is received, there is truly exhibited also the body and blood itself of the Lord, to be received by faith. For whilst the ministers distribute the sacrament of the body and blood of Christ, Christ himself communicates himself to be spiritually enjoyed, that the pious may have communion with him and live by him." *Hosp. Hist. Sac. Part II.* p. 157, 158.

The Synod of Dort.

This venerable body was convened in the year 1618, with reference particularly to the errors introduced by Arminius. It was composed of delegates, not only from the United Provinces, but also from England, Switzerland, the Palatinate, Hessia, Nassau, East Friesland, and Bremen; forming in fact an œcumenical council of the entire Reformed Church. It was not called of course to express any direct judgment on the sacramental question. It may be said to have done this indirectly however, by solemnly endorsing both the Belgic Confession and the Heidelberg Catechism, as true and faithful expositions in full of the general faith of the Church. The first having been submitted previously to a particular examination on the part of the different national delegations, was unanimously approved in the 146th session; as containing nothing at variance with the word of God, or needing in any way to be changed. The other was afterwards laid before the body, with the request that it might be tried in the same way. As the result, a declaration was filed in the name of all present, that "the doctrine contained in the Catechism of the Palatinate was found to be conformable at all points to the word of God; that there was nothing in it that needed in this view to be changed or corrected; and that altogether it formed a most accurate compend of the orthodox Christian faith, being with singular skill not only adjusted to the apprehension of tender youth, but so framed also as to serve the purpose of instruction at the same time in the case of older persons."—*Acta Syn. Nat. Dord. Sess. CXLVI. p.* 302.

Westminster Confession.

This belongs to the middle of the seventeenth century. It has a different character in some respects, from that which distinguishes the older confessions of the Reformed Church; the result, at least in part, of the Puritanic principle, under whose influence, in some measure, it was formed. This involved from the beginning a tendency, that might be considered unfavourable to the idea of the objective and mystical in the life of the Church, as it prevailed with both Protestant confessions in the age of the Reformation; and which has since in fact contributed largely to the production of that false form of thinking, that has come to be so general, at the present time, in the opposite direction. But notwithstanding all this, the doctrine of the real presence, in the form now under consideration, appears here in its full force. The testimony of course is only of secondary weight, in any view, as compared with the symbolical authorities of the sixteenth century, to which we have already referred. It is still however of special interest, as showing how deeply the old Calvinistic doctrine had lodged itself in the heart of the Church; and how full and distinct must have been its proclamation in the beginning, to which at the distance of a hundred years, so clear an echo at least is still returned, from the very bosom of the Puritan Revolution itself. Let the Confession speak for itself.

> "Worthy receivers, outwardly partaking of the visible elements in this sacrament, do then inwardly also by faith, really and indeed, yet not carnally and corporally, but spiritually, receive and feed upon Christ crucified and all benefits of his death; the body and blood of Christ being then not corporally or carnally in, with, or under the bread and wine; yet as *really* but *spiritually present* to the faith of believers in that ordinance, as the elements themselves are to their outward senses." Chap. 29, § 7.

Compare with this, as confirming and illustrating still farther the same view, the following questions from the Larger Catechism.

> "Quest. 168. *What is the Lord's Supper?*
>
> "Ans. The Lord's Supper is a sacrament of the New Testament, wherein by giving and receiving bread and wine, according to the appointment of Jesus Christ, his death is showed forth; and they that worthily communicate, feed upon his body and blood, to their spiritual nourishment and growth in grace; have their union and communion with him confirmed; testify and renew their thankfulness and engagement to God, and their mutual love and fellowship with each other, as members of the same mystical body."
>
> "Quest. 170. *How do they that worthily communicate in the Lord's Supper feed upon the body and blood of Christ therein?*

"Ans. As the body and blood of Christ are not corporally or
carnally present in, with, or under, the bread and wine in the Lord's
Supper; and yet *are spiritually present* to the faith of the receiver, no
less truly and *really* than the elements themselves are to their outward
senses; so they that worthily communicate in the sacrament of the
Lord's Supper, do therein feed upon the body and blood of Christ, not
after a corporal or carnal, but in a spiritual manner; yet truly and really,
while by faith they receive and apply unto themselves Christ crucified,
and all the benefits of his death."

This, it must be admitted, is not entirely free from ambiguity, as compared with the language of the sixteenth century. Taken by itself, it might
be held to mean nothing more than such a presence of Christ's body as is
involved in the lively *conception* of it in the worshipper's mind; though
all must feel, that a strange abuse of language would be employed, in that
case, to express so plain a thought. But we need only some tolerable
familiarity with the Calvinistic theory of the Lord's Supper, as held before
this time in the Reformed Church, to be fully satisfied that no such poor
construction as that now mentioned can be entitled to any respect. It is not
simply a real *spiritual* presence that is here affirmed as belonging to the
sacrament, but a spiritual real presence; a communication by faith with the
body and *blood* of Christ, which involves union and communion with his
person under such view, and on the ground of this only, a full interest at
the same time in all the benefits of his death. The term *spiritual* as here
used, it must always be borne in mind, carries in it no opposition to the
idea of substance; nor does it refer to the person of Christ simply as it is
spirit, and not body. On the contrary, it has regard to the inmost substance
of his body itself. All imagination of a material intermingling of Christ's
flesh with ours is indeed carefully removed; but it is only to assert the
more positively a *real* participation in the true life of his flesh as such.
The communion is with the Saviour's body and blood, the very essence
of which under a spiritual form, is carried over into the believer's person.
If this be not the meaning of the Westminster Assembly; if in the use of
language, borrowed here so plainly from the creed of Calvin and the
Reformed Church generally in the sixteenth century, the Assembly
intended to signify after all something quite different from that creed, a
mere moral union with Christ for instance, a communication with him in
his divine nature simply, or an appropriation only of the merits of his life
and death; it will be found very hard, in the first place, to put any
intelligible sense whatever into their words, and more difficult still, in the
second place, to vindicate the interpretation as worthy either of their
wisdom or their truth.*

*In appealing to the authority of the several Reformed Confessions, notice has been
taken directly of the Thirty-nine Articles of the Church of England. As this branch of the

Hooker and Owen.

In conclusion, let me be allowed to refer to the authority of two of the most eminent English divines, who lived close upon the age of the Reformation, and who may be taken as the most prominent representatives of the two great contrary tendencies, which the Reformed Church may be said to have involved in its constitution from the very start. Hooker and Owen! How different in their whole spiritual conformation, and yet how closely bound together, notwithstanding, in the last ground of their religious life. The one stands forth to our view, the deeply earnest, most learned and most indefatigable champion, of all that is comprehended in the idea of the *Church.* The other is known as the no less indefatigable champion of all that is included in the idea of religious *freedom* and *individual* responsibility. Hooker is the great ornament of the English Episcopacy. Owen has been styled the prince, the oracle, and the metropolitan of the English Independency and Puritanism. The one belongs to the close of the sixteenth century; the other flourished amid the revolutionary storms of the period that followed. I refer to them both as witnesses merely, not as sources of authority in themselves. Hooker was an Episcopalian, with high views of the Church; but, as a man of learning, he must be supposed to have understood the doctrine of the Reformed Church, as it stood in his own time. Owen was a Puritan, with low views of the Church; but this only serves to render the more striking his response to the same truth, in a case where its last echo has ceased to be heard with the Puritans of a later day.

Protestant communion is considered by many to be somewhat tainted, in its very constitution, with the errors of Rome, it seemed best not to lay much stress upon its testimony in the present discussion. It is remarkable, however, that what may be styled the *high* sacramental doctrine, is not put forward with any special prominence in the teachings of this Church, as compared with the view held by the Reformed Church generally in the sixteenth century. We find the doctrine, indeed, clearly proclaimed. How could it be otherwise, in the period to which we refer? "Sacraments ordained of Christ." it is said, "be certain sure witnesses and effectual signs of grace, and God's good will towards us, *by the which* he doth work invisibly in us, and doth not only quicken, but also strengthen and confirm our faith in him." *Art.* XXV. Though only after an heavenly and Spiritual manner, as distinguished from a mere corporeal eating, still "the body of Christ is *given, taken* and *eaten* in the Supper." *Art.* XXVIII. So in the Communion Service, believers in receiving the elements are represented as partaking of Christ's most blessed body and blood, at the same time. Undoubtedly the doctrine of the *real presence* of Christ *by the Spirit*, in the Holy Eucharist, is plainly taught by the English Church; and it is only strange that any question should ever be made with regard to the point, in the Church itself. But it is no less certain, that it has no claim to be considered a distinctively Episcopal doctrine, so far at least as the past history of the Reformed church is concerned, in any sense. Among all the early Reformed Confessions, there is hardly one in which it is not even more distinctly affirmed than it is in the Thirty-nine Articles. The Confession of the Reformed Dutch Church, in particular, is decidedly more high-toned here than the formulary of the Church of England; and we may say as much also even of the Westminster Confession itself.

The following passages are extracted from Hooker's great work, the *Ecclesiastical Polity.*

"It is too cold an interpretation, whereby some men expound our being in Christ, to import nothing else, but only that the self-same nature which maketh us to be men, is in him, and maketh him man as we are. For what man in the world is there, which hath not so far forth communion with Jesus Christ? It is not this that can sustain the weight of such sentences as speak of the mystery of our coherence with Jesus Christ. The Church is in Christ as Eve was in Adam. Yea, by grace, we are every of us in Christ and in his Church, as by nature we are in those our first parents. God made Eve of the rib of Adam. And his Church he frameth out of the very flesh, the very wounded and bleeding side of the Son of man. His body crucified and his blood shed for the life of the world, are the true elements of that heavenly being, which maketh us such as himself is of whom we come. For which cause the words of Adam may be fitly the words of Christ concerning his Church, 'flesh of my flesh, and bone of my bones,' a true native extract out of mine own body. So that in him even according to his manhood, we according to our heavenly being, are as branches in that root out of which they grow." *Book V. chap.* LVI. § 7.

"These things St. Cyril duly considering reproveth their speeches, which taught that only the deity of Christ is the vine whereupon we by faith do depend as branches, and that neither his flesh nor our bodies are comprised in this resemblance. For doth any man doubt, but that even from the flesh of Christ our very bodies do receive that life which shall make them glorious on the latter day, and for which they are already accounted parts of his blessed body? Our corruptible bodies could never live the life they shall live were it not that here they are joined with his body which is incorruptible, and that his is in ours as a cause of immortality, a cause by removing through the death and merit of his own flesh that which hindered the life of ours. Christ is therefore, both as God and as man, that true vine, whereof we both spiritually and corporally are true branches. He mixture of his bodily substance with ours is a thing which the ancient Fathers disclaim. Yet the mixture of his flesh with ours, they speak of, to signify what our very bodies, through mystical conjunction, receive from that vital efficacy which we know to be in his; and from bodily mixtures they borrow divers similitudes rather to declare the truth than the manner of coherence between his sacred and the sanctified bodies of saints." B. V. c. LVI. § 9.

"This was it that some did exceedingly fear, lest Zuinglius and Œcolampadius would bring to pass, that men should account of this sacrament but only as of a shadow, destitute, empty, and void of Christ. But seeing that by opening the several opinions which have been held, they are shown for aught I can see on all sides at the length to a general agreement concerning that which alone is material, namely the *real participation* of Christ, and of life in his body and blood *by means of this sacrament;* wherefore should the world continue still distracted and rent with so manifold contentions, when there remaineth now no controversy saying only about the subject *where* Christ is? Yea, even in this point no side denieth but that the *soul of man* is the receptacle of Christ's presence. Whereby the question is yet driven to a narrower issue, nor doth any thing rest doubtful but this, whether when the sacrament is administered Christ be whole *within man only*, or else his body and blood be also externally seated in the very consecrated elements themselves; which opinion they that defend, are driven either to *consubstantiate* and incorporate Christ with elements sacramental, or to *transubstantiate* and change their substance into his; and so the one to hold him really but invisibly moulded up with the substance of those elements, the other to hide him under the only visible show of bread and wine, the substance whereof, as they imagine, is abolished, and his succeeded in the same room." B. V. c. LXVII. § 2.

"It is on all sides plainly confessed, first, that this sacrament is a true and a real participation of Christ, who thereby imparteth himself, even his whole entire person as *a mystical Head* unto every soul that receiveth him, and that every such receiver doth incorporate or unite himself unto Christ as *a mystical member* of him, yea of them also whom he acknowledgeth to be his own; secondly, that to whom the *person of Christ* is thus communicated, to them he giveth by the same sacrament his Holy Spirit to sanctify them as it sanctifieth him which is their head; thirdly, that what *merit, force, of virtue soever there is in his sacrificed body and blood*, we freely, fully, and wholly have it by this sacrament; fourthly, that the *effect thereof in us is a real transmutation of our souls and bodies* from sin to righteousness, from death and corruption to immortality and life; fifthly, that because the sacrament being of itself but a corruptible and earthly creature, must needs be thought an unlikely instrument to work so admirable effects in man, we are therefore to rest ourselves altogether upon *the strength of his glorious power*, who is able and will bring to pass that the bread and cup which he giveth us shall be truly the thing he promiseth.

"It seemeth therefore much amiss that against them whom they term *Sacramentaries*, so many invective discourses are made, all running on two points, that the Eucharist is not a bare sign or figure only, and that the efficacy of his body and blood is not all we receive in this sacrament. For no man having read their books and writings which are thus traduced, can be ignorant that both these assertions they plainly confess to be most true. They do not so interpret the words of Christ, as if the name of his body did import but the figure of his body, and to *be* were only to signify his blood. They grant that these holy mysteries received in due manner do instrumentally both make us partakers of the grace of that body and blood which were given for the life of the world, and besides also impart unto us even in true and real though mystical manner the very person of our Lord himself, whole, perfect, and entire, as hath been showed." B. V. c. LXVII. § 7, 8.

Let us now turn to Dr. Owen. It is easy to feel ourselves in a different element here, from that which formed the inward life of Hooker. The whole system of the great nonconformist tended to carry him towards an incorporeal spiritualism in religion, that might be counted particularly unfavourable to a right estimate of the sacraments. Still, however, when we contrast his language with the frigid, rationalistic style in which the same system is accustomed to express itself on this subject at the present day, we can hardly fail to be surprised with the difference. The following passages are taken from his "Sacramental Discourses," as contained in Vol. XVII. of his Works, Russel's London edition.

"Christ is present with us in an especial manner in this ordinance. One of the greatest engines that ever the devil made use of to overthrow the faith of the Church, was by forging such a presence of Christ as is not truly in this ordinance, to drive us off from looking after that presence which is true. I look upon it as one of the greatest engines that ever hell set on work. It is not a corporeal presence; there are in-numerable arguments against that; every thing that is in sense, reason, and the faith of a man, overthrows that corporeal presence."—"Christ is present in this ordinance in an especial manner in three ways: by representation; by exhibition; by obsignation or sealing." *Disc.* X., *p.* 209, 210.

"Christ is present with us by way of *exhibition;* that is, he doth really tender and exhibit himself unto the souls of believers in this ordinance, which the world hath lost, and knows not what to make of it. They exhibit that which they do not contain. This bread doth not contain the body of Christ, or the flesh of Christ; the cup doth not contain the blood of Christ; but they exhibit them; both do as really exhibit them to believers, as they partake of the outward signs. Certainly we believe that our Lord Jesus Christ doth not invite us unto this table for the bread that perishes, for outward food; it is to feed our souls. What do we think then? doth he invite us unto an empty, painted feast? do we deal so with our friends? Here is something really exhibited by Jesus Christ unto us to receive, beside the outward pledges of bread and wine. We must not think the Lord Jesus Christ deludes our souls with empty shows and appearances. That which is exhibited is himself, it is his 'flesh as meat indeed, and his blood as drink indeed;' it is himself as broken and crucified that he exhibits unto us."—"Christ doth exhibit himself unto our souls, if we are not wanting unto ourselves, for these two things, incorporation and nourishment; to be received into union; and to give strength unto our souls." *Ib. p.* 211, 212.

"As it is plain from the sign and the thing signified that there is a real grant, of a real communication of Jesus Christ unto the souls of them that believe, so it is evident from the nature of the exercise of faith in this ordinance; it is by eating and drinking. Can you eat and drink unless something be really communicated? You are called to eat the flesh and drink the blood of the Son of Man; unless really com-municated, we cannot eat it nor drink it. We may have other appre-hensions of these things, but our faith cannot be exercised in eating and drinking, which is a receiving of what is really exhibited and communicated. As truly my brethren as we do eat of this bread and drink of this cup, which is really communicated to us, so every true believer doth receive Christ, his body and blood, in all the benefits of it, that are really exhibited by God unto the soul in this ordinance, and it is a means of communicating to faith." *Disc.* XXIII. *p.* 265.

"It is a common received notion among Christians, and it is true, that there is a peculiar communion with Christ in this ordinance, which we have in no other ordinance; that there is a peculiar acting of faith in this ordinance which is in no other ordinance. This is the faith of the whole Church of Christ, and has been so in all ages. This is the greatest mystery of all the practicals of our Christian religion, a way of receiving Christ by eating and drinking, something peculiar that is not in prayer, that is not in the hearing of the word, nor in any other part of divine worship whatsoever; a peculiar participation of Christ, a peculiar acting of faith towards Christ. This participation of Christ is not carnal, but spiritual. In the beginning of the ministry of our Lord Jesus Christ, when he began to instruct them in the communication of himself, and the benefit of his mediation, to believers, because it was a new thing, he expresses it by eating his flesh and drinking his blood, John VI. 53, 'Unless ye eat the flesh and drink the blood of the Son of man, ye have no life in you.' This offended and amazed them. They thought he taught them to eat his natural flesh and blood. 'How can this man give us his flesh to eat?' They thought he instructed them to be cannibals. Whereupon he gives that everlasting rule for the guidance of the Church, which the Church forsook, and thereby ruined itself; saith he, 'It is the Spirit that quickens; the flesh profits nothing. The words that I speak, they are spirit, and they are life.' It is a spiritual communication, saith he, of myself unto you; but it is as intimate, and gives as real an incorporation, as if you did eat my flesh and drink my blood."—*Disc.* XXV. *p.* 268.

"The fourth thing is the *mysteriousness*, which I leave to your experience, for it is beyond expression, the mysterious reception of Christ in this peculiar way of exhibition. There is a reception of Christ as tendered in the promise of the Gospel, but here is a peculiar way of his exhibition under outward signs, and a mysterious reception of him in them really, so as to come to a real substantial incorporation in our souls." *Ib. p.* 270.

All this, it must be confessed, is not without some measure of ambiguity, as it regards a real participation in the substance of Christ's humanity. It falls short altogether of the firm, clear utterances of Calvin and the Church of the sixteenth century. But it is full of force from such a man as Owen, in the age of Cromwell and the English Commonwealth. Here we have at least, in strong terms, the sense of an objective force, a true exhibition of the thing signified, in the sacrament. The communion, moreover, is specific, mystical, bound to the ordinance as its medium and instrument. Then it involves a real incorporation into Christ; and it is plainly felt, that this includes a special respect to his human nature, his flesh and blood, as given for the life of the world. But just at this point the representation is found to waver. The truth that struggles for utterance, is still embarrassed by the abstractions of the understanding, and is not permitted to come to a full, unfaltering expression.

CHAPTER II.

THE MODERN PURITAN THEORY.

SECTION I.

HISTORICAL EXHIBITION

IT cannot be denied that the view generally entertained of the Lord's Supper at the present time, in the Protestant Church, involves a wide departure from the faith of the sixteenth century with regard to the same subject. The fact must be at once clear to every one at all familiar with the religious world as it now exists, as soon as he is made to understand in any measure the actual form in which the sacramental doctrine was held in the period just mentioned.

This falling away from the creed of the Reformation is not confined to any particular country or religious confession. It has been most broadly displayed among the continental churches of Europe, in the form of that open, rampant rationalism, which has there to so great an extent triumphed over the old orthodoxy at so many other points. But it is found widely prevalent also in Great Britain and in this country. It is especially striking, of course, as has been already remarked, in the case of the Lutheran Church, which was distinguished from the other Protestant confession, in the beginning, mainly by its high view of the Lord's Supper, and the zeal it showed in opposition to what it stigmatized reproachfully as sacramentarian error. In this respect, it can hardly be recognized indeed as the same communion. The original name remains, but the original distinctive character is gone. Particularly is this the case, with a large part at least, of the Lutheran Church in our own country. We cannot say of it simply, that it has been led to moderate the old sacramental doctrine of the church, as exhibited in the *Form of Concord*; it has abandoned the doctrine altogether. Not only is the true Lutheran position, as occupied so violently against the Calvinists in the sixteenth century, openly and fully renounced; but the Calvinistic ground itself, then shunned with so much horror as the very threshold of infidelity, has come to be considered as also in unsafe contiguity with Rome. With no denomination do we find the anti-mystical tendency, usually charged upon the Reformed Church, more decidedly developed. Methodism itself can hardly be said to make less account of the sacraments, practically or theoretically. A strange contradiction surely, which, we may trust, is not destined always to endure. For it is not to be imagined that such an utter abandonment of the Lutheran principle in the case of the Lord's Supper, can be confined to this single point. Central as the doctrine of the sacrament is to the whole Christian system, (so felt to be especially by Luther,) such a change necessarily implies a change that extends much farther. The whole life of the Church, in these circumstances, must be brought into contradiction to its own proper principle. It cannot be true to itself. This of course we regard as a fit subject for lamentation. Never was there a time when it was more important, that this Church should understand and fulfil her own mission; and in no part of the world perhaps is this more needed than just here in America, where the tendency to undervalue all that is sacramental and objective in religion, has become unhappily so strong.*

*It is not intended, of course, to involve all connected with the Church, indiscriminately, in this censure. There are many excellent men belonging to it, no doubt, who feel and deplore the very evil which is here brought into view; and it is to be trusted, that these will yet cause their influence to be felt, in such a way as to roll off at last, in some measure at least, the reproach now resting upon the Church. For that room exists in fact for this reproach, cannot be seriously questioned by any one acquainted with the religious posture of the country, and it cannot be taken amiss therefore that it should be noticed in this public way. It is notorious that the American Lutheran Church, under its principal and most influential exhibition at least, has given up altogether the sacramental doctrine of Luther, and along with this, (for the two things can never be sundered,) the original genius and life of the Lutheran Confession. It is regarded by others as an evangelical *improvement* in the character and state of the Church, that it has become in this respect hopefully conformed to what may be styled the Modern Puritan theory of religion, with a strong inclination even to Methodism; and the same idea would seem to be very extensively entertained in the bosom of the Church itself. We have a right to take the so called *Lutheran Observer*, as an index of the prevailing tone of thinking in the Church, in this case. It is not, indeed, strictly speaking, under any ecclesiastical direction and control. The editor's responsibilities are all his own. Still, however, the mere fact that the paper is allowed to represent the Church before the world, constitutes it properly the organ of the body, and the accredited interpreter of its views. But now the Observer, besides being characteristically un-Lutheran in other respects, openly derides the whole idea of a real communion with the humanity of Christ as an exploded superstition! Thus, for instance, referring to the *Reformed* of Calvinistic view as asserted at Mercersburg, the editor does not hesitate, in his paper of Dec. 5, 1845, to use such language as the following: "Dr. N.'s doctrine of Con-corporation, alias his semi-Romanism in relation to the Eucharist."—"The Mercersburg effort to revive the errors of by-gone ages, from which it was fondly hoped our American Churches had finally and forever escaped."—"That figment of the imagination, that poor, low, mystical, confused, carnal and antiquated doctrine, yclept con-corporation! Only think of it—the literal communication of Christ's glorified humanity to the believer, thus confounding the natures of believers and of Christ, and actually predicating *ubiquity* of humanity! The glorified body of Christ received by the believer with the bread and wine! If this be not a *corporeal* presence, what meaning is there in

But it is not the Lutheran Church only, which has fallen away from its original creed, in the case of the Lord's Supper. Though the defection may not be so immediately palpable and open to all observation, it exists with equal certainty, as was said before, on the part of the Reformed Church. It does so for the most part in Europe; and in this country the case is, to say the least, no better. Our sect system must be considered, in its very nature, unfavourable to all proper respect for the sacraments. This may be taken, indeed, as a just criterion of the spirit of *sect*, as distinguished from the true spirit of the Christian church. In proportion as the sect character prevails, it will be found that Baptism and the Lord's Supper are looked upon as mere outward signs, in the case of which all proper efficacy is supposed to be previously at hand in the inward state of the subject by whom they are received. It is this feeling which leads so generally to the rejection of infant baptism, on the part of those who affect to improve our Christianity in the way of new schisms. It is particularly significant, moreover, in the aspect now considered, that the *Baptist* body, as such, is numerically stronger than any other denomination in the country. But the *baptistic* principle prevails more extensively still; for it is very plain that all true sense of the sacramental value of baptism is wanting, in large portions of the church, where the ordinance is still retained; and the consequence is, that it is employed to the same extent as a merely outward and traditional form. Along with this, of course, must prevail an unsacramental feeling generally, by which the Lord's Supper also is shorn of all its significance and power. Methodism, in this way, may be said to wrong, the sacraments, (as also the entire idea of the *Church*,) almost as seriously as the Baptist system itself. The general evil, however, reaches still farther. Even those denominations among us which represent the Reformed Church by true and legitimate descent, such as the Presbyterian in its different branches, and the Reformed Dutch, show plainly that they have fallen away, to some extent, from the original faith of the church, in the same direction. Remains of it indeed may still be found in the private piety of many, the result, in part, of their special advantage in the way of early traditional education, and in part the

language? If this is not equal to Puseyism, and an immense stride toward Romanism, we would like to know what is?"—"It grates upon the ear, jars the feelings, offends the understanding, and unhinges the holiest associations of many of the best and most spiritual [*sic!*] men, in the most evangelic churches."—Such is the style in which, not the old *Lutheran*, but the old *Reformed* doctrine of the Lord's Supper, is profanely abused by the principal paper in the present American Lutheran Church! Multitudes in that Church. of course, have been pained and mortified by such bare-faced ecclesiastical infidelity. They disclaim all sympathy with it in their hearts, and protest against it quietly as downright treason to all true Lutheranism. Still, the paper is endured, as the organ, in fact, of the Church; and until something more effectual than a mere silent protest is exhibited, we must mourn over the Church itself as being, it is to be feared, but too faithfully represented by the so-called *Lutheran Observer*.

product of their own religious life itself;* but, so far as the general reigning belief is concerned, the old doctrine may be said to be fairly suppressed by one of a different character. It is so theoretically, to a great extent, in our systems of theology, biblical expositions, sermons, and religious teaching generally, so far as the sacramental question is concerned. It is so practically, to an equal extent, in the corresponding views and feelings with which the use of the sacraments is maintained on the part of professing Christians. Not only is the old doctrine rejected, but it has become almost lost even to the knowledge of the Church. When it is brought into view, it is not believed, perhaps, that the Reformed Church ever held or taught, in fact, any doctrine of the sort; or if it be yielded at length, that Calvin and some others maintained some such view, it is set down summarily as one of those instances in which the work of the

*There is much comfort in this thought. The same reflection, only in somewhat stronger terms, is made by *Prof. Tayler Lewis*, of New York, in his admirable article on the Church Question, published in the *Bib. Repository, for Jan.*, 1846. The idea of the mystical union, he says correctly, is, and ever must be, a living principle in the hearts of all evangelical Christians. He appeals, accordingly, to the devotional books of the Scottish Church, and even to the common phraseology of Wesleyan prayer meetings, as serving to show a more active sense of truth itself in the form of life, than is to be found under all the outward display which may be made of the tenet by Rome or Oxford, as a dead relic of antiquity. "The life may be stronger than the dogma. Even in the absence of definite conceptions, the extreme fondness of a certain class of minds for this language, manifests the current of the affections in distinction from the speculative views maintained, and a consciousness, that even if there be a figure, it is figurative of a reality more precious and glorious than was ever set forth in any form of rationalism." This is very true. Dr. Lewis, however, himself admits, that there has been a great failing away on the part of the Church at large, from the faith, of the Reformation as well as of primitive Christianity, with regard to this point; and that, as a dogma at least, the truth is not now generally maintained. I must believe, too, that he overrates, in some measure, the extent to which it is practically felt. It is to be borne in mind always, that every truth in Christianity finds its counterfeit and shadow, in the religious life contemplated under a lower view. It is the *absolute* reality of what we meet elsewhere, under the form of mere prophecy or nisus. Now the very idea of religion, no matter how defective, involves a demand for union with God. Of course, when powerfully excited, in connection with Christianity, it can hardly fail to make this thought prominent in some way. And all this certainly constitutes a strong argument for the truth itself which it is thus attempted to reach. But there in a constant tendency, within the Christian sphere as well as beyond it, to substitute here the phantasm for the reality itself; as we may see in the case of the Anabaptists and Quakers. Much of the *experience* of Methodist prayer meetings, it in to be feared, labors under the same defect of *unreality*; and, universally, there is danger of this, where religion is suffered to run out into the simply subjective form, with little or no regard to the sacraments and the true idea of the Church. The piety of the old Scotch divines, is of a far more substantial order; and we have reason to be thankful that the life and power of it are still *felt*, in the case of this doctrine of the mystical union, far more extensively than the doctrine itself is either understood of acknowledged. But this want of proportion between life and doctrine, is itself a great evil; especially now when the strong tide of rationalistic error, arrogating to itself the title of Protestant orthodoxy, is threatening to rarefy and spiritualize the whole truth into a sheer moral abstraction.

Reformation appears still clogged with a measure of Popish superstition, brought over from that state of darkness and bondage which had just been left behind. In this view, the doctrine is considered to be of no force whatever for the Church, in her present condition of gospel light and liberty. It is unintelligible and absurd; savors of transubstantiation; exalts the flesh at the expense of the spirit. A real presence of the whole Christ in the Lord's Supper, under any form, is counted a hard saying, not to be endured by human reason, and contrary to God's word. Thus it stands with our churches generally. Even in the Episcopal Church, with all the account it professes to make of the sacraments, few are willing to receive in full such representations of the eucharistic presence, as are made either by Hooker or Calvin.

To feel at once the full force of the representation now made, it is only necessary to observe the style in which it is usual, at the present time, to speak of the sacraments in general, and of the Lord's Supper in particular, as compared with the language of the Church on the same subject in the period of the Reformation. The following extracts, taken from several of our popular modern theological writers, will be acknowledged, no doubt, to be a fair representation of the view, which is now too commonly entertained among us, on the subject to which they refer.

"The sacraments are also said to seal the blessings that they signify; and accordingly they are called not only signs but seals. It is a difficult matter to explain, and clearly to state the difference between these two words, or to show what is contained in a seal that is not in a sign. Some think that it is distinction without a difference."—"if we call them confirming seals, we intend nothing else hereby but that God has, to the promises that are given to us in his word, added these ordinances; not only to bring to mind this great doctrine, that Christ has redeemed his people by his blood, but to assure them that they who believe in him shall be made partakers of this blessing; so that these ordinances are a pledge thereof to them, in which respect God has set his seal, whereby in an objective way he gives believers to understand, that Christ and his benefits are theirs; and they are obliged at the same time by faith, as well as in an external manner, to signify their compliance with his covenant, which we may call their setting to *their* seal that God is true."—*Ridgely's Body of Divinity (Philadelphia edition of* 1815,) *Vol. IV. p.* 163, 165.

—

"Thus concerning Christ's death, showed forth or signified in this ordinance. We are farther, under this head, to consider *how* he is present, and they who engage in it aright feed on his body and blood by faith. We are not to suppose that Christ is present in a corporal way, so that we should be said to partake of his body in a literal sense; but he being a divine person, and consequently omnipresent, and having promised his presence with his Church in all ages and places, when met together in his name; in this respect he is present with them, in like manner as he is in other ordinances, to supply their wants, hear their prayers, and strengthen them against corruption and temptation, and remove their guilt by the application of his blood, which is presented as an object for their contemplation in a more peculiar manner in this ordinance.

"As for our feeding on, or being nourished by the body and blood of Christ, these are metaphorical expressions, taken from and adapted to the nature and quality of the bread and wine by which it is signified; but that which we are to understand hereby is, our graces being farther strengthened and established, and we enabled to exercise them with greater vigour and delight; and this derived from Christ, and particularly founded on his death. And when we are said to feed upon him in order hereunto, it denotes the application of what be has done and suffered to ourselves; and in order hereunto we are to bring our sins, with all the guilt that attends them, as it were, to the foot of the cross of Christ, confess and humble our souls for them before him, and by faith plead the virtue of his death, in order to our obtaining forgiveness, and at the same time renew our dedication to him, while hoping and praying for the blessing and privileges of the covenant of grace, which were purchased by him."—*Ibid. p.* 215.

—

"There is in the Lord's Supper a mutual solemn profession of the two parties transacting the covenant of grace, and visibly united in that covenant; the Lord Christ by his minister on the one hand, and the communicants (who are professing believers) on the other. The administrator of the ordinance acts in the quality of Christ's minister, acts in his name, as representing him; and stands in the place where Christ himself stood, at the first administration of this sacrament, and in the original institution of the ordinance. Christ, by the speeches and actions of the minister, makes a solemn profession of his part in the covenant of grace; he exhibits the sacrifice of his body broken and his blood shed; and in the minister's offering the sacramental bread and wine to the communicants, Christ presents himself to the believing communicants as their propitiation and bread of life; and by these outward signs confirms and seals his sincere engagements to be their Saviour and food, and to impart to them all the benefits of his propitiation and salvation. And they, in receiving what is offered, and eating and drinking the symbols of Christ's body and blood, also profess their part in the covenant of grace; they profess to embrace the promises and lay hold of the hope set before them, to receive the atonement, to receive Christ as their spiritual food, and to feed upon him in their hearts by faith."—"The sacramental elements in the Lord's Supper do represent Christ as a party in covenant, as truly as a *proxy* represents a prince to a foreign lady in her marriage; and our taking those elements is as truly a professing to accept Christ, as in the other case the lady's taking the proxy is her professing to accept the prince as her husband. Or the matter may be more fitly represented by this similitude:—it is as if a prince should send an ambassador to a woman in a foreign land, proposing marriage, and by his ambassador should send her his *picture*, and should desire her to manifest her acceptance of his suit, not only by professing her acceptance in words to his ambassador, but in token of her sincerity, openly to take or accept that picture, and to seal her profession by thus representing the matter over again by a symbolical action."—*President Edwards. On Full Communion. Works, (New York,* 1844,) *Vol. I. p.* 145, 146.

—

"The elements of this ordinance are bread and wine. The bread consecrated and broken represents the broken body of Christ, in his death on the cross. The wine poured out represents his blood in his death, which was shed for the remission of sins. The professed followers of Christ, by eating the bread and drinking the wine, when consecrated and blessed by prayer and thanksgiving, and distributed to them by the officers of the church, do by this transaction profess cordially to receive Christ by faith, and to live upon him, loving him, and trusting in him for pardon and complete redemption, consecrating themselves to his service. And by the ministers of the gospel consecrating those elements, and ordering them to be distributed to the communicants, Christ is exhibited as an all-sufficient Saviour, and the promise of salvation is expressed and sealed to all his friends. This is therefore a covenant transaction, in which those who partake of the bread and wine express their faith in Christ, that they are his friends, and devoted to his service, and their cordial compliance with the covenant of grace, and solemnly seal this covenant by partaking of these elements. And at the same time they are a token and seal of the covenant of grace on the part of Christ."—*Dr. Samuel Hopkins. System of Theology, Second edition, Boston,* 1811. *Vol. II. p.* 343.

—

"At the Lord's table Christ, by the mouth of his minister says, *This is my body, take ye, eat ye all of it. This is my blood, take ye, drink ye all of it.* Hereby sealing to the truth contained in the 'written instrument.' But it is therein written in so many words: 'I am the living bread which came down from heaven; if any man eat of this bread, he shall live forever; and the bread that I will give him is my flesh, which I will give for the life of the world. He that eateth my flesh and drinketh my blood, dwelleth in me, and I in him.' John VI. 51, 56. Thus it is written, and thus it is sealed on Christ's part. On the other hand, the communicant by his practice declares: 'I take his flesh, and eat it; I take his blood and drink it;' and seals the covenant on his part. And thus the 'written instrument' is externally and visibly sealed, ratified, and confirmed, on both sides, with as much formality as any 'written instrument' is mutually sealed by the parties in any covenant among men. And now if both parties are sincere in the covenant thus sealed, and if both abide by and act according to it, the communicant will be saved."—*Bellamy. Works, Vol. III. p.* 166.

—

Dr. Dwight has much to say of the Lord's Supper. In speaking of its design, he tells us that it is intended, first, *to represent the great sacrifice of Christ on the cross.* Sensible impressions go far beyond those made directly on the understanding. In no other ordinance is this truth so fully realized as in the Lord's Supper. "The breaking of the bread, and the pouring out of the wine, exhibit the sacrifice of Christ with a force, a liveliness of representation, confessed by all Christians, at all times; and indeed by most others also; and unrivalled in its efficacy even by the Passover itself. All the parts of this service are perfectly simle, and are contemplated by the mind without the least distraction or labour. The symbols are exact, and most lively portraits of the affecting original, and present to us the crucifixion, and the sufferings of the great subject of it, as again undergone before our eyes. We are not barely taught; we see and hear, and of consequence feel, *that Christ our Passover was slain for us, and died on the cross that we might live.*"—"So those doctrines of the Christian system, which are most intimately connected with it, are here exhibited with a corresponding clearness."—" In this solemn ordinance, these truths are in a sense visible. The guilt of sin is here *written with a pen of iron and with the point of a diamond.* Christ in a sense ascends the cross; is nailed to the accursed tree; is pierced with the spear; and pours out his blood to wash away the sins of men. Thus, in colours of life and death, we here behold the wonderful scene in which *was laid on him the iniquity of us all.*" The other purposes of the institution, treated of at length, are as follows: It is a standing proof of Christ's mission; it exhibits the purity of Christ's character; it admonishes Christians of the second coming of Christ; it unites them in a known, public, and efficacious bond of union; it is a visible and affecting pledge of Christ's love to his followers; it is suited also to edify Christians in the divine life; "The edification of Christians is the increase of justness in their views, of purity and fervour in their affections, and of faithfulness in their conduct, with regard to the objects of religion. To this increase, in all respects, the Lord's Supper naturally and eminently contributes."—*Dwight's Theology, Serm.* CLX.

The *motives* which should influence us to the celebration of the Lord's Supper are stated to be—1. The command of Christ; 2. The honour of Christ; 3. The benefits derived from it by the Church; 4. Our own personal good. "At the table of Christ chiefly, after their baptism, Christians are seen, and see each other, as a public body, as mutual friends, and as followers of the Lamb. Here, mutually, they and receive countenance and resolution; worship together as Christians only; rejoice together; weep together; and universally exercise the Christian graces, invigorated, refined, and exalted by the sympathy of the gospel. Here the social principle of the intelligent nature ascends to the highest pitch of dignity and excellence, of which in this world it is capable. Mind here refines, enlarges, and ennobles mind; virtue purifies and elevates virtue; and evangelical friendship not only finds and makes friends, but continually renders them more and more worthy of the name."—"No exercises of the Christian life are ordinarily more pure, vigorous, and evangelical, than those which are experienced at the sacramental table.

The sense which we here feel of our guilt, danger, and helplessness, is apt to be vivid and impressive in an unusual degree. Equally impressive are the views which we form of forgiving, redeeming, and sanctifying love. Here godly sorrow for sin is powerfully awakened. Here are strongly excited complacency in the divine character, admiration of the riches of divine grace, and gratitude for the glorious interference of Christ in becoming the propitiation of our sins. Here brotherly love is kindled into a flame; and benevolence, warm, generous, and expansive, learns to encircle the whole family of *Adam*. Here, more perhaps than any where else, Christians *have the same mind which was also in Christ*, and prepare themselves *to walk as he walked*. Every evangelical affection becomes vigorous and active, virtuous resolutions stable, and the purposes of the Christian life exalted."—"The ends proposed in the institution of the Lord's Supper by the Redeemer of mankind, are certainly of a most benevolent and glorious nature, and peculiarly worthy of the All-perfect Mind. They are the enlargement and rectification of our views concerning the noblest of all subjects, the purification of our affections, and the amendment of our lives. The means by which these ends are accomplished, are equally efficacious and desirable. They are at the same time simple, intelligible to the humblest capacity, in no respect burdensome, lying within the reach of all men, incapable of being misconstrued without violence, and therefore not easily susceptible of mystical or superstitious perversion. In their own proper, undisguised nature, they appeal powerfully to the senses, the imagination, and the heart, and at the same time enlighten, in the happiest manner, the understanding. Accordingly, Christians in all ages have regarded this sacrament with the highest veneration; have gone to the celebration with hope; attended it with delight; and. left it with improvement in the evangelical character."—*Dwight's Theology. Serm*. CLXI.

—

Dr. Dick endorses and accepts in full the opinion of Zuingli on the Lord's Supper, which he affirms to have been this: "That the bread and wine were no more than a representation of the body and blood of Christ; or in other words, the signs appointed to denote the benefits that were conferred upon mankind in consequence of the death of Christ; that therefore Christians derive no other fruit from the participation of the Lord's Supper, than a mere commemoration and remembrance of the merits of Christ, and that there is nothing in the ordinance but a memorial of Christ." There seems to have been a disposition in that age, he thinks, "to believe that there was a presence of Christ in the eucharist, different from his presence in the other ordinances of the gospel; an undefined something which corresponded to the strong language used at the institution of the Supper, *This is my body—this is my blood*. Acknowledging it to be figurative, many still thought that a mystery was couched under it. It was not indeed easy for those who had long been accustomed to the notion of the bodily presence of Christ, at once to simplify their ideas; and perhaps too they were induced to express themselves as they did, with a view to give less offence to the

Lutherans. Whatever was their motive, their language is not always sufficiently guarded." Calvin was one of the brightest ornaments of the Reformation, and in learning genius, and zeal, had few equals, and no superior. Yet *he* too falls into this condemnation. A passage is quoted, which it is found impossible to understand. "It supposes a communion of believers in the human nature of our Saviour, in the eucharist; and endeavours to remove the objection arising from distance of place, by a reference to the almighty power of the Spirit, much in the same way as Papists and Lutherans solve the difficulty attending their respective systems. If Calvin had meant only that in the Sacred Supper believers have fellowship with Christ in his death, he would have asserted an important truth, attested by the experience of the people of God in every age; but why did he obscure it, and destroy its simplicity, by involving it in ambiguous language? If he had any thing different in view; if he meant that there is some mysterious communication with his human nature, we must be permitted to say that the notion was as incomprehensible to himself as it is to his readers."—"Stript of all metaphorical terms, the action must mean, that in the believing and grateful commemoration of his death, we enjoy the blessing which were purchased by it, in the same manner in which we enjoy them when we exercise faith in hearing the gospel. Why then should any man talk as Calvin does, of some inexplicable communion in this ordinance with the human nature of Christ; and tell us that although it seems impossible, on account of the distance to which he is removed from us, we are not to measure the power of the Divine Spirit by our standard? I am sure that the person who speaks so, conveys no idea into the minds of those whom he addresses; and I am equally certain that he does not understand himself."—"There is an absurdity in the notion, that there is any communion with the body and blood of Christ, considered in themselves; that he intended any such thing; of that it could be of any advantage to us."—"When our Church therefore says, that 'the body and blood are as really, but spiritually, present to the faith of believers in that ordinance, as the elements themselves are to their outward senses,' and that they 'feed upon his body and blood to their spiritual nourishment and growth in grace,' it can mean only, that our incarnate suffering Saviour is apprehended by their minds, through the instituted signs; and that by faith they enjoy peace and hope; or it means something unintelligible and unscriptural." This looks to the Westminster Confession. The language of the Gallic or French Confession is then quoted, only to be condemned in still more explicit terms. Still the presence of Christ in the eucharist must be admitted. But then it is only as he is present in religious services generally. "In all these ordinances he is present; and he is present in the same manner in them all, namely, by his Spirit, who renders them effectual means of salvation."—*Lectures on Theology, by the late Rev. John Dick, D.D.*, Lect. XCI. XCII.

—

"By the body and blood of Christ, figuratively represented in the Lord's Supper, we are undoubtedly to understand his whole work of satisfying the justice of God in behalf of his peculiar people, which was consummated or completed, when his body was broken and his blood shed on the cross of Calvary; together with the privileges and blessings resulting, both in this life and that which is to come, from their Saviour's finished work. All these rich and inestimable gifts of divine grace, faith receives and applies in the proper celebration of this holy rite."—"Justly does our Confession of Faith declare, when speaking of this sacrament, that 'the body and blood of Christ are as really, but spiritually, present to the faith of believers, in this ordinance, as the elements themselves are to the outward senses.' O, my young friends! what blessed visions of faith are those, in which this precious grace creates an ideal presence of the suffering, bleeding, dying, atoning Saviour. When Gethsemane, and Pilate's hall, and the cross, the thorny crown, the nails, the spear, the hill of Calvary, are in present view; when the astounding cry of the co-equal Son of the Father, *My God, my God, why hast thou forsaken me*, thrills through the ear to the heart; when the joyous voice quickly follows, proclaiming, *It is finished! Father, into thy hands, I commend my spirit.* Yes, it is here that faith sees the sinner's ransom amply paid, &c. &c. Well may it be added, that 'spiritual nourishment and growth in grace' must be the result of views and exercises such as these."—*Lectures on the Shorter Catechism, by Dr. Green*, vol. II. p. 338–340.

—

"*John* VI. 53–56. The plain meaning of the passage is, that by his bloody death, his body and his blood offered in sacrifice for sin, he would procure pardon and life for man; and that they who partook of that, or had an interest in that, should obtain eternal life. He uses the figure of eating and drinking, because that was the subject of discourse, because the Jews prided themselves much on the fact that their fathers had eaten *manna*; and because, as he had said that he was the *bread* of life, it was natural to *carry out the figure*, and say that that bread must be eaten, in order to be of any avail in supporting and saving men."—"*Is meat indeed.* Is truly food. My *doctrine* is truly that which will give life to the soul."—"*Dwelleth in me.* Is truly and intimately connected with me. To dwell or abide in him is to remain in the belief of his doctrine, and in the participation of all the benefits of his death."—"*I in him.* Jesus dwells in believers by his spirit and doctrine. When his spirit is given them to sanctify them, and his temper, his meekness, humility, love, pervades their hearts; and when his doctrine is received by them and influences their life, and when they are supported by the consolations of his gospel, it may be said that he *abides* or dwells in them."—"*Matthew* XXVI. 26. *This is my body.* This *represents* my body. This broken bread shows the manner in which my body will be broken; or this will serve to call my dying sufferings to your *remembrance*."—"So Paul and Luke say of the bread, 'this is my body broken for you; this do *in remembrance* of me.' This expresses the whole design of the sacramental bread. It is by a striking emblem to call to *remembrance* in a vivid manner the dying sufferings of our Lord."—*Barnes, Notes on the Gospels.*

These are respectable authorities. They are quoted with respect. They will be acknowledged generally no doubt to be a fair representation of the predominant modern view, with regard to the Lord's Supper; particularly as it prevails in New England, and throughout the Calvinistic Churches of this country in general. The extracts are made various and full, as the best means of producing a clear and distinct impression of the sense that runs through them as a whole. It would be easy of course to multiply them almost to any extent. But this is not necessary. All that the case requires is simply such a picture as may be acknowledged to furnish a proper exhibition of the general view it is intended to represent. For this, the extracts now offered are sufficient.

SECTION II.

CONTRAST.

Now the first point that claims attention in the case, is the fact of such a difference between the view here exhibited and the Reformed doctrine of the sixteenth century, as has been already affirmed. So far as this goes, it is not necessary to decide absolutely on the nature of the difference. We may call it a change for the worse or a change for the better, as it may happen to strike our judgment. But the *fact* of the difference itself all must allow. The theology of New England, in the case before us, is not the theology of the Reformed Church of the sixteenth century. This Puritan theory of the power and virtue of the sacraments, is not the theory that was held by Calvin and that appears in the symbolical books of the first Calvinistic Churches.

We need only to make ourselves at home in the first place among the opinions of the sixteenth century, as presented for instance in Hospinian or Planck, and then pass over suddenly to the thinking of our own time, as revealed in such works as have now been quoted, in order to *feel* the full force of the difference. It is a transition into another spiritual element entirely. The difference is not simply in words and forms of expression. It extends to thoughts themselves. A different view prevails, in the two cases, of the nature of the sacraments, and of their relation to the ends for which they have been instituted; and along with this, the fact cannot be disguised, a different view also of the nature of the Christian salvation itself, in its relation to the person of the glorious Redeemer. Calvin could not possibly have approved what appears to have been the sacramental doctrine of Edwards. Ursinus must have openly condemned the style in which the subject is presented by Ridgely. Dr. Dick virtually pronounces himself at variance with all the early Reformed symbols. Even Owen himself could hardly have endured with patience, the language of Dr. Dwight. The difference is real and serious. The doctrine that runs through these extracts, is not the doctrine of the Reformed Church as it stood in the beginning.

To make the case more plain, let the following particulars be noticed, as characterizing in general the departure of the modern Puritan from the old Reformed view. They will show that it is a question of something more than mere words.

1. In the old Reformed view, the communion of the believer with Christ in the Supper is taken to be *specific* in its nature, and *different* from all that has place in the common exercises of worship. The sacrament, not the elements of course separately considered, but the ordinance as the

union of element and word, is held to be such an exhibition of saving grace, as is presented to the faith of the Church under no other form. It is not simply the word brought to mind in its ordinary force. The outward is not merely the occasion by which the inward, in the case, is made present to the soul as a separate existence; but inward and outward, by the energy of the Spirit, are made to flow together in the way of a common life; and come thus to exert a peculiar, and altogether extraordinary power, in this form, to the benefit of the believer. "There is a peculiar communion with Christ," says Dr. Owen, "which we have in no other ordinance;" and this, he adds, has been the faith of the whole Church in all ages. "A way of receiving Christ by eating and drinking; something peculiar, that is not in prayer, that is not in the hearing of the word, nor in any other part of divine worship whatever; a peculiar participation of Christ, a peculiar acting of faith towards Christ;" —In the modern Puritan view, on the contrary, this specific peculiar virtue of the sacraments is not recognized. Christ is present, we are told by Dr. Dick, in all ordinances; "and he is present in the same manner in them all, namely by his Spirit, who renders them effectual means of salvation." So with Dr. Dwight the entire force of the institution, is made to consist in the occasion it affords, for the affections and exercises of common religious worship. The idea of a peculiar sacramental power, belonging to this form of worship as such, seems to have no place at all in his system.

2. In the old Reformed view, the sacramental transaction is a *mystery*; nay, in some sense an actual *miracle*. The Spirit works here in a way that transcends, not only the human understanding, but the ordinary course of the world also in every other view. There is a form of action in the sacraments, which now belongs indeed to the regular order of the life that is comprehended in the Church, but which as thus established still involves a character that may be denominated *supernatural*, as compared with the ordinary constitution, not only of nature, but even of the Christian life itself. "Not without reason," says Calvin, "is the communication, which makes us flesh of Christ's flesh and bone of his bones denominated by Paul *a great mystery*. In the sacred Supper, therefore, we acknowledge it a *miracle*, transcending both nature and our own understanding, that Christ's life is made common to us with himself and his flesh given to us as aliment." "This *mystery* of our coalition with Christ," says the Gallic Confession, "is so sublime, that it transcends all our senses and also the whole course of nature." "The mode is such," according to the Belgic Confession, "as to surpass the apprehension of our mind, and cannot be understood by any." "The *mysteriousness*," we are told by Dr. Owen, "is beyond expression; the *mysterious* reception of Christ in this peculiar way of exhibition."

Contrast with this now the style in which the ordinance is represented, from the proper Puritan stand-point, in the extracts already quoted.

Modern
Puritans!

We find it spoken of, it is true, with great respect, as full of interest, significance and power. But it is no mystery; much less a miracle. As little so, it would seem, in the view of Dr. Dwight, as a common fourth of July celebration. The ends contemplated in the one case are religious, in the other patriotic; but the institutions as related to these ends are in all material respects of one and the same order. The ends proposed in the Supper "the enlargement and rectification of our *views*—the purification of our *affections*—the amendment of our lives. The means are efficacious and desirable; at the same time simple; *intelligible to the humblest capacity*; in no respect burdensome; lying within the reach of all men; incapable of being misconstrued without violence; and therefore not easily susceptible of *mystical* or superstitious perversion. In their own proper, undisguised nature, they appeal powerfully to the *senses*, the *imagination*, and the *heart*; and at the same time enlighten in the happiest manner, the *understanding*." All this is said to show "the *wisdom* of this institution." "There seems to have been a disposition in that age," says Dr. Dick, with reference to the sixteenth century, "to believe that there was a presence of Christ in the eucharist *different* from his presence in the other ordinances of the gospel; an undefined something, which corresponded to the strong language used at the institution of the Supper: *This is my body,—this is my blood.* Acknowledging it to be figurative, many still thought that a *mystery* was couched under it." Dr. Dick himself of course finds no mystery in the case. Calvin's doctrine accordingly is rejected, as *incomprehensible*; not understood by himself, (as the great theologian indeed humbly admits,) and beyond the understanding also of his readers. "Plain, literal language is best, especially on spiritual subjects, and should have been employed by Protestant Churches with the utmost care, as the figurative terms of Scripture have been so grossly mistaken." To this we may add, that the very reason why *such* plain, simple language as might have suited Dr. Dick has *not* been employed by the Protestant Churches in their symbolical books, is to be found in the fact that these Protestant Churches believed and intended to assert the presence of a mystery in the sacrament, for the idea of which no place is allowed in *his* creed, and that could not be properly represented therefore by any language which this creed might supply.

3. The old Reformed doctrine includes always the idea of an *objective force* in the sacraments. The sacramental union between the sign and the thing signified is real, and holds in virtue of the constitution of the ordinance itself, not in the faith simply of inward frame of the communicant. Without faith indeed this force which belongs to the sacrament cannot avail to the benefit of the communicant; faith forms the indispensable condition, by whose presence only the potential in this case can become actual, the life that is present be brought to take effect in the interior man. But the condition here, as in all other cases, is something different

Objective
force

from the thing itself, for which it makes room.* The grace of the sacrament comes from God; but it comes as such under the sacrament as its true and proper form; not inhering in the elements indeed, outwardly considered; but still mysteriously lodged, by the power of the Holy Ghost, in the sacramental transaction as a whole. The grace is truly present, according to Calvin, even where it is excluded from the soul by unbelief; as much so as the fertilizing qualities of the rain, that falls fruitless on the barren rock. Unbelief may make it of no effect; but the intrinsic virtue of the sacrament itself still remains the same. The bread and wine are the sure pledge still of the presence of what they represent, and "a true exhibition of it on the part of God." "The symbols," say Beza and Farel, "are by no means naked; but so far as God is concerned, who makes the promise and offer, they always have the thing itself truly and certainly joined with them, whether proposed to believers or unbelievers." —"We do utterly condemn the vanity of those who affirm, that the sacraments are nothing else but mere naked signs." *Old Scotch Confession.*—"Those signs then are by no means vain or void." *Belgic Confession.* —"We teach that the things signified are together with the signs in the right use exhibited and communicated." *Ursinus.* The sacrament in this view, not only signifies, but *seals* to believers, the grace it carries in its constitution. It is not simply a pledge that the blessings it represents are sure to them, in a general way, apart from this particular engagement itself; as when a man by some outward stipulation binds himself to fulfil the terms of a contract in another place and at another time. The sacramental transaction certifies and makes good the grace it represents, as actually communicated

*It is strange how much difficulty some persons seem to find in making this plain distinction. Because faith is necessary to the right use of the Lord's Supper, they will have it forthwith that all the force of it must resolve itself into the exercise of this grace on the part of the worshipper; and when they hear of an *objective* virtue in the sacrament itself, the presence of a real spiritual energy belonging to it in its own nature, whether apprehended by the communicant or not, and altogether independent of his faith, they are ready to exclaim against it at once an the very *opus operatum* of Popery itself. But the difference between *condition* and *principle*, is one that meets us on all sides, in every sphere of life. The plant cannot vegetate and grow without the presence of certain conditions, earth, moisture, heat, light, &c., required for its development. Are these conditions then, in any sense, the principle or ground of its life as such? Shall we say of the seed that it has no life in itself till it is thus called out in an actual way? On the contrary, we affirm the life to be in the seed objectively, even though it should never have an opportunity to make its appearance. And so we say, the sacrament of the Lord's Supper—not the *elements*, of course, as such, but the *transaction*, the sacramental mystery as a whole—includes, or makes present objectively the true life of Christ, which, when it meets with the proper conditions in the believer's soul, will there reveal itself in the same character, as something quite different from the mere working of the conditions themselves by which this is accomplished. To the unbeliever the same life is exhibited under the same form, but he does not accept it in his soul. He eats and drinks judgment to himself, not discerning the Lord's body.

at the time. So it is said to *exhibit* also the thing signified. The thing is *there*, not the name of the thing only, and not its sign of shadow; but the actual substance itself. "The sacrament is no picture," says Calvin, "but the true, veritable pledge of our union with Christ." To say that the body of Christ is adumbrated by the symbol of bread, only as a dead statue is made to represent Hercules or Mercury, he pronounces profane. The signs, Owen tells us, "*exhibit* that which they do not contain. It is no empty, painted feast. Here is something really exhibited by Jesus Christ unto us, to receive besides the outward pledges of bread and wine."

How different from all this again, the light in which the subject is presented in our modern Puritan theology. Here too the sacraments are indeed said to seal, and also to exhibit, the grace they represent. But plainly the old, proper sense of these terms, in the case, is changed. The *seal* ratifies simply a covenant, in virtue of which certain blessings are made sure to the believer, on certain conditions, under a wholly different form. Two parties in the transaction, Christ and his people, stipulate to be faithful to each other in fulfilling the engagements of a mutual contract; and in doing so, they both affix their seal to the sacramental bond. Such is the view presented very distinctly by Edwards, Hopkins, and Bellamy. The contract of salvation according to this last, is in the Lord's Supper, "externally and visibly sealed, ratified, and confirmed, on both sides, with as much formality as any written instrument is mutually sealed by the parties, in any covenant among men. And now if both parties are sincere in the covenant thus sealed, and if both abide by and act according to it, the communicant will be saved." So the sacrament is allowed to be exhibitional; not however of any actual present substance, as the old doctrine always held; but only in the way of figure, shadow or sign. A picture or statue may be said to exhibit their original, to the same extent. The sacramental elements are Christ's *proxy*. "Or the matter may be more fitly represented by this similitude: it is as if a prince should send an ambassador to a woman in a foreign land, proposing marriage, and by his ambassador should send her his *picture*, &c." *Edwards.* —With Dr. Dwight the sacrament is reduced fully to the character of a mere occasion, by which religious affections are excited and supported in the breast of the worshipper. He seems to have no idea at all of an objective force, belonging to the institution in its own nature. All is subjective, and subjective only. All turns on the adaptation of the rite to instruct and affect. He measures its wisdom and power, wholly by this standard. It is admirably *contrived* to work upon "the senses, the imagination, and the heart," as well as to "enlighten the understanding." Its whole force, when all is done, is the amount simply of the good thoughts, good feelings, and good purposes, that are brought to it, and made to go along with it, on the part of the worshippers themselves.

4. According to the old Reformed doctrine the invisible grace of the sacrament, includes a real participation in his *person*. That which is made present to the believer, is the very life of Christ himself in its true power and substance. The doctrine proceeds on the assumption, that the Christian salvation stands in an actual union between Christ and his people, mystical but in the highest sense real, in virtue of which they are as closely joined to him, as the limbs are to the head in the natural body. They are in Him, and He is in them, not figuratively but truly; in the way of a growing process that will become complete finally in the resurrection. The power of this fact is mysteriously concentrated in the Holy Supper. Here Christ communicates *himself* to his Church; not simply a right to the grace that resides in his person, or an interest by outward grant in the benefits of his life and death; but his person itself, as the ground and fountain, from which all these other blessings may be expected to flow. This idea is exhibited under all forms in which it could well be presented, and in terms the most clear and explicit. Christ first, and *then* his benefits. Calvin will hear of no other order but this. The same view runs through all the Calvinistic symbols. Not a title to Christ *in* his benefits, the efficacy of his atonement, the work of his spirit; but a true property in his life itself, out of which only that other title can legitimately spring. "We are quickened by a real participation of him, which he designates by the terms *eating* and *drinking* that no person might suppose the life which we receive from him to consist in simple knowledge." *Calvin.* We communicate with Christ's *substance.* "A substantial communication is affirmed by me everywhere." *Id.* —"He nourishes and vivifies us by the substance of his body and blood." *Gallic Confession.* —"It is *not only* to embrace with a believing heart all the sufferings and death of Christ, and thereby to obtain the pardon of sin and life eternal; but also *besides that* to become more and more united to his sacred body, by the Holy Ghost, &c." *Heidelberg Catechism.* —"We teach that he is present and united with us by the Holy Ghost, albeit his body be far absent from us." *Ursinus.* —"In the Supper we are made partakers, not only of the Spirit of Christ, and his satisfaction, justice, virtue, and operation; but also of the very substance and essence of his true body and blood, &c." *Id.* —"*Christ crucified, and* all benefits of his death." *Westminster Confession.* —"It is on all sides plainly confessed, that this sacrament is a true and a real participation of Christ, who thereby imparteth himself, even his whole entire person, as a mystical head, unto every soul that receiveth him, and that every such receiver doth incorporate or unite himself unto Christ as a mystical member of him." *Hooker.* —A peculiar exhibition of Christ under outward signs, "and a mysterious reception of him in them really, so as to come to a real substantial incorporation in our souls." *Owen.*

As the modern Puritan theory eviscerates the institution of all objective force, under any view, it must of course still more decidedly refuse to admit the idea of any such virtue belonging to it as that now mentioned. The union of the believer with Christ it makes to be moral only; or at least a figurative incorporation with his Spirit!* The sacred Supper forms an occasion, by which the graces of the pious communicant are called into favourable exercise; and his faith in particular is assisted in apprehending and appropriating the precious contents of the Christian salvation, as wrought out by the Redeemer's life and death! He participates in this way in the fruits of Christ's love, the benefits of his mediatorial work, his imputed righteousness, his heavenly intercession, the influences of his Spirit, &c.; but in the substantial life of Christ himself he has no part whatever. "A mutual solemn profession of the two parties transacting the covenant of grace, and visibly united in that covenant." *Edwards.* —So also *Hopkins* and *Bellamy.* "Sensible impressions are much more powerful than those which are made on the understanding, &c." *Dwight.* —"The ends proposed in the institution of the Lord's Supper are, the enlargement and rectification of our views concerning the noblest of all subjects, the purification of our affections and the amendment of our lives." *Id.* —"Stript of all metaphorical terms, the action must mean that in the believing and grateful commemoration of his death, we enjoy the blessings which were purchased by it, in the same manner in which we enjoy them when we exercise faith in hearing the Gospel." *Dick.* —"No man who admits that the bread and wine are only signs and figures, can consistently suppose the words, 1 Cor. X. 16, to have any other meaning, than that we have communion with Christ in the fruits of his sufferings and death; or that receiving the symbols we receive by faith the benefits procured by the pains of his body and the effusion of his blood." *Id.* —Christ's "*doctrine* is truly that which will give life to the soul." *Barnes.* —"To dwell or abide in him, is to remain in the belief of his doctrine and in the participation of all the benefits of his death." *Id.* —"The whole design of the sacramental bread, is by a striking emblem to call to *remembrance*, in a vivid manner, the dying sufferings of our Lord." *Id.*

5. In the old Reformed view of the Lord's Supper, the communion of the believer in the true person of Christ, in the form now stated, is supposed to hold with him especially as the Word made *flesh*. His humanity forms the medium of his union with the Church. The life of which he is the fountain, flows forth from him only as he is the Son of Man. To have part in it at all, we must have part in it as a real human life; we must eat his flesh and drink his blood; take into us the substance of what he was as

---

*The insufficient and contradictory character of the representations by which it is attempted in part to uphold the idea of a *real* union with Christ, on the basis of this theology, will be noticed in another place. To a great extent, the idea seems not to be acknowledged at all. The whole is made to be a sort of biblical figure, which only the most mystical imagination might be expected to understand in any literal sense.

man; so as to become flesh of his flesh and bone of his bones. "The very flesh in which he dwells is made to be vivific for us, that we may be nourished by it to immortality." *Calvin.* —"This sacred communication of his flesh and blood, in which Christ transfuses his life into us, just as if he penetrated our bones and marrow, he testifies and seals also in the Holy Supper." *Id.* —"I do not teach that Christ dwells in us simply by his Spirit, but that he so raises us to himself as to transfuse into us the vivific vigor of his flesh." *Id.** —"The very substance itself of the Son of Man." *Beza and Farel.* —"That same substance which he took in the womb of the Virgin, and which he carried up into heaven." *Beza and Peter Martyr.* —"As the eternal deity has imparted life and immortality to the flesh of Jesus Christ, so likewise his flesh and blood, when eaten and drunk by us, confer upon us the same prerogatives." *Old Scotch Confession.* —"That which is eaten is the very, natural body of Christ, and what is drunk his true blood." *Belgic Confession.* —"Flesh of his flesh and bone of his bone . . . . We are as *really* partakers of his true body and blood, as we receive these holy signs." *Heidelberg Catechism.* —"We are in such sort coupled, knit, and incorporated into his true, essential human body, by his Spirit dwelling both in him and us, that we are flesh of his flesh and bone of his bones." *Ursinus.* —"They that worthily communicate in the sacrament of the Lord's Supper, do therein feed upon the body and blood of Christ—truly and really." *Westminster Catechism.*

All this the modern Puritan view utterly repudiates, as semi-popish mysticism. It will allow no real participation of Christ's person in the Lord's Supper, under any form: but least of all under the form of his humanity. Such communion as it is willing to admit, it limits to the presence of Christ in his divine nature, of to the energy he puts forth by his Spirit. As for all that is said about his body and blood, it is taken to be mere figure, intended to express the value of his sufferings and death. With his body in the strict sense, his life as incarnate, formerly on earth and now in heaven, we can have no communion at all, except in the way of remembering what was endured in it for our salvation. The *flesh* in any other view profiteth nothing; it is only the Spirit that quickeneth. The language of the Calvinistic confessions on this subject, is resolved into bold, violent metaphor, that comes in the end to mean almost nothing. "If he (Calvin) meant that there is some mysterious communication with his

---

*Vitam quam nobis Christus largitur, non in eo, duntaxat sitam esse confitemur, quod spiritu suo vivificat, sed quod spiritus etiam sui virtute carnis suæ vivificæ nos facit participes, qua participatione in vitam æternam pascamur. Itaque cum de communione quam cum Christo fideles habent loquimur, non minus carni et sanguini ejus communicare ipsos intelligimus quam spiritui, ut ita totum Christum possideant.—Hanc autem carnis et Sanguinis sui communionem Christus sub panis et vini symbolis in sacro sancta sua cœna offert et exhibet omnibus, qui eam rite celebrant juxta legatimum ejus institutum. *Confessio Fidei de Eucharistia*, exhibited by *Farel, Calvin* and *Viret*, a. 1537.

human nature, we must be permitted to say the notion was as incomprehensible to himself as it is to his readers." *Dick.* —"There is an absurdity in the notion that there is any communion with the body and blood of Christ, considered in themselves." *Id.* —"Justly does our Confession of Faith declare, that the body and blood of Christ are as *really*, but spiritually present to the faith of believers, &c. . . . . What blessed visions of faith are those, in which this precious grace creates an *ideal* presence of the suffering, bleeding, dying, atoning Saviour! Then Gethsemane, and Pilate's hall, and the cross, the thorny crown, the nails, the spear, the hill of Calvary, are in present view!" *Green.* —"This broken bread shows the manner in which my body will be broken; or this will serve to call my dying sufferings to your *remembrance.*" *Barnes.*

Let this suffice in the way of comparison. The two theories, it is clear, are different throughout. Nor is the difference such as may be considered of small account. It is not simply formal or accidental. The modern Puritan view evidently involves a material falling away, not merely from the form of the old Calvinistic doctrine, but from its inward life and force. It makes a great difference surely, whether the union of the believer with Christ be regarded as the power of one and the same life, or as holding only in a correspondence of thought and feeling; whether the Lord's Supper be a sign and seal only of God's grace in general, or the pledge also of a special invisible grace present in the transaction itself; and whether we are united by means of it to the person of Christ, or only to his merits; and whether finally we communicate in the ordinance with the whole Christ, in a real way, or only with his divinity. Such, however, is the difference that stares us in the face, from the comparison now made. All must see and feel that it exists, and that it is serious.

Under this view then simply the subject is entitled to earnest attention. Apart from all judgment upon the character of the change which has taken place, the fact itself is one that may well challenge consideration. We have no right to overlook it, or to treat it as though it did not exist. We have no right to hold it unimportant, or to take it for granted with unreflecting presumption that the truth is all on the modern side. The mere fact is serious. For the doctrine of the eucharist lies at the very heart of christianity itself; and the chasm that divides the two systems here is wide and deep. For churches that claim to represent, by true and legitimate succession, the life of the Reformation under its best form, the subject is worthy of being laid to heart. Only ignorance or frivolity can allow themselves to make light of it.

SECTION III.

FAITH OF THE EARLY CHURCH.

A strong presumption is furnished *against* the modern Puritan doctrine, as compared with the Calvinistic or Reformed, in the fact that the first may be said to be of yesterday only in the history of the Church, while the last, so far as the difference in question is concerned, has been the faith of nearly the whole Christian world from the beginning. It included indeed a protest against the errors with which the truth had been overlaid in the church of Rome. It rejected transubstantiation and the sacrifice of the mass; and refused to go with Luther in his dogma of a local presence. But in all this it formed no rupture with the original doctrine of the Church. That which had constituted the central idea of this doctrine from the first, and which appears even under the perversions that have just been named, it still continued to hold with a firm grasp. It is this central idea, the true and proper substance of the ancient church faith precisely, that created the difference between the Reformed doctrine and the modern Puritan. In the Reformed system it is present in all its force; in the other it is wanting. The voice of antiquity is all on the side of the Sixteenth Century, in its high view of the sacrament. To the low view which has since come to prevail, it lends no support whatever.

It is granted readily, that the view taken of the Lord's Supper in the early Church, as represented to us in the writings of the fathers, is by no means free from obscurity and contradiction. It is not from the infancy of the Church in any case, that we are to look for clear and satisfactory statements of theological truth. The fathers form no binding authority for the faith of later times in this view; although it does not follow immediately from such a concession, that we are at liberty to despise or overlook their authority entirely; just as little as it could be counted rational for a man in advanced life, to affect an utter independence of his own childhood, because it is found to have been characterized by all manner of imperfections and mistakes. Doctrines, in the Church, have their separate history. The life and power of the truth they express has been present from the beginning; but centuries have been needed to give them their proper form for the understanding. It constitutes then no objection whatever to an established article of the Christian creed, the doctrine of the true and proper divinity of Christ for instance, or the doctrine of total depravity and free grace, that testimonies may be gathered from the earlier fathers, which seem to conflict with it, or at least to show it of uncertain authority. All such confusion and contradiction serve only to show, that the article in question had not at the time evolved itself for the consciousness of the Church into the clear theological form, in which it was subsequently held. The confusion impairs not on the one hand the credit of the doctrine, and brings no fair reproach upon the witnessing authorities in the case on the other. It is enough that we find them true to the inward soul and substance of the Christian faith; though they may fall short of its full and proper expression; while it must be regarded always as a fair test of the correctness of any later statement, claiming to be the expression required, that it shall be found to take up and preserve the substance at least of the same life that is presented in the earlier creed. Thus in the case before us, the weight and significance of the Lord's Supper are not to be measured precisely, by the terms in which we find it spoken of in the early Church. We need not be surprised either to meet with some confusion and contradiction, in the testimony furnished by the fathers on the subject of the ordinance, its nature and design. The doctrine of the eucharist, like every other Christian doctrine, has a history. Its history moreover has proceeded through error; and it must be allowed, that the principle of this error began to work at a very early period. All this is to be taken into consideration, when we carry our appeal in the present case to the first ages of the Church. But all this can never form a sufficient reason, for treating the authority of these ages with indifference or contempt. Allowing their testimony to be imperfect, confused, and not always consistent with itself, admitting too that as we advance into the fourth and fifth centuries, we are met with forms of thinking and speaking that look directly towards the great error of transubstantiation; we have still no right to assume that the Church in the beginning had no faith that could be counted real and substantial, in the case of the eucharist, or that this faith included in no sense the truth as it has been of force for the Church since. In the midst of all errors and contradictions, the early Church must have been in possession of the truth, here as at other points, at least in its essential power and life. Running through all, there must be a certain fundamental substratum, in which the true idea of the sacrament was always at hand, and which the Church is bound accordingly, through all ages, to respect in this light.

Now it is very certain that the early fathers do not teach either transubstantiation or consubstantiation. There is not a passage which can be quoted from the first three centuries, that yields the least support, on any fair interpretation, to either of these dogmas; while the general testimony of the period contradicts both in explicit terms. We may say too, that in the period following, on to the time of Paschasius Radbert, in the ninth century, the case continues the same; although undoubtedly a style of speaking was now introduced, that seems often to countenance in full, if not pointedly to affirm, the superstition that was afterwards openly proclaimed as the creed of the Church. The sacramental doctrine of the early Church recognized no local presence of Christ's body in the

elements, no merely oral communication, nothing like a magical virtue in
the use of the ordinance outwardly considered. But just as little, on the
other hand, did it fall over to the opposite extreme of making the ordinance a mere representation of spiritual blessings to the mind of the
worshipper. From the beginning evidently it was *felt* to be more than this.
It was regarded as a mystery, in which was involved the inmost life of the
gospel, and a form of communion with the Saviour altogether peculiar
and extraordinary. We find it accordingly exalted and honoured as the
central service in the Christian worship, around which all other services
were made to revolve, and from which they might be said to borrow all
their light. The elements were more than memorials simply and signs.
They were made to bear the designation of the Lord's body and blood, in
the way of common liturgical expression; which could not have been the
case, if they had not been regarded as the actual exhibition of his person,
in a mystery, under this form. The same thing is clear from utterances of
a more direct nature, with regard to the peculiar power of the institution;
all serving to show in the breast of the Church, from the first, the feeling
that the eucharist includes in its very constitution a real communion with
the whole person of Christ, as the ground of all interest on the part of the
believer in his benefits. This idea, in the course of time, carried the faith
of Christendom quite over to the absurdity of transubstantiation; which
itself, however, only serves to illustrate the force with which it wrought
as an essential, constituent part of the Christian consciousness from the
beginning. If Christianity had not included in its very nature the idea of
a true substantial union with the human life of Christ, not only signified
but embodied and made actual in the mystery of the Supper, such a
superstition as that maintained by the Church of Rome could never have
come to prevail. The simple fact that the early sacramental doctrine *was*
carried regularly forward, by perversion, to this extraordinary and monstrous result, is itself evidence satisfactory that the doctrine always contained the idea, out of which only it was possible for any such abuse to
spring. Had the low view of the sacraments with which many are satisfied
at the present time prevailed in the faith of the primitive Church, such an
error as that which supposes an actual change of the elements into the
body and blood of Christ could never have appeared.

The early fathers speak of the eucharist frequently as an *offering* or
oblation; never, however, in the sense in which it came to be so regarded
in the later Catholic Church. It was viewed in this case merely as an act
of Christian worship, in which the congregation joyfully recognized the
goodness of God as displayed in the natural creation, and rendered praise
to him especially for the grace of redemption bestowed upon the world
through his Son Jesus Christ. In this last direction, it was regarded, of
course, also as a memorial of the Saviour, by which the lively recollection
of his person, and particularly of his sufferings and death, was to be

perpetuated in the Church to the end of time. But this all formed only one side of the Christian consciousness in the case. Even as an act of thanksgiving and commemoration, the service included a special reference to the death of Christ as a *propitiation* for sin; something therefore to be reached and appropriated by the spirit of the worshipper, as the indispensable condition of his own life. It was felt to be more then than a mere occasion for the exercise of common recollection of imagination; it demanded *faith* on the part of the worshipper, and was felt at the same time to embody an objective exhibition of the great Christian sacrifice in the way of actual pledge and seal, for the benefit of the soul in which such faith was at hand. This relation, however, was found to involve, to the apprehension of the Church, a connection with the Saviour still more intimate and close. To have part truly and fully in the virtue of his atonement, it was felt that there must be a real participation also in the *life* of his person. This formed accordingly the other side of the Christian consciousness, in the period to which we refer; and both conceptions must be joined together, in order that we may understand and interpret it fairly, in relation to the point with which we are now concerned.

It will be found now, on proper investigation, that the view of the eucharist held in the early Church includes throughout, along with that reference to the virtue of Christ's atonement which has been mentioned, this idea also of a real communication with his *person*, as the only ground on which the other benefit can become available. The idea in some cases may be in a measure thrown into the shade; but it never passes wholly out of sight; while for the most part it stands forth with such prominence, as to leave no room whatever to question its presence.*

*For an able and full exposition of this point, the reader is referred to a recent work, *Das Dogma vom heiligen Abendmahl und seine Geschichte, von* Dr. August Ebrard. *Frankfurt a M.* 1845. Dr. Ebrard is Professor of Theology, at Zurich, in the service, of course, of the *Reformed* Church. His work is intended to be a vindication of the Reformed or Calvinistic theory of the Eucharist, in its substance, as distinguished from what is styled the Old Lutheran view; and it carries throughout, on this account, a somewhat polemical reference in this direction. The ultimate design of it, however, is irenical; as the author supposes that the case is one which admits of reconciliation, and that all that is needed for this purpose is such a statement of the doctrine as may relieve it from what may be regarded as merely accidental objections on both sides. He, of course, maintains a real communion with Christ's *whole* life, in the new nature of the Christian generally, and in the transaction of the sacrament in particular. This is something certainly that deserves to be noted, as proceeding from the very heart of the original Swiss Reformation, and the theological chair, we may say, of Zuingli himself. It serves to show how powerfully the tide of evangelical thinking has come, to set in, at this time in the direction here taken. I need not say, that it has been particularly encouraging to me, to meet with this publication in the course of the present work; maintaining as it does, substantially, the same view of Christ's presence in the Eucharist, though constructed on a wholly different plan, and in view also of altogether different relations. I regret, however, that the second volume, which was to have appeared some months ago, exhibiting the history of the doctrine *since the Reformation*, has not yet come into my hands.

Ignatius speaks of the eucharist (*ep. ad Smyrn. c.* 7,) as the flesh of Christ, that suffered for our sins and was raised again by the goodness of the Father. This does not imply that he supposed the body of Christ to be in the bread. We know he did not. But the language here employed, which must be considered true to the general view of the Church at the time, serves to show with what force the feeling prevailed that the things represented by the signs in the Lord's Supper were so bound to them inwardly, as to form in some sense one and the same presence. So when he styles the bread (*ep. ad Ephes. c.* 20,) "the medicine of immortality, the antidote of death," it does not indeed imply that he considered the reception of Christ's body into the believer's person the means physically of his resurrection; but it certainly does show this much at least, that something more was felt to be involved in the sacramental service, than a mere thinking of Christ and his mediatorial work. The sacrament is viewed as carrying in itself objectively the power to unite us with the atonement of Christ, by making us one with him in his life. It is the antidote of death, as it causes us to "live always in Jesus Christ."

Justin Martyr (*Apol. I. c.* 66,) tells us that the eucharist was not received by Christians as *common* bread or *common* drink; but that as Jesus Christ himself became flesh for our salvation, so it was held that the consecrated food in this solemnity is his flesh and blood. His meaning is, that in partaking of the one, we partake of the other also in a mystery, to the sustentation of that new life which is communicated to us by Christ.

Irenœus seems to go farther still, and to teach that the bread and wine in the eucharist are so pervaded with the very body and blood of Christ, as to become by physical incorporation the source of immortality to the body of the believer. By a proper comparison, however, of one passage with another, it appears that this could not have been his meaning. But it is thus made only so much the more certain, that he considered the participation of the sacramental bread and wine to be a participation, at the same time, of the person of Christ, in virtue of which the body itself, in the case of the true Christian, is made to have part in his nature, and so in that eternal life of which he is the fountain. "As the bread out of the earth," he tells us, (Adv. hær. IV. 18, 5,) "after its consecration, is no longer common bread, but the *eucharist*, consisting of two things, an earthly and a heavenly; so also our bodies, when they partake of the eucharist, are no longer mortal, having the hope of the resurrection to life everlasting." Again (Adv. hær. V. 2, 3): "As the slip of the vine inserted in the ground has in its own time brought forth fruit, and the grain of wheat falling into earth and undergoing dissolution has been raised up with multiplication by the Spirit of God, through whom all things consist; and these, made meet afterwards, in God's wisdom, for man's use, and having added to them the word of divine consecration, become the *eucharist*, which is Christ's body and blood; so in like manner our bodies are nourished by this, and after they are buried and dissolved in the earth, shall in their own time rise again, the divine word imparting to them the resurrection." Here he seems to identify the elements absolutely with Christ's body and blood, and has been supposed by some to teach that the mere oral or corporeal reception of them served to convey into the bodies of believers, in a physical way, the virtue of immortality. But other passages show that such was not his meaning; and, even in these quotations, it is clear that all is referred to the word of God, the presence of a higher life, that is felt to be mystically joined with the sacramental symbols. Hence he styles the bread and wine elsewhere the *antitypes* of Christ's body and blood, in the participation of which we are made to receive the remission of sins and life everlasting. This term (ἀντίτυπα) was frequently applied to the elements in the early Church.

The view represented by Ignatius, Justin Martyr, and Irenæus, was that which prevailed most generally, according to Neander, in their time.* In the north of Africa, as represented by Tertullian and Cyprian, we find a more guarded phraseology in relation to the whole subject. The bread and wine are more distinctly exhibited in the character of symbols, and no room is given for the imagination to confound them with the actual body and blood of Christ. Still they are not dead symbols. Along with their sacramental use, a real communication with the body and blood they represent is also supposed to have place; the visible and the invisible com-

---

Allg. Gesch. der Chr. Religion und Kirche. 2d edit. *Hamburg*, 1843. Vol. II. p. 1117–1120. Neander tells us that the view represented by these fathers involved the supposition of an actual corporeity assumed by the Logos immediately in the sacrament itself, in conjunction with the elements, and in such way as to be carried over with them into the bodies of believers as a φάρμακον ἀθανασίας or pabulum of immortality; an idea which he admits, however, was not *distinctly* uttered till a later time. It lies, he thinks, particularly in the passage of *Justin*, to which reference has already been made, (Apol. I. 66,) where we have the words: Την δι᾽ εὐχῆς λόγου τοῦ παρ᾽ αὐτοῦ εὐχαριστηθεῖσαν τροφὴν, ἐξ ἧς αἷμα καὶ σάρκες κατὰ μεταβολὴν τρέφονται ἡμῶν, ἐκείνου τοῦ σαρκωποιηθέντος Ἰησοῦ καὶ σαρκά καὶ αἷμα ἐδιδάχθημεν εἶναι. It must be confessed, however, that this is very obscure evidence of any such opinion. Ebrard, in the work already quoted, shows very clearly that these early fathers, in the use of such language, did not intend to assert, what their language at times might seem to imply, an actual corporealizition of Christ in any way in the elements, but simply the presence of his body mystically in the sacramental transaction. The elements were constituted, by consecration, the "body and blood" of Christ, and were so styled in the general liturgical phraseology; they received a new character under the eucharistic benediction, and became the present pledge of what they represented; but still, they remained, in their own substance, bread and wine. All goes to show, however, how deep was the feeling, that the ordinance comprehended in it a *real* communion with the life of Christ; and with this life, it may be added, under its *human* form. For even the conception mentioned by Neander, would resolve itself at last simply into this, that Christ's humanity must extend itself, not by any division of his individual person but in the way of organic reproduction into the persons of all whom he will thus raise up at the last day. His life, in this form, is the true φάρμακον ἀθανασίας, as he says expressly himself (John VI. 54).

prehended in the same transaction. The practice of the Church may itself be taken as an evidence, that a high sense was entertained of the objective virtue of the sacrament; for it was in Northern Africa particularly, that daily communion prevailed, and for a time also the custom of extending the ordinance even to infants. *Tertullian,* indeed, tells us that the words "My body," in the form of institution mean, "The figure of my body;" and this is sufficient to show, that he had no thought of any thing like an actual inclusion of Christ's body in the bread.* But he tells us elsewhere again, that we partake in the Supper of "the fatness of the Lord's body" (De pudic. cap. 9,) and that the flesh is fed with the sacramental body and blood of Christ, in order that the soul also may be fat from God." (De resur. carn. cap. 8.) While in another connection he makes this spiritual nourishment to be the very life of Christ himself, when he teaches, (De orat. c. 6,) that the petition for daily bread must be taken mainly in a spiritual sense; as Christ is the proper bread of life according to his own word, and as signified in the bread of the eucharist; so that, in praying, Give us our daily bread, "perpetuitatem postulamus in Christo, et individuitatem a corpore ejus."

The Alexandrian fathers, *Clement,* and more particularly *Origen,* separate of course still more widely between the inward and the outward, in the case of the sacraments, as in every other case. Their tendency was always to an extreme spiritualism; which, with Origen especially, came near to making the whole Christian revelation little better than a splendid philosophical allegory. He disparages the letter continually, for the purpose of exalting the spirit. So in the case of the eucharist, he goes so far as to make the body and blood of Christ nothing more than his word.†
"His great object," says Neander, "was to withstand the idea of a magical efficiency in the Supper, separately considered—which however the other church teachers were far from holding; but his view opposed in fact every

---

*Rudelbach, in his work, "Reformation, Lutherthum und Union," Leipzig, 1839, devotes a special excursus to Tertullian's doctrine of the Lord's Supper; in which he labours with all his might to make him out a sound Lutheran, of the old stamp. He will have it that the term *figure,* in the passage here referred to (Adv. Marc. IV. 40), denotes the actual form of the body itself, in the sense of its reality! This, however, would be nothing less than transubstantiation itself. Ebrard exposes the extravagance of Rudelbach with just severity, (p. 294–298.) The whole style of Tertullian's thinking stands opposed to every such construction of his words. He, and Cyprian, and Augustin, the founders and fathers, we may say, of the whole Western Latin theology, occupy here the very same ground, so far as we can judge, that was afterwards taken by the *Reformed* Church, in distinction both from the Lutheran and the Church of Rome.

†Nam corpus Dei Verbi aut sanguis, quid aliud esse potest, nisi verbum quod nutrit, et verbum quod lætificat cor?—Pursuing his allegorical exegesis, he makes the *body* to be the word of the Old Testament, and the *blood* the word of the New! See Ebrard, p. 274–277.

conception of any sort of higher meaning of force in the outward signs, even such as was admitted by the African Church."

It is hardly necessary to say that this view found comparatively small favour in the Church. The tendency, indeed, was already towards an extreme the other way. We cannot say, that the presence of Christ was as yet confounded with the presence of the symbols, by which it was represented; but the feeling was strong, that the two were mystically bound together, and the language employed to express this thought became always more bold and absolute; till in the end the liturgical appellation Christ's "body and blood," applied to the bread and wine, might almost seem to have been taken by many, even long before the time of Paschasius Radbert, in a strictly literal and proper sense.

Thus we hear *Cyril*, of Jerusalem, in the fourth century, insisting on the words of institution in such style as this: "When he himself has plainly said in relation to the bread, *This is my body*, who will presume to have any farther doubt? And when he has solemnly assured us, *This is my blood*, who will hesitate ever to say that it is his blood? He changed water before into wine resembling blood, in Cana of Galilee; and shall we distrust him here as changing wine into blood?"* This sounds like transubstantiation itself in the fullest sense; and yet there is good reason to believe, that such was not the meaning of the worthy father himself, after all.

Chrysostom uses very strong language too in the same direction; but he is, on the whole, more guarded, and less liable to misconstruction. He makes the sensible elements in the Supper to be indeed the form, under which its proper spiritual grace is brought near to the believer; as the washing with water in Baptism, is the outward exhibition of the grace of regeneration. But still the outward and inward are not made to flow absolutely together. The first is something, αἰθητόν, for the senses; the other is νοητόν, not a mere thought, certainly, but something to be received by the soul, and not simply by the mouth. "If thou hadst been without a body," he says, "the grace might have come to thee in the same naked form; but since the soul is interwoven with the body, he gives thee the spiritual in forms of sense (ἐν αἰθητοῦς τὰ νοητά σοι παραδίδωσι)."†

Cateches. 4. The terms μεταβολή, μετάβάλλεσθαι, μεταμορφοῦσθαι, &c., were familiarly applied at this time to the change which was supposed to take place in the elements, by their consecration. A new character was held to be imparted to them by the influence of the Holy Ghost, which made them to be what they were not before, in a sacramental sense. Still no idea was entertained of an actual transmutation of the bread and wine into Christ's body and blood. They were regarded only as having a supernatural character communicated to them, in virtue of which they served to bring those who partook of them into communion with Christ's true body and blood.

†Hom. 82, in Matthaei evangelium.

Among the Latin fathers of the same period, we find *Ambrose* almost as bold in his representations as Cyril himself. "The sacrament you receive is wrought by the word of Christ. The word of Elias had power to bring down fire from heaven; and shall not the word of Christ avail to change the character (speciem) of the elements? You have read, in relation to the whole work of creation, He spake and it was done, he commanded and it stood fast; and shall not the word of Christ, which could thus call out of nothing that which was not, be able also to change things that are into what they were not before?"* And yet he says, in his exposition of Luke, again, "Tangimus Christum non corporali tactu, sed fide tantum." The change, then, which he supposed to be wrought in the bread by its consecration, was not such as to transmute it, in his view, actually into Christ's body; but served only to clothe it with a new power or virtue by the Holy Ghost, (Cyril's divine μεταβολὴ,) that made it for the recipient the true medium of an actual communication with the body it represented.

We have a much better representative of the faith of the Western Church, during this period, in *Augustine*, the great theological successor of Cyprian in the North of Africa. He distinguishes clearly between the outward and inward, in the sacramental transaction, the form of the sacrament and its substance; and says of the bread, separately considered, that it is simply the sign of Christ's body.† In the sacraments, "aliud videtur, aliud intelligitur." He will hear of no oral communication; "quia gratia ejus non consumitur morsibus." Still, as Neander remarks, Augustine held a real conjunction, in the case of the Lord's Supper, between the signs and the things signified; in virtue of which believers, (not unbelievers,) along with the outward form, were made to partake of its proper contents, the "res sacramenti" itself. And this *res sacramenti* he held to be the union of believers with their one head Christ, and their closer union thus with one another, as members of his glorious mystical body, the Church. He asserts as clearly as Calvin the local circumscription of Christ's proper body in heaven; and of course makes our communion with him to be wholly by the Spirit. Still be represents it to be always a *real* communion. "Habe fidem, et tecum est, quem non vides."‡

It is not necessary here to refer to other authorities. Nor does the subject call us to trace, even in a general way, the course of the sacramental doctrine, as corrupted by the Catholic Church, in later times.¶

---

*De initiandis, cap. 9.

†Non enim Dominus dubitavit dicere: Hoc est corpus meum, cum *signum* daret corporis sui.

‡See Neander's Kirchengesch. Bd. 2, Abth. 3, p. 1399–1401.

¶This is done at length by *Prof. Ebrard*, in the work which has been already mentioned. The progress of error, in this case, was very slow and insidious. It may be traced particularly in the gradual differences of representation, that appear in the different ancient

As before remarked, the gross errors of transubstantiation and the sacrifice of the mass, only serve to show more impressively the truth of the position now insisted upon; that the sacrament was felt, from the beginning, to involve not simply a memorial of Christ's sacrifice, but the very power of the sacrifice itself, as made present in his glorified life. To the consciousness of the early Church, the solemn ordinance was an exhibition immediately of the offering for sin made once for all by Christ's death; in the participation of which, the believer was considered to receive the full benefit of it, as of a living atonement brought before God at the time. This, however, was felt to comprehend an actual reception of the life itself, in whose presence only such living and enduring virtue could be supposed to reside. The mere recollection of the atonement as a past fact, was not enough for the Christianity of those days; it must be apprehended and appropriated as a present reality, under a living form. Christ must himself animate the sacrament, and be received in it as the soul of the sacrifice it represented. All this, however, according to the faith of the first centuries, in a purely spiritual way. We hear of no transubstantiation of the elements into Christ's body and blood, as afterwards taught by the Church of Rome. They are called, indeed, his body and blood; but only in a sacramental or liturgical sense. We hear of no material or local presence of his flesh, in the Lutheran sense; no tactual communication with his glorified body; no reception of his life in a simply oral way. But the fact of a real communication with this life, in its strictly human character, as comprehended in the sacramental *transaction*, (actio in actione,) is none the less, but only the more distinctly asserted, we may say for this very reason. All Christian antiquity stands opposed here to the low rationalistic idea of a merely moral virtue in the eucharist. The faith of the Church became afterwards, it is true, the occasion of superstitious error, which had well nigh proved its own grave. The doctrine of the real presence ἐν πνευματι, degenerated into transubstanti-

---

liturgies. In time, the false view, which existed at first only in the form of feeling, began to claim authority also in the form of distinct logical expression for the understanding. This, however, called forth, even in the ninth century, a very active protest. The doctrine of *Paschasius Radbert*, caused at first much commotion, and was strongly opposed by the monk *Ratramn, Rabanus Maurus, John Scotus Erigena,* and many others. "They did not deny," says *Knapp, (Chr. Theol. Wood's Trans.* vol. II. p. 571,) "the *presence* of the body and blood of Christ; but they taught that this *conversio* or *immutatio* of the bread and wine is not of a *carnal*, but of a *spiritual* nature; that these elements are not transmuted into the real body and blood of Christ, but are signs or symbols of them. In many points they approximated to the opinion of the Reformed theologians." That is, they insisted on what had been the general doctrine of the Church from the beginning, namely, that the elements were the body and blood of Christ, not literally, but mystically, as serving after their consecration to make them present in fact, though in a spiritual way, to the communicant. Any view lower than this was out of the question, as the Church then stood; and even this was borne down at last by the force of the corruption that had now begun to usurp its place.

ation, or the real presence ἐν σαρκί. The living memorial of Christ's one sacrifice, was converted itself into the new, continually repeated sacrifice of the mass. But the corruption of a great truth, may never be urged reasonably against the authority of the truth itself. And of all forms of fanaticism, there is none more poor than the zeal, which in such circumstances seeks to rectify a gross extreme in one direction, by throwing itself blindly into the arms of an extreme equally gross in the other; and to revenge itself upon an acknowledged abuse, is ready to demolish along with it the whole form of existence out of which it has grown. To clear ourselves of transubstantiation and the mass, is it necessary that we should strip the sacrament of *all* mystery, and refuse to allow it any objective force whatever? So thought not the Reformers, as we have already seen. Not only Luther and Melancthon, but Calvin also, and Beza and Ursinus, and the fathers of the *Reformed* Church generally, discovered a proper anxiety here to save the substance of the primitive faith, while they endeavoured to rescue it from the errors with which it had become overlaid in the Church of Rome. They honoured, in this case as in other cases also, the authority of the ancient fathers, and the life of the early Church; and they took pains accordingly to show, as far as they could, that this testimony, rightly interpreted and understood, was on *their* side, and not on the side of Rome. It was reserved for a later time, and for a theology of different spirit from that which generally prevailed in the sixteenth century, to treat this whole appeal with contempt, by charging the Church with corruption and superstition from the very start, and pretending to construct the entire scheme of Christianity *de novo* from the scriptures, without any regard to the primitive faith whatever.

SECTION IV.

RATIONALISM AND THE SECTS.

The modern Puritan theory of the Lord's Supper, as it involves a falling away from the general faith of the Reformation, finds at the same time no sanction whatever in the faith of the primitive Church. This of itself constitutes certainly a powerful presumption against it. What right, we may ask, has Puritanism had to depart thus from the creed of the sixteenth century, and the creed of whole ancient Christianity, at the same time? The right of private judgment, it may be replied, against the authority of tradition. But is not tradition itself in this case the judgment merely, which has been entertained of the sense of the bible by the Reformers and the early Church? Why then should the particular judgment of Puritanism, as such, be allowed to carry with it any such weight as is needed to bear down the judgment of the universal Church besides from the beginning? In the very nature of the case, strong grounds and solid arguments should be exhibited, to justify this modern particularity of faith, in its palpable defection from the general creed of Christendom, with regard to an article so momentous as the one now under contemplation. The presumption here, I repeat it, is *against* modern Puritanism. The simple statement of the case, is adapted *prima facie*, when fairly understood, to create an impression unfavourable to its claims.

But this is not all. A still farther presumption against the same view, is created by the fact that in departing from the faith of the Reformation, it is found to be in full harmony with the false Pelagian tendency, by which the truth under other forms, as originally held by the Reformers, has been so widely subverted in different Protestant lands. The modern Puritan view of the Lord's Supper, is constitutionally rationalistic.

As a matter of course, the Socinians of the sixteenth century sunk the conception of the sacraments to the general level of their false theological system. As they denied the divinity of the Saviour, and reduced the whole Christian salvation to a mere system of morality, they could see in the sacraments naturally, nothing more than external, simply human ceremonies. Their idea was, that Christianity, as a *spiritual* religion, had no dependence on forms and rites as such; and hence in this case, they made no account whatever of any virtue or force, that might be supposed to belong to the sacraments themselves, considered as divine institutions. To attribute to them any objective value, they counted mere Jewish ritualism. "For how," it is asked, "can that serve to confirm us in faith, which we do ourselves, and which though commanded of God is still our own work, including or exhibiting nothing remarkable, and having no fitness to convince or persuade us of the truth of any of those things, by which our faith is confirmed." (*F. Soc. Opp. I. p.* 753.) The sacraments are made to be, "mutuæ inter Deum ac homines sacræ confœderationis *tesseræ.*" The idea of a real presence of any sort in the Lord's Supper, is held to be a mere superstition; all is turned into a naked commemoration of Christ's benefits.

> In the Lord's Supper, we receive according to the Lord's own word, *nothing* from the ordinance itself save bread and wine; but we commemorate past favours and give thanks for them." *F. Soc. Opp. I. p.* 753.

> "Quest. *What is the Lord's Supper?*

> "Ans. The appointment of Christ that his saints should break and eat bread and drink of the cup, in order to show forth his death; which is to continue till his advent.

> "Quest. *But what is it to show forth the Lord's death?*

> "Ans. Publicly and solemnly to give thanks to Christ, that out of his ineffable love towards us, he suffered his body to be tortured, and in a sense broken, and his blood to be shed; and to extol and magnify the kindness he has shown to us in this way." *Rac. Cat. Qu.* 334, 335.

> "Quest. *Is there no other reason for the institution?*

> "Ans. There is no other (nulla prorsus); though many have been imagined, &c." *Ib. Qu.* 337.

> "Quest. *What is the meaning of the words,* This is my body?

> "Ans. They are variously understood, for some suppose that the bread is changed really into the body and the wine into the blood; which they call transubstantiation. Others imagine the body of the Lord to be in the bread, under the bread, with the bread. There are those finally, who believe that they partake of the Lord's body and blood in the Supper, though only in a spiritual way. But *all* these opinions are fallacious and erroneous." *Ib. Qu.* 340.

With the rise of Arminianism in the following century, in the bosom of the Reformed Church, we find a similar undervaluation of the sacraments, reducing them in the end again to mere signs.

> "We hold the sacraments to be sacred and solemn rites, by which as covenant signs and seals, God not only represents and adumbrates, but *in a certain sense* also exhibits and confirms, his benefits promised especially in the gospel covenant." *Confess. Remonst.* XXIII. 1. *Drawn up by Simon Episcopius A.D.* 1622.

> "We may say that God exhibits his grace to us through the sacraments, not as conferring it by them actually, but by employing them as clear signs to *represent* it and set it before our eyes. They operate upon us as signs, that represent to our mind the thing whose signs they are. Nor should any other efficacy be sought in them.—They

promote piety besides on our part, as involving an obligation to duty, of the same nature with a soldier's oath." *Limborch Theol. Chr.* v. 66, 31, 32.

"The Lord's Supper is the other sacred rite of the New Testament, instituted by Jesus Christ, on the night in which he was betrayed, for the eucharistic and solemn commemoration of his death; in which believers, after proper self-examination and assurance of their own faith, eat sacred bread publicly broken in the congregation, and drink wine publicly poured out, to show forth with solemn action of thanks, the Lord's bloody death endured for our sake, (by which our hearts, as the body is nourished by meat and drink, are fed and strengthened to the hope of eternal life); and also to testify publicly before God and the Church, their living spiritual communion with Christ's crucified body and shed blood, (or with Jesus Christ himself as crucified and dead for us,) and so with all the benefits procured by his death, as well as their love to one another." *Conf. Remonst.* XXIII. 4.*

The triumph of Rationalism, during the eighteenth century, in Germany and throughout Europe generally, brought with it of course a still more extensive degradation of religious views. It is not necessary here to trace the rise of this apostasy and its connection with the previous state of Protestantism.† Enough to say, that it grew out of a tendency involved in the very nature of Protestantism from the beginning; the opposite exactly of that by which the Catholic Church previously had been carried into an equally false extreme, on the other side. As Romanism had sacrificed the rights of the individual to the authority of the general,—the claims of the subjective to the overwhelming weight of the objective; so the tendency of Protestantism may be said to have been from the very start, to assert these same rights and claims in the way of violent reaction, at the cost of the opposite interest. In the age of the Reformation itself, deeply imbued as it was with the positive life of truth and faith, this tendency was powerfully held within limits. With Luther, and Calvin, and the Reformers generally, the principle of freedom was still held in check by the principle of authority, and the reason of the individual was required to bend to the idea of a divine revelation as something broader and more sure than itself. It came not however in all this, it must be confessed, to a true inward reconciliation of these polar forces. The old orthodoxy, it is now generally allowed, particularly under the form it carried in the Lutheran Church, involved in itself accordingly the necessity of such a process of inward conflict and dissolution, as it has since been called to pass through; in

---

*"Hac in re," says Episcopius, "assentientes sibi habent non paucos Reformatos, inter quos *Zwinglius*, optimus hujus ceremoniæ doctor, princeps est." Limborch expressly opposes the Calvinistic theory.

†For a brier but clear sketch of this, the reader is referred to Prof. Schaf's *Principle of Protestantism*, p. 98–102.

order that the contradiction which was lodged in its bosom, might come fairly into view, and the way be opened thus for its reconstruction, under a form at once more perfect and more true to its own nature. The characteristic tendency of Protestantism already mentioned, burst finally through all the counteracting force, with which it had been restrained in the beginning. Religion ran out into sheer subjectivity; first in the form of Pietism, and afterwards in the overflowing desolation of Rationalism, reducing all to the character of the most flat natural morality. The eighteenth century was characteristically infidel. As an age, it seemed to have no organ for the supernatural. All was made to shrink to the dimensions of the mere human spirit, in its isolated character. Theology of course was robbed of all its higher life. Even the supernaturalism of the period was rationalistic; and occupying as it did in fact a false position with regard to the truth, by which a measure of right was given to the rival interest, it proved altogether incompetent to maintain its ground against the reigning spirit. The views of rationalism may be said to infect the whole theology of this period, and also of the first part of the present century, openly heretical and professedly orthodox alike.

In the nature of the case, this may be expected to show itself in low views of the sacraments, Baptism and the Lord's Supper. Rationalism is too *spiritual*, to make much account of outward forms and services of any sort in religion. All must be resolved into the exercises of the worshipper's own mind. The subjective is every thing; the objective next to nothing. Hence the supernatural itself is made to sink into the form of the simply moral. The sacraments of course become signs, and signs *only*. Any power they may have is not to be found in them, but altogether in such use merely as a pious soul may be able to make of them, as *occasions* for quickening its own devout thoughts and feelings.

Under the force of this predominant spirit, even the more sound theologians of the period now in view, are found lamentably defective in their representations of the Lord's Supper, as compared with the true Protestant fathers of the Sixteenth Century. Such men as *Zachariä, Mursinna, Döderlein, Knapp, Steudel,* &c.,* no longer venture to speak

---

*Nor can any exception he made, with regard to this point, even in favor of *Storr* and *Reinhard*. They do indeed employ language, which seems at times to imply a participation in the very substance of Christ's life; but this is so qualified and modified again by a different phraseology, that all runs out at last into the idea of mere supernatural influence of power. *Reinhard* pretends, indeed, to censure the Reformed view as too low; but he misrepresents it by charging it with the error of holding the elements to be *mere* signs; whereas they should be regarded, he says, as *exhibitive* also of what they represent. This, however, as we have seen, was always the true doctrine of the Reformed Church itself. Then he affirms that we receive in, with and under the bread and wine, the true body and blood of Christ; but immediately explains this to be, in other words, "that the exalted God-man Jesus *works*, (exerts an influence,) by his body and blood, on all who make use of this ceremony." Again, by "presence," he understands simply, "nothing more than the power

of a *real* communication with Christ's body and blood in the old sense. For the old doctrine, they substitute at best a simple *præsentiam operativam*; by which all is resolved in the end into the idea of a mere heavenly efficacy; supernatural it is true, but still *moral* only, as being nothing more than an occasion to call out pious exercises on the part of the worshipper himself. Men of less pretension to orthodoxy, and for this reason more consistently rationalistic in their thinking, *Henke, Eckermann*, the elder *Nitzsch, Hase, De Wette, Wegscheider*, &c., discard the idea of a celestial substance in the sacrament entirely, and find its whole meaning at once in the sphere of mere nature and common life.

—

"The design of the Holy Supper is this; that all who profess the name of Christ, while they partake of the broken bread as a sign of his crucified body, and of the wine as the symbol of his shed blood, may thankfully remember the benefits which they owe to their Redeemer, and so be incited to fulfil all the duties to which they are bound. Along with this main end Paul mentions another also, 1 Cor. x. 17, namely, that when we come to the table in common, we call to mind the natural love that is required of those who profess the same religion, and show ourselves ready to maintain it."—*Mursinna. Lehrb. der Dogm.* p. 267, 268.

—

to exert an influence at a particular place." *Dogmatik*, §. 162. *Storr*, in the judgment of *Bretschneider*, does not get beyond the same view; and to be satisfied of this, we need only to read attentively all that he says on the subject, in §. 114 of his *Dogmatik*. The words of institution mean, be tells us, "This bread makes you *participant* of my body—this wine hands over to you my blood," and argues at large against the figurative interpretation of *Zuingli* and *Œcolampadius*. But all comes at last to this, that the Lord Jesus, in whose person humanity and divinity are inseparably united, is actually present at the celebration of the Supper, and "*exerts his influence* there in an incomprehensible manner." The believer derives actual nourishment from Christ, more than is comprehended in the simple exercise of his own faith and trust; but still it is in the form of a "salutary influence," mysteriously proceeding from his person, rather than by an actual participation in his very life itself. In this respect, the doctrine of *Storr* and *Reinhard*, undoubtedly falls short of the doctrine taught by *Calvin*; for it is not to be questioned, that this last had in his mind always, as much as Luther himself, the idea of a true reproduction of Christ's life in the believer, an actual extension of its very substance into the believer's soul, and not simply an *operation* proceeding from this *life*, under however high a form.—Professor *Schmucker*, of this country, in his translation of the Biblical Theology of *Storr* and *Flatt*, 1826, has an appendix to this section on the Eucharist, in which he brings forward the concurrent view of *Reinhard*, backed by the authority of Mosheim, as a fair exhibition of the proper Lutheran doctrine. And yet it was considered by many an evidence of the strong power of sectarian prejudice, that the *American* Lutheran Professor should have allowed himself at the time, to go so far as to endorse, apparently, the doctrine of the *real presence*, even in the convenient sense of these "sober and judicious" divines!

"Nor is it difficult to understand and show, what force this sacrament has in itself to *affect the mind.*—Its efficacy, in the way of exciting and quickening *faith*, and for the purposes of *piety*, is clear. —Some however may say, if the eucharist furnish nothing more than this opportunity of calling to mind Christ's benefits, as already before us in the word, it seems to be a superfluous rite. So far am I however from thinking any institution to be superfluous which brings the truth, though otherwise known, with new force before the mind, it appears to me suitable to the gravity and dignity of the subject rather, that it should be presented to the understanding and memory, not in one way only, but in manifold ways.—The virtue of the Lord's Supper, therefore, like that of Baptism, does not differ from the power of the divine word. Like this it is logico-moral, worthy thus of the divine wisdom and of the christian religion, including also the influence of the Holy Spirit, who makes use of the bread and wine as instruments to excite such affections as are pious and pleasing to God." *Döderlein. Inst. Theol. Ch.* p. 691–694.

—

"The Holy Spirit acts upon the hearts of men through the Supper, or through the bread and wine, and by this means produces faith and pious dispositions. But he produces this effect through the word, or through the truths of Christianity, exhibited before us and presented to us in this ordinance. The effect of the Lord's Supper is therefore an effect, which is produced by God and Christ, through his word, or the truths of his doctrine, and the use of the same. In this sacrament of the Supper, the most important truths of Christianity, which we commonly only hear or read, are visibly set before us, made cognizable to the senses, and exhibited in such a way as powerfully to move the feelings, and make an indelible impression on the memory."—*Knapp. Lect. on Chr. Theol., Wood's Translation,* vol. II. p. 562.

"Hence it appears that the internal efficacy of the Lord's Supper, or of the word of God through the Supper, is two-fold.

FIRST. This ordinance is the means of exciting and strengthening the *faith* of one who worthily celebrates it, &c.—For we are reminded by it, 1st. Of the *death* of Christ, &c. 2d. Of the *causes*, &c. &c.

SECONDLY. In this way does this ordinance contribute to maintain and promote *piety* among believers, &c." *Ibid.* p. 563.

"The better way, therefore, in exhibiting either the Lutheran or Reformed doctrine, is, to avoid these subtleties, and merely take the general position, that Christ, as man and as the Son of God, may exert his agency, may act, whenever and in whatever manner he pleases. He therefore may *exert his power* at his table, as well as elsewhere. This is perfectly scriptural; and it is also the sense and spirit of the Protestant theory. And this doctrine concerning the *nearness* of Christ, his *assistance*, and *strengthening influence*, in his present exalted state, secures eminently that proper inward enjoyment, which Lutheran and Reformed christians, and even Catholics, with all their diversity of speculation on this point, may have alike in the Lord's Supper. Christ, when he was about to leave the world, no more to be seen by his followers with the mortal eye, left them this Supper, as a pledge of his presence, his protection, and love." *Ibid.* p. 577.

—

"The meaning of Christ seems to have been, that the close intimacy which had subsisted thus far between him and his friends, should not be interrupted by his death; but that it was his desire now especially to give himself to them as he was, to be and remain wholly theirs in the most intimate conjunction. As therefore they were now taking bread and wine, so he ought to be himself received by his disciples, his whole discipline, his spirit and example, with all the benefits about to be procured by his death, so as to be converted as it were into their very flesh and blood, &c."—*Henke. Lin. Fid. Chr.* p. 252.

—

"The sacred Supper is the solemn participation of bread and wine, as symbols of Christ's death, by which such as attend upon it, being impressively reminded of this death and of the general merit of Christ, but especially of his instruction and example, are excited and engaged to true piety towards God and Christ, as also to kindness towards others, and are imbued at the same time with the hope of obtaining by their virtue the pardon of sin and everlasting felicity. Thus the bread and wine in the eucharist, are not only properly called signs *significant*, but also signs or symbols *exhibitive*; inasmuch as they do in a certain moral way represent to communicants the whole Christ, such and so great as that divine teacher was who sealed his doctrine with his blood, and forcibly press upon them the duty of following him with decision, so as not to shrink even from enduring death, after his example, for what is true and right. Although the rite, regarded as a manducation of human flesh and potation of human blood, whether really or symbolically, is not so suitable to the views and manners of the modern world, as to those of antiquity; still, even for our age, if administered with becoming regard to its advanced cultivation, it is capable of being turned to excellent moral account. Hence it is greatly to be wished, that its more frequent use might be encouraged, &c."—*Wegscheider. Inst. Theol.* § 180.*

*Even the more sound theologians of this period, *Reinhard, Knapp,* &c., hold that the salutary influence of the sacrament does not depend at all on the view that may be taken of its nature; a judgment that may be allowed to be correct within certain limits, though not in the form, nor to the extent exactly, in which it is to be understood, probably, with these divines. *Bretschneider,* according to whom the original institution was simply a solemn covenant meal, designed to proclaim, symbolically, the introduction of the new dispensation, to which other references and uses were subsequently attached, considers that the benefit to be derived from it is not suspended absolutely even on a full faith in Christ's death as the ground of our salvation. "For one who does not honour Jesus as a Mediator, but simply as a teacher of divine truth and a benefactor of mankind, who sacrificed his life to the noblest ends, may still, by the celebration of his death, be excited to like zeal for

These extracts may suffice to illustrate the genius of Rationalism, as it regards the point now under consideration. Let us rejoice, that its iron sceptre is at length broken, for the territory of theological *science* at least, where not a great while since all seemed to acknowledge its sway; and that a new and brighter era has already begun to dawn auspiciously on the history of the Protestant Church. The authority of interpreters, like *Paulus* and *Quinöl*, and theologians such as *Ammon, Wegscheider* and *Bret-schneider*, God be praised, has become to the religious world like the idle wind which no man regards. Along with it, however, the authority of what may be styled the relative orthodoxy of the same period has in like manner passed away. *John David Michaelis* is felt to be as little worthy of confidence as the unfortunate *Semler*. The supernaturalism of the school of *Ernesti* and *Morus*, cool, mechanical, external, the product of the understanding only, is found almost as unreal and unsubstantial, as the openly infidel theology with which it waged unsuccessful war. Who now, of any true theological culture, thinks of taking the *Rosenmüllers*, or *Koppe* and his continuators, for his guides in the study of the scriptures? Who that is aware at all of the true historical stand-point of the age, can sit at the feet of such men as *Mursinna*, and *Döderlein*, and *Flatt*, and *Storr*, and *Reinhard*, and *Knapp*, for instruction in the mysteries of the Christian faith? They are all indeed venerable names, and they are entitled to the lasting respect of the Church for their fidelity to Christ in a time of general apostacy and defection. The results of their learning too will always continue to be of value for Christianity, at least in an indirect way. But they stood themselves in a false position with regard to the truth; and they were not able accordingly to stem the tide, which was bearing all thought and all life the contrary way. So far as any better order of religion has come to prevail, it must be referred to other influences altogether. The salvation of theology has sprung from a different quarter. The very orthodoxy of the school now noticed was itself rationalistic; and we may say of it, in this view, that it served only to precipitate the catastrophe which it sought to avert. For its conception of the supernatural was always external and abstract; placing it thus in the same false relation precisely to nature and humanity, which was established by Rationalism itself. This was to justify the wrong issue on which the controversy had been made to hang, and to make common cause in a certain sense with the enemy, by consenting to meet him on his own ground, the arena of the mere finite understanding. No wonder, that the supernatural *thus* defended, was found

truth and virtue, to improvement, and to perseverance in the conflict with superstition and vice, and be tilled thus with the presentiment also of a better world. The great design of Christianity, which is to free men from sin and to prepare them for a higher life, is in that case advanced in *him* as well as in others, though in a different way; and hence the Lord's Supper becomes for him too a salutary sacrament." *Dogmatik*, §. 200.

unable to sustain itself against the reigning tendency of the age. No wonder, that it yielded to this tendency more and more itself, and went finally to swell the triumphant stream with which all was carried in this downward direction."*

Parallel to a real extent with the development of the subjective principle in the false form now noticed, runs the revelation also of the same tendency in the equally false form of Sectarism and schism. No one can study attentively the character of either, without being led to see that the two tendencies are but different phases of one and the same spiritual obliquity.† No one, in reading the history of the Church, can well fail to be struck with the many points of correspondence, which are found universally to hold between the two forms of life, in spite of the broad difference by which they might seem to be separated, in many cases, on a superficial view. The spirit of sect is characteristically full of religious pretension; and professing to make supreme account of religion as something personal and experimental, it assumes always a more than ordinarily spiritual character, and moves in the element of restless excitement and action. Hence it is often, generally indeed at the start, fanatical and wild; especially in the way of opposition to outward forms and the existing order of the Church generally. And yet how invariably it falls in with the rationalistic way of thinking, as far as it may *think* at all, from the very beginning; and how certainly its principles and views, when carried

---

*It deserves to be well considered, that it is mainly the theology of this rationalistic period, which has been derived from Germany thus far into our American divinity, so far as any such importation may have taken place. Those among us who have had some acquaintance with German learning, and to whom we are indebted, it may be, for translations of German theological works, show themselves unfortunately, for the most part, at least twenty years, if not a full half century, *behind* the true scientific stand-point of the present time; by exhibiting principles of interpretation and theological views, in the name of *theology* properly so styled, which in Germany itself are acknowledged to be shorn of all their force. Nor is the error helped materially, by making a supposed judicious distinction, in this case, between the orthodoxy of the period and its avowed religious infidelity. The whole posture of the time was rationalistic. Ernesti, for instance, is entitled to no confidence whatever, as a guide to the true sense of God's word, as it is *spirit* and *life*. Knapp, with all his orthodoxy, comes short, perpetually, of the true depth of Christianity as a science. When we find *this* school of theology recognized and honoured by a wide section of the American Church, as the only valuable and only safe form of German thinking in the sphere of religion; while the far deeper and infinitely more spiritual efforts, by which the theology of the present time, in the hands of such men as *Dorner, G. A. Meier, Julius Müller*, and others of like spirit, is struggling to surmount forever the contradictions of the old stand-point, are superciliously condemned as transcendental nonsense; it is certainly not easy to possess one's soul in proper patience. Alas, it is but too plain, that with all our boasted orthodoxy, the coils of Rationalism have fastened themselves with deadly embrace on the *thinking* at least, (though not on the hearts we may trust,) of hundreds, who are the last to dream of any such thing.

†On this subject, the reader is referred again to Scharf's *Principle of Protestantism*, p. 107–121.

out subsequently to their legitimate results, are found to involve in the end the worst errors of Rationalism itself. Both systems are antagonistic to the idea of the *Church*. Both are disposed to trample under foot the authority of *history*. Both make the *objective* to be nothing, and the *subjective* to be all in all. Both undervalue the *outward*, in favour of what they conceive to be the *inward*. Both despise *forms*, under the pretext of exalting the *spirit*. Both of course sink the *sacraments* to the character of mere outward rites; or possibly deny their necessity altogether. Both affect to make much of the *bible*; at least in the beginning; though sometimes indeed it is made to yield, with Sectarianism, to the imagination of some superior inward light more directly from God; and in all cases, it is forced to submit, to the tyranny of mere private interpretation, as the only proper measure of its sense. With both forms of thinking, the idea of Christianity, as a permanent order of life, a real supernatural constitution unfolding itself historically in the world, is we may say wanting altogether. All at last is flesh, the natural life of man as such; exalted it may be in its own order, but never of course transcending itself so as to become *spirit*. The sect principle may indeed affect to move in the highest sphere of the heavenly and divine; carrying it possibly to an absolute rupture even with all that belongs to the present world. But in this case it begins in the spirit, only to end the more certainly in the flesh. Hyper-spiritualism is ever fleshly pseudo-spiritualism; that is sure to fall back sooner or later impotent and self-exhausted, into the low element from which it has vainly pretended to make its escape. Anabaptism finds its legitimate, natural end in the excesses of Munster; as Mormonism in the like excesses of Nauvoo. What a difference apparently between the inspiration of George Fox, and the cold infidelity of Elias Hicks. And yet the last is the true spiritual descendant of the first. The inward light of the one, and the light of reason as held by the other, come to the same thing at last. Both contradict the true conception of religion. Both are supremely subjective, and in this view supremely rationalistic at the same time.

It is by no fortuitous coincidence then, that we find the spirit of *sect* since the Reformation, (as indeed before it also,) in close affinity with the spirit of theoretic rationalism, in its low estimate of the Christian sacraments. The relationship of the two systems, in the case, is inward and real. The Anabaptists and Socinians of the sixteenth century, go here hand in hand together; as do also the Mennonites and Arminians of Holland, in the century following. All hold the sacraments to be signs only for the understanding and heart of the pious communicant, without any objective value or force in their own nature. All alike reduce them to the character of something outward and accidental only to the true Christian life. The Quakers, more consistently true than all sects besides to the spiritualistic theory out of which the sect life springs, agree with infidelity itself, in rejecting the sacraments altogether.* Not from the Christ without, the objective historical Christ, as revealing himself in the Church and exhibited in the sacramental symbols, but only from the Christ within, the interior spiritual life of the believer himself, is any true salvation to be expected. "Whenever the soul is turned towards the light of the Lord within, and is thus made to participate of the celestial life that nourishes the interior man, (the privilege of the believer at any time,) it may be said to enjoy the Lord's Supper, and to partake of his flesh and blood." To insist upon the outward sacraments is to fall back to Judaism, and to magnify rites and forms at the cost of that spiritual worship, which alone is worthy of our own nature, or suitable to the character of God.

The anti-sacramental tendency of the sect spirit is strikingly revealed under its true rationalistic nature, in the disposition so commonly shown by it to reject infant baptism. If the sacraments are regarded as in themselves outward rites only, that can have no value or force except as the grace they represent is made to be present by the subjective exercises of the worshipper, it is hard to see on what ground infants, who are still without knowledge or faith, should be admitted to any privilege of the sort. If there be no objective reality in the life of the Church, as something more deep and comprehensive than the life of the individual believer separately taken, infant baptism becomes necessarily an unmeaning contradiction. Hence invariably, (as already remarked in the first part of the present chapter,) where the true church consciousness is brought to yield to the spirit of sect, the tendency to depreciate the ordinance in this form is found to prevail to the same extent; and so on the other hand, there is no more sure criterion and measure of the presence of the sect spirit, as distinguished from the true spirit of the Church, than the tendency now mentioned, wherever it may be exhibited. The baptistic principle, whether carried out fully in practice or not, constitutes the certain mark of sectarianism all the world over.† It may be controlled in

---

*"Nihil aliud hæreditatis nostræ signaturam et arrhabonem nominat scriptura præter spiritum Dei." *Barcl. Apol.* The Lord's Supper, originally observed, "imbecillium causa," was only a shadow, he tells us, that is no longer needed for those who have the substance.

†"Why are the Congregationalists, or Baptists, any more a sect than the German Reformed or the Episcopalians?" Thus asks the *Biblical Repertory*, in its review of Schaf on Protestantism, (Oct. 1845,) charging the author with being vague in what he says on the subject of sectarism. The question is certainly very striking, in view of the quarter from which it comes. Only think of Baxter, or any sound Presbyterian of the seventeenth century, asking such a question in relation even to Congregationalism! But here the very *Baptists* themselves, whom the New England Congregationalists of that period could not tolerate in their midst, are exalted to the same church level with the churches of the Reformation generally. This, of itself, betrays a most low conception of the Church, and a strange confusion in relation to the idea of *sect*. Neither Calvin nor Luther could have endured the thought, of being associated in this way with a spirit so utterly unhistorical, unchurchly, and unsacramental, as that which is presented to us in the Anabaptist schism from beginning to end.

many cases by outward influences, or by some remnant possibly of church feeling still preserved, so as not to come openly into view; but it will be found then as a worm at least at the root of the institution here in view, consuming all its vigor, and turning it in fact into the powerless form for which it is unbelievingly and rationalistically taken. Where it comes, however, to a full triumph of the sect character, the baptistic principle, for the most part, asserts its authority in a more open way. Infant baptism is discarded as a relic of Roman superstition. Here again the Anabaptists and Mennonites appear in close connection with Socinians and Arminians; whose judgment at least with regard to the point in hand, though not their practice, has ever been substantially the same. According to the Racovian Catechism, the baptism of infants is without authority and without reason, and to be tolerated only as a harmless inveterate prejudice.* The Remonstrants of Holland, (Arminians,) much in the same way, declare the rite worthy of being continued to avoid scandal, but hold it to be of no binding authority in its own nature.† In our own country, as was remarked before, we have, at the present time, an exemplification of the sect feeling at this point, on a large scale. The Baptists, as they are called, including all the sects that reject the baptism of infants, form, it is said, the most numerous religious profession in the United States: and the baptistic principle, it is plain, prevails still more widely, where the practice, through the force of denominational tradition, remains of an opposite character.

It appears then that the spirit of heresy, and the spirit of *schism*, in the case before us, are substantially one and the same. Both are unchurchly and anti-sacramental, to the same extent. It is not an accidental resemblance simply, that connects them together in this view; but the inward power of a common life. It belongs to the very genius of sect to be rationalistic.‡

---

*Errorem adeo inveteratum et pervulgatum christiana charitas tolerare suadet. *Rac. Cat.*

†Remonstrantes ritum baptizandi, infantes ut perantiquum haud illubenter etiam in cœtibus suis admittunt, adeoque vix sine offensione et scandalo magno intermitti posse statuunt; tantum abest ut eum seu illicitum aut nefastum improbent ac damnent. *Apolog. Remonst.*

‡Ronge, the famous head of the "German Catholic" movement, now engaging so much attention, shows here also his true theological stand-point. Christ laid down his life, according to this man, to open the way for the more rapid spread of his salutary *doctrine* in the world; and the Supper was instituted to keep up his *memory*, and to be the standing *"brother-meal of humanity,"* in all times. See a notice of the Easter Service held last year in Berlin, by Ronge and Czersky, in the correspondence of *Krummacher's Palmblætter, for June*, 1845. How invariably the rationalistic and sectaristic spirit betrays itself just at this point, and always in the same way! This Ronge, it will be remembered, was hailed by our religious papers generally, at first, as a second Huss or Luther. But it is in the highest degree dishonourable to the Reformation, to think of it as parallel, in any measure, with such a movement. Ronge is no Reformer, but a Radical only, of the worst stamp. Like

And now it cannot be denied, that the modern Puritan theory of the Lord's Supper, as it has been presented to us in contrast with the old Calvinistic doctrine, is strikingly in harmony with the whole style of thinking here offered to our view. This must be apparent at once to any one, who will only take the trouble to refer again to the illustrations of the Puritan theory that have been already quoted, and to compare them with the modes of thought and language employed by the rationalistic school on the same subject. The ground on which much of our American theology is here standing at the present time, is palpably the same with that occupied by the old rationalistic supernaturalism of Germany; which was found so insufficient, as we have just seen, to maintain itself scientifically against the neology with which it was called to contend. It is the orthodoxy at best of such men as Ernesti and Morus, Reinhard and Knapp; only with a very small part of their learning. Its safety is found in the fact, that it has for the most part no power to perceive the contradiction it carries in its own bosom. But with all this, the false element works itself out in many practical consequences, alike mischievous for theology and for the religious life in general.

It is not necessary that we should be able to trace any outward connection between the two forms of theology thus compared, to establish their actual affinity. It is enough that they are inwardly connected, and that they belong to the same general development of a false tendency comprehended in Protestantism itself. This tendency has shown its power from the beginning, as a spirit of heresy in one direction, and a spirit of schism in another; but it may be said to have come to the fullest revelation of its bad life, during the last century and the first part of the present. That the modern Puritan theology should be deeply affected by its influence, might seem to be in the circumstances precisely what was to be expected. Puritanism, as all know, involves in its original constitution a large

Luther, he has indeed cast off the authority of Rome. But the resemblance of the two cases is merely in outward form. Luther was full of positive life; Ronge is negative wholly, and destitute of all faith in Christianity as a real life-revelation in the world. Luther stood in the element of the *objective*, and felt himself to be the passive organ only of the true and proper *historical* life of the *Church* itself; Ronge is supremely *subjective*, unhistorical, and full of blind *self-will*. Luther was himself the first, central, and in some sense *fontal*, product of the vast spiritual revolution in which he led the way; it came to the birth with deep, convulsive throes, in his separate personal consciousness, before it revealed itself in the rest of the Church, already ripe for the change. Ronge stands in no such relation to the inmost religious life of the age, in which he affects to play the spiritual hero. No world-convulsion has gone forward, in the first place, in his own soul. His vocation is evidently superficial and outward, in the fullest sense; and the movement over which he presides is as plainly distinguished throughout by the same character. God may make it indirectly subservient at last, in some way, to the advancement of his kingdom; but, in its own nature, it belongs not at all to this kingdom but to the world only.—See an excellent article on the whole subject, by Professor *Ullmann*, characterized by his usual caution, moderation, and profound historical wisdom, in the *Studien und Kritiken*, for the last year.

measure of the tendency which has just been mentioned. It formed from the start, a marked advance, in this direction, upon the character of the Reformed Church, as it stood in the beginning; showing itself more decidedly independent of all objective authority, and more favourable by far to a mere abstract spiritualism in religion. The danger to which the Reformed Church might be said to have been most liable, in its very nature, from the first, came here to be something more than danger; it appeared as actual ultra-protestantism itself, hostile to the proper idea of the Church, and irreverent towards all history at the same time. Nor has the history of this system of thinking since furnished any reason to suppose in its case a change of character, in the respect here noticed. On the contrary, it is clear that the wrong element which was embodied in it at the beginning, has been only confirmed and consolidated since, under the same character; for to this very influence must be referred, to a great extent, more or less directly, the curse of sectarism, as it has now become so widely established both in Great Britain and in this country. That some leaven of rationalism then enter into its theology, in these circumstances, must appear, after what has already been said, a matter of course. This may be, notwithstanding the presence of a large amount of religious life in connection with the same system.

Be all this as it may, however, it must at all events be regarded as a presumption against the modern Puritan view of the Lord's Supper, that, in departing from the doctrine of the Reformation, it is found to fall in so strikingly with what may be styled the apostacy of Rationalism in the same direction. It might seem sufficiently startling to be sundered, in such a case, from the general faith of Christendom as it has stood from the beginning. But still more startling, certainly, is the thought of such separation in *such* company. This much is clear. The Reformation included in its original and proper constitution, two different elements or tendencies; and it was felt that it could be true to itself, only by acknowledging the authority of both, as mutually necessary each for the perfection and proper support of the other. In the nature of the case, however, there was a powerful liability in the movement to become ultraistic and extreme, on that side which seemed to carry the most direct *protest* against the errors of the Church, as it stood before. In the course of time, undeniably, this became, as we have already seen, its general character. The simply Protestant tendency was gradually sundered, in a great measure, from its true Catholic complement and counterpoise; and in this abstract character it has run out into theoretical and practical rationalism, to a fearful extent, in all parts of the Church. The low view of the sacraments, which we have now under consideration, came in with this unfortunate obliquity. It belongs historically and constitutionally to the bastard form, under which the original life of Protestantism has become so widely caricatured in the way of heresy and schism. Its inward affinity with the spirit of Rationalism, in one direction, and the spirit of Sect in another, (two different phases only of the same modern Antichrist,) is too clear to be for one moment called in question. In this character, it forms most certainly, like the whole system with which it is associated, a departure from the faith, not only of the Lutheran, but of the Reformed Church also, as it stood in the sixteenth century. It involves in this respect, what would have been counted, at that time, not only a perversion, but a very serious perversion of the true Protestant doctrine. Now, with this neological and sectarian view, we find the modern Puritan theory of the Lord's Supper to be in full agreement. Both sink its objective virtue wholly out of sight. Both do this, on the principle of making the service spiritual and rational, instead of simply *ritual*. Both, in this way, wrong the claims of Christianity as a supernatural *life*, in favour of its claims as a divine doctrine. Both proceed on the same false abstraction, by which soul and body, outward and inward, are made to be absolutely different, and in some sense really antagonistic, spheres of existence. Both show the same utter disregard to the authority of a previous history, and affect to construct the whole theory of the Church, doctrine, sacraments, and all, in the way of independent private judgment, from the Bible and common sense. Both, in all this, involve a like defection, and substantially to the same extent, from the creed of the Reformation; and would have been regarded accordingly, not only by Luther, but by Calvin also, and Beza, and Ursinus, and the fathers of the Reformed Church generally, as alike treasonable to the interest, which has become identified with their great names.

This much, we say, is clear. Let it carry with it such weight as may of right belong to it; and no more. The question is not to be decided, we all know, by church authority and mere blind tradition. The primitive Church may have gone astray from the very start. The fathers of the Reformation were not infallible; and it must be allowed, that the life of the Reformation, in its *first* form, was the product or birth spiritually of the Catholic Church as it stood before, and not of the sects that broke away from it in the middle ages. If the Reformers had sprung from this line of witnesses on the outside, it is quite likely their Protestantism would have been something vastly different from the gigantic new creation we find it to be in fact. The birth, it may be taken for granted, *did* partake largely of the character of the womb, in which it had been carried for so many centuries before. These *Catholic* Reformers *may* have been wrong, in the case now before us, as in many other points. Whole Christendom *may* have been wrong, not only in the form, but in the very substance of its faith, with regard to the sacraments, for more than fifteen hundred years; till this modern view began to reveal itself in the Protestant world, partly in the form of infidelity, and partly in the form of a claim to superior evangelical piety. The coincidence in this case too *may* be accidental only, and not natural or necessary. With regard to all this, we utter here no positive judgment. We wish simply to exhibit facts as they stand. But in this character, they have their solemn weight. They create a powerful presumption, as I before said, *against* the modern Puritan view, and impose upon all an *à priori* obligation of great force, not to acquiesce in it without examination.

CHAPTER III.

AN ATTEMPT TO PLACE THE DOCTRINE IN ITS PROPER SCIENTIFIC FORM.

IT has been already admitted that the Calvinistic theory of the Eucharistic Presence, as exhibited more or less distinctly in all the Reformed symbols of the sixteenth century, is embarrassed with some difficulties. These however concern at last not so much the fact itself, which may be said to constitute the true and proper substance of the doctrine, as the defective form in which it was attempted to bring it before the understanding. It was always held indeed that the fact was in its own nature a mystery, not to be reduced to any clear explanation in this way: but still it became necessary in the controversy with Romanism and Lutheranism on the one side and the Socinanizing tendency on the other, not only to define and describe the limits of the fact itself at every point, but also to go a certain length at least, in endeavouring to beat down popular objections, and meet the demands of the common reason. The success of such an effort hung necessarily, to a greater or less extent, on the general theological and philosophical culture of the time. As this has been in some measure superseded by later intellectual advances, it ought not to be counted strange that the doctrine now before us, as well as the entire religious system of the same period, should be found to exhibit some vulnerable points as it regards form and outward representation. This we find to be the case in fact.

SECTION I.

PRELIMINARY POSITIONS.

Calvin's theory seems to labor particularly at three points; all connected with a false psychology, as applied either to the person of Christ or the persons of his people.

In the *first* place he does not make a sufficiently clear distinction, between the idea of the organic *law* which constitutes the proper identity

of a human body, and the material volume it is found to embrace as
exhibited to the senses. A true and perfect body must indeed appear in the
form of organized matter. As a *mere* law, it can have no proper reality.
But still the matter, apart from the law, is in no sense the body. Only as it
is found to be transfused with the active presence of the law at every
point, and in this way filled with the form of life, can it be said to have
any such character; and then it is of course as the medium simply, by
which what is inward and invisible is enabled to gain for itself a true
outward existence. The principle of the body as a system of life, the
original salient point of its being as a whole, is in no respect material. It
is not bound of course, for its identity, to any particular portion of matter
as such. If the matter which enters into its constitution were changed
every hour, it would still remain the same body; since that which passed
away in each case would have no more right to be considered a part of the
man than it had before entering the law of life in his person, and the
demands of this law would always be abundantly satisfied by the matter
that might fill it at each moment. A real communication then between the
body of Christ and the bodies of his saints, does not imply necessarily the
gross imagination of any transition of his flesh as such into their persons.
This would be indeed of no meaning or value. For how could the flesh of
Christ as something sundered from the law of life in the presence of
which only it can have any force, and in this form supernaturally inserted
into my flesh under the like abstract view, bring with it any advantage or
profit? In such sense as this, we *may* say, without wresting our Saviour's
words, "the flesh profiteth nothing." And here precisely comes into view,
one of the most valid and forcible objections to the dogma of the Roman
Church, as well as to the kindred doctrine of Luther; in both of which so
much is made to hang on a sort of tactual participation of the matter of
Christ's body in the sacrament, rather than in the law simply of his true
human life. This is urged in fact by Calvin himself, with great force,
against the false theories in question. This shows of course that he was not
insensible to the idea of the distinction now mentioned; a point
abundantly manifest besides from his whole way of representing the
subject in general. Still it seems to have been a matter of correct feeling
with him, rather than of clear scientific apprehension. Hence he never
brings it forward in a distinct way, and never turns it to any such account
in the service of his theory, as in the nature of the case he might have
done. Thus too much account is made perhaps of the flesh of Christ under
a local form, (there confined to the right hand of God in heaven,) as the
seat and fountain of the new life which is to be conveyed into his people;
and the attempt which is then made to bring the two parties together,
notwithstanding such vast separation in space, must be allowed to be
somewhat awkward and violent. No wonder that men of less dialectic
subtlety than the great theologian himself, were at a loss to make any

thing out of such a seeming contradiction in terms. In this case he may be said to cut the knot, which his speculation fails to solve. Christ's body is altogether in heaven only. How then is its vivific virtue to be carried into the believer? By the miraculous energy of the Holy Ghost; which however cannot be said in the case so much to bring his life down to us, as it serves rather to raise us in the exercise of faith to the presence of the Saviour on high. The result however is a real participation always in his full and entire humanity. But the representation is confused, and brings the mind no proper satisfaction. If for the "vivific virtue" of Christ's flesh Calvin had been led to substitute distinctly the idea of the organic law of Christ's human life, his theory would have assumed at once a much more consistent and intelligible form. For in this view, it cannot be said that local, material contact is necessary, to sustain a true and strict continuity of existence, either in the sphere of nature or in that of grace.

A *second* point of difficulty in the case of Calvin's theory is, that he fails to insist, with proper freedom and emphasis, on the absolute *unity* of what we denominate *person*, both in the case of Christ himself and in the case of his people. Hence he dwells too much on the life-giving virtue of Christ's *flesh* simply; as if this were not necessarily and inseparably knit to his soul, and to his divinity too, as a single indivisible life; so that where the latter form of existence is present in a real way, the other must be really present too, so far as its inmost nature is concerned, to the same extent. When I travel, whether by the eye or in thought simply, to the planet Saturn, the act includes my whole person; not the body as such of course, but just as little the soul under the like abstraction; it is the act of that single and absolutely one life which I call myself, as the unity of both soul and body. And if it were possible in any way that the thought which carries me to Saturn, could be made to assume there a real concrete existence, holding in organic connection with my own life, it must as a *human* existence appear under a human form; which in such a case would be as strictly a continuation of my bodily as well as spiritual being, as though it had sprung immediately from the local presence of my body itself. So the acts of the incarnate Word belong to his person as a whole. Not as though his humanity separately considered could be said to exercise the functions of his divinity; for this is a false distinction in the case; and we have just as little reason to say that the divinity thus separately considered ever exercises the same functions. They are exercised by the theanthropic Person of the Mediators as one and indivisible. If then Christ's life be conveyed over to the persons of his people at all, in a real and not simply figurative way, it *must* be so carried over under a human form, including both the constituents of humanity, body as well as soul; and the new bodily existence thus produced, must be considered, independently of all local connection, a continuation in the strictest sense of Christ's life under the same form. This point does not

appear to have been apprehended, with sufficient distinctness, by Calvin
and the Reformers generally. Hence more or less confusion, and at times
some apparent contradiction, in tracing the derivation of Christ's human
life into the person of the believer. Bound as he felt himself to be to resist
everything like the idea of a local presence, he found it necessary to
resolve the whole process into a special supernatural agency of the Holy
Ghost, as a sort of foreign medium introduced to meet the wants of the
case. Thus the view taken of Christ's human nature becomes altogether
too abstract, and it is made difficult to keep hold of the idea of a true
organic connection between his life in this form, and that of his people.
It is not easy then of course to maintain a clear distinction between such
a communication of the substance of Christ's life, and an influence in the
way of mere spiritual power; to which conception Calvin's theory was in
fact always made to sink by his high-toned Lutheran adversaries; although
he never failed to protest against this as grossly perverse and unjust, and
has taken the greatest pains indeed to save himself at this point from
misconstruction.* But his theory it must be allowed, carries here a

---

*It is wonderful, with what pertinacity the view of Calvin has been misrepresented
at this point. Rigid Lutherans have charged him with a sort of theological duplicity, as
pretending to differ from Zuingli, while he agreed with him in fact; and modern Calvinists,
who have fallen away entirely from the sacramental doctrine of the sixteenth century,
would fain bring him down too, if it were possible, from the high position which it is
acknowledged his language sometimes *seems* to imply. Even the *Form of Concord* is
chargeable here with great injustice. It divides the Sacramentarians into two classes; the
more *gross*, who openly profess what they believe in their hearts; and the *politic*, who use
something like Lutheran language only to cover the same error. These last representing of
course the Calvinistic or proper Reformed view, are made to be "*omnium nocentissimi
sacramentarii*;" because, it is said, they pretend themselves to allow a "true presence of the
true substantial and living body and blood of Christ in the Lord's Supper," and yet declare
it to be spiritual only, and by faith. Under these high sounding terms, they in fact will have
nothing to be present but mere bread and wine. "For the term *spiritually*, signifies with
them only Christ's Spirit, or the virtue of his absent body, and his merit," &c. So such
writers of the present day as *Guerike*, (Symbolik, p. 452–458,) *Rudelbach*, (Ref. Luth. und
Union, p. 188ff.) and *Scheibel*, (Das Abendmahl, p. 331ff.) spare no pains, in their zeal for
Lutheranism, to establish the same representation. They insist upon it that Calvin only plays
with words, in pretending to go beyond Zuingli in his theory of Christ's presence in the
Supper; that all comes at last to the conception of mere *power* and *effect*, as it regards
communion with his person, and that the sacrament is *significative* simply of the grace it
represents, and nothing more. But it is easy to see that such judgment rests altogether, in
this case, on the fixed prejudice already established, that any communion with the life of
Christ's *body*, in order to be real, *must* hold in some bodily way, and not by the soul. Grant
this, and Calvin's theory, of course, leaves no room for any communion of the sort. But
this, Calvin, at least, did not grant. On the contrary he held, that to make the communion
dependent on any merely corporeal act, considered as *such* only, was in the nature of the
case to deprive it of all reality or value. The more spiritual, in his view, the more real. All
that Luther aimed to secure by his theory of an oral communication, (for with him too this
must be *hyperphysical* to be of any account,) Calvin proposed to reach more satisfactorily
by pressing the idea of a spiritual communication. He declared himself of one mind with
Luther as to the *fact*; the only difference between them was as to the *mode*. This was the

Individual & corporate personality →

somewhat fantastic character. So on the other hand the relation of soul and body in the person of the believer appears too abstract also, according to his view. He will hear of no translation of the material particles of Christ's body into our bodies. The vivific virtue of his flesh can be apprehended on our part only by faith, and in this form of course by the soul only, through the power of the Holy Ghost. Still it extends to the body also, in the end. But all this, it would seem, in a way transcending all known analogies, in virtue of an extraordinary divine power present for the purpose, rather than as the natural and necessary result of the new life lodged in the soul itself. This is not satisfactory. Christ's Person is one, and the person of the believer is one; and to secure a real communication of the whole human life of the first over into the personality of the second, it is only necessary that the communication should spring from the centre of Christ's life and pass over to the centre of ours. This can be only by the Holy Ghost. But the Holy Ghost in this case is not to be sundered from the Person of Christ. We must say rather that this, and no other, is the very form in which Christ's life is made present in the Church, for the purposes of the christian salvation.

The *third* source of embarrassment belonging to the form in which Calvin exhibits his theory, is found in this that he makes no clear distinction between the individual personal life of Christ, and the same life in a *generic* view. In every sphere of life, the individual and the general are found closely united in the same subject. Thus, in the vegetable world, the acorn, cast into the ground, and transformed subsequently into the oak of a hundred years, constitutes in one view only a

position taken also by the Reformed Church in general. Did not Calvin *know* what Luther meant by his doctrine? And shall we not believe him when he professes to hold a sacramental union with Christ's body and blood, in the same sense, simply because he conceives it to take place in a different way? There is no reason to question that he held and taught a real communication, not with the power and operation of Christ's body merely, but with its true substantial life itself. The elements, as such, were signs, and might be separated from the *res sacramenti*, as Augustine also explicitly teaches; but the sacramental transaction, as a whole, was no such sign or symbol only. It was held to *exhibit* what is represented; as much so as the *dove*, to borrow his own illustration, in whose form the Holy Ghost descended upon the Saviour at his baptism. "It is perfectly plain." says *Bretschneider*, "that Calvin's theory includes what with Luther was the main object, namely, the true, full participation of Christ's body and blood, to the strengthening and quickening of the soul; and that the question, whether this take place *under* the bread, or at the same time with it, by the mouth or by the soul, does not touch the substance of the case. For unless we conceive of the body of Christ as something *sensible*, and thus allow a Capernaitic eating, the oral participation must become at last nothing else than a participation through the soul, and it is not necessary that the Lord's spiritual body could be taken in by the mouth, in order to have effect upon the soul." See the judgment of *Schleiermacher*, with regard to the same point, as already quoted on page 70. *Knapp, Reinhard*, &c., of course, try to sink the Calvinistic theory somewhat below the level of their own, as they pretend to uphold the Lutheran view in opposition to it. But, as we have seen, they come short, in fact, both of Calvin and Luther, in the case.

single existence. But in another, it includes the force of a life that is capable of reaching far beyond all such individual limits. For the oak may produce ten thousand other acorns, and thus repeat its own life in a whole forest of trees. Still, in the end, the life of the forest, in such a case, is nothing more than an expansion of the life that lay involved at first in the original acorn; and the whole general existence thus produced is bound together, inwardly and organically, by as true and close a unity as that which holds in any of the single existences embraced in it, separately considered. So among men, every parent may be regarded as the bearer not only of a single individual life, that which constitutes his own person, but of a general life also, that reveals itself in his children. Thus especially, in an eminent sense, the first man Adam is exhibited to our view always under a twofold character. In one respect he is simply *a* man, to be counted as one amongst men since born, his sons. In another he is *the* man; in whose person was included the whole human race. Thus he bears the name, (in Hebrew,) of the race itself; and it is under this generic title particularly that he is presented to our notice in the sacred history of the Bible. His individual personality of course was limited wholly to himself. But a whole world of like separate personalities lay involved in his life, at the same time, as a generic principle or root. And all these, in a deep sense, form at last but one and the same life. Adam lives in his posterity, as truly as he has ever lived in his own person. They participate in his whole nature, soul and body, and are truly bone of his bone and flesh of his flesh. So in the case before us, the life of Christ is to be viewed also under the same twofold aspect. Not indeed as if the individual and general here, might be supposed to hold under the same form exactly, as in the cases which have been mentioned. The relation of the single oak to its offspring forest, is not the same fully with that of the first man to his posterity. Nor is this last at all commensurate with the relation of Christ to his Church. This will appear hereafter. Still, however, for the point now in hand, the cases are parallel. The distinction of an individual and a general life in the person of Christ, is just as necessary as the same distinction in the person of Adam; and the analogy is at all events sufficient to show, that there may be a real communication of Christ's life to his people, without the idea of any thing like a local mixture with his person. In one view the Saviour is *a* man, Jesus of Nazareth, partaking of the same flesh and blood with other men, though joined at the same time in mysterious union with the everlasting Word. But in another view he is again *the* man; in a higher sense than this could be said of Adam; emphatically the SON OF MAN, in whose person stood revealed the true idea of humanity, under its ultimate and most comprehensive form. Without any loss or change of character in the first view, his life is carried over in this last view continually into the persons of his people. He lives in himself, and yet lives in them really and truly at the same time. This distinction between the individual and the general in the life of Christ, Calvin does not turn to account as he might have done. That the force of it was, in some measure, present to his mind, seems altogether clear. But it is not brought out in a distinct, full way; and his system is made to labour under some unnecessary difficulty on this account.

It is easy to see that the three scientific determinations to which our attention has now been directed, when taken together and clearly affirmed, must serve to modify and improve very materially the Calvinistic doctrine of Christ's union with his people, an far as the mode of its statement is concerned; relieving it in fact from its most serious difficulties, and placing it under a form with which even the abstract understanding itself can have no good right to find fault. For the positions here applied to the case are in no sense arbitrary or hypothetical. They belong to the actual science of the present time, and have a *right* to be respected in any inquiry which has this question for its object. No such inquiry can deserve to be considered scientific, if it fail to take them into view. At the same time it is equally clear, that in all this the true and proper substance of the old doctrine is preserved. Here we stand divided from Rationalism and modern Puritanism. We agree with them, that the doctrine under its old form has difficulties, with which the understanding had a right to quarrel. But, to get clear of these, *they* have thought good to cast away the whole doctrine, substance and form together. A process of pure negation and destruction, which, in such a case, can *never* be right. *We* hold fast to the substance, while, for the very sake of doing so, we endeavour to place it in a better form. Of this none can have a right to complain; and least of all those who have given up the whole doctrine. They are negative only, in the case. We are positive. We cling to the old; in its life, however, rather than by slavish adhesion to its letter. So it must be indeed in the case of all religious truth, dogmatically considered. It cannot hold in the form of dead tradition. But neither can it be disjoined from the life of the past. Its true form is that of *history*; in which the past, though left behind in one view, is always in another taken up by the present, and borne along with it as the central power of its own life.

When we speak, however, of putting the doctrine in question into a form more satisfactory to the understanding, it is not to be imagined of course that we consider it to be any the less a mystery, on this account, in its own nature. The mystical union of Christ with his Church is something, that, in the very nature of the case, transcends all analogies drawn from any lower sphere of life; which it is vain to expect, therefore, that the finite understanding as such can ever fathom or grasp. Still, however, much depends on the statement even of what is incomprehensible, for its being brought to stand at least in a right relation to the understanding. The understanding may be reconciled, relatively, to that which it cannot comprehend absolutely. It may be set right in relation to a mystery negatively, where it has no power still to grasp it in a positive way, but can only fall back for relief at last on the *reason*, as a deeper and more comprehensive power. But it is much that false conceptions be taken out of the way, and that no room be given for objections that lie in the end, not against the truth itself, but only against the form of its representation. It is much also that this last be made to stand in true correspondence with known analogies in other spheres of life, and especially with the organic idea of the new creation itself; which, with all its supernatural character as a whole, must always be regarded as a continuation still of the natural creation in its highest form, and as such most perfectly symmetrical and self-consistent in all its parts. It is only in such view, that we may be allowed to speak of bringing the doctrine before us nearer to the understanding, by any improvement that may be possible in the mode of its exhibition.

Taking advantage then of the scientific truths which have been already mentioned and which Calvin failed at least to apply to the subject in their full force, and keeping in view always the authority of God's most holy revelation, (not so much single abstract texts as the life and power of the word rather as a whole). I will now endeavour to throw the doctrine comprehensively into the form which the nature of the case seems to me to require. The way will then be open for the actual trial of the doctrine, by the Scriptures themselves. These form of course the last and only conclusive measure of truth in the case. But before we make our appeal to them, it is important that we should have clearly in view the precise object for which they are to be consulted.

The subject may be exhibited, to the best advantage perhaps, in the way of successive theses or propositions, accompanied with such illustration as each case may seem to require in order to be made clear. These will have respect first to the Mystical Union, and then to the question of the Eucharist.

SECTION II.

THE MYSTICAL UNION.

1. *The human world in its present natural state, as descended from Adam, is sundered from its proper life in God by sin, and utterly disabled in this character for rising by itself to any higher position.* The fall of Adam was the fall of the race. Not simply because he represented the race, but because the race was itself comprehended in his person. The terrible fact of sin revealed itself in him as a world-fact, that was now incorporated with the inmost life of humanity itself, and became from this point onward an insurmountable law in the progress of its development. The ruin under which we lie is an organic ruin; the ruin of our nature; universal and whole, not simply because all men are sinners, but as making all men to be sinners. Men do not make their nature, their nature makes them. To have part in the human nature at all, we must have part in it primarily as a fallen nature; a spiritually impotent nature; from whose constitution the principle of life has departed in its very root. Not by accident or bad example only, as the Pelagians vainly dream, are we all in the same condemnation. There is a law of sin at work in us from our birth. The whole Pelagian view of life is shallow in the extreme. It sees in the human race only a vast aggregation of particular men, outwardly put together; a huge living sand-heap, nd nothing more. But the human race is not a sand-heap. It is the power of a single life. It is bound together, not outwardly, but inwardly. Men have been one before they became many; and as many, they are still one. We have a perfect right then to say that Adam's sin is imputed to all his posterity. Only let us not think of a mere outward transfer in the case. Against *such* imputation the objection commonly made to the doctrine has force. It would be to substitute a fiction for a fact. No imputation of that sort is taught in the Bible. But the imputation of Adam's sin to his posterity involves no fiction. It is counted to them simply because it is theirs in fact. They are born into Adam's nature, and for this reason only, as forming with him the same general life, they are born also into his guilt.

2. *The union in which we stand with our first parent, as thus fallen extends to his entire person,* BODY *as well as* SOUL. He did not fall in his soul simply, nor in his body simply, but in both at once. The *man* fell. So the humanity of which he was the root fell in him and with him, to the same extent. The *whole* became corrupt. And now as such it includes in

all his posterity, a real and true perpetuation of his life under both forms on to the end of time. They partake of his body as well as of his soul. Both are transmitted by ordinary generation, the same identical organic life-stream, from one age onward always to another. We are bone of his bone, and flesh of his flesh, and blood of his blood. And still there is no material communication, no local contact. Not a particle of Adam's body has come into ours. The identity resolves itself at last into an invisible law; and it is not one law for the body, and another law for the soul; but one and the same law involves the presence of both, as the power of a common life. Where the law works, there Adam's life is reproduced, body and soul together. And still the individual Adam is not blended with his posterity in any such way, as to lose his own personality or swallow up theirs. His identity with his posterity is generic; but none the less real or close on this account. We are all familiar with the case, and if we stop to think of it at all can hardly feel perhaps that it calls for any explanation. And yet of a truth, it is something very wonderful. A mystery in fact, that goes quite beyond the region of the understanding.

3. *By the hypostatical union of the two natures in the person of* JESUS CHRIST, *our humanity as fallen in Adam was exalted again to a new and imperishable divine life.* That the race might be saved, it was necessary that a work should be wrought not beyond it, but in it; and this inward salvation to be effective must lay hold of the race itself in its organic, universal character, before it could extend to individuals, since in no other form was it possible for it to cover fully the breadth and depth of the ruin that lay in its way. Such an inward salvation of the race required that it should be joined in a living way with the divine nature itself, as represented by the everlasting Word or *Logos*, the fountain of all created light and life. The Word accordingly became flesh, that is assumed humanity into union with itself. It was not an act, whose force was intended to stop in the person of one man himself to be transplanted soon afterwards to heaven. Nor was it intended merely to serve as the necessary basis of the great work of atonement, the power of which might be applied to the world subsequently in the way of outward imputation. It had this use indeed, but not as its first and most comprehensive necessity. The object of the incarnation was to couple the human nature in real union with the Logos, as a permanent source of life. It resulted from the presence of sin only, (itself no part of this nature in its original constitution,) that the union thus formed called the Saviour to suffer. As the bearer of a fallen humanity he must descend with it to the lowest depths of sorrow and pain, in order that he might triumph with it again in the power of his own imperishable life. In all this, he acted for himself and yet for the race he represented at the same time. For it was no external relation simply, that he sustained to this last. He was himself the race. Humanity dwelt in his

person as the second Adam, under a higher form than ever it carried in the first.

4. *The* VALUE *of Christ's sufferings and death, as well as of his entire life, in relation to men, springs wholly from the view of the incarnation now presented.* The assumption of humanity on the part of the *Logos* involved the necessity of suffering, as the only way in which the new life with which it was thus joined could triumph over the law of sin and death it was called to surmount. The passion of the Son of God was the world's spiritual *crisis,* in which the principle of health came to its last struggle with the principle of disease, and burst forth from the very bosom of the grave itself in the form of immortality. This was the atonement, Christ's victory over sin and hell. As such it forms the only medium of salvation to men. But how? Only as the value of it is made over in each case to the subject, who is to be saved. This we are told is by imputation. But does the act of imputation reckon to us as ours, that which is not ours in fact? Does it proceed upon a fiction in the divine mind? Just as little as in the case of our relation to the sin of Adam. This last is not a foreign evil arbitrarily set over to our account. It is immanent to our nature itself. Just so here. The atonement as a foreign work, could not be made to reach us in the way of a true salvation. Only as it may be considered *immanent* in our nature itself, can it be imputed to us as ours, and so become available in us for its own ends. And this is its character in truth. It holds in humanity, as a work wrought out by it in Christ. When Christ died and rose, humanity died and rose at the same time in his person; not figuratively, but truly; just as it had fallen before in the person of Adam.

5. *The Christian Salvation then, as thus comprehended in Christ, is a new* LIFE, *in the deepest sense of the word.* Not a doctrine merely for the mind to embrace. Not an event simply to be remembered with faith, as the basis of piety in the way of example of other outward support; the sense of some, who have much to say of Christianity as a *fact* in their own shallow way. Not the constitution only of a new order of spiritual relations, or a new system of divine appliances, in the case of fallen, helpless man. But a new *Life* introduced into the very centre of humanity itself. In this view, though bound most closely with the organic development of the world's history as it stood before, it is by no means comprehended in it, or carried by it, as its proper product and fruit. Christianity is more than a continuation simply of Judaism. It claims the character of a *creation*, by which old things in the end must pass away, and all things become new. This indicates, however, its relation to the old order. That is not to be annihilated by it, but taken up into it as a higher life. The incarnation is supernatural; not magical, however; not fantastic or visionary; not something to be gazed at as a transient prodigy in the world's history. It is the supernatural linking itself to the onward flow of the world's life, and becoming thenceforward itself the ground and

principle of the entire organism, now poised at last on its true centre. In this sense Christianity is indeed a *fact*; even as the first creation was a Fact; a Fact for all time; a WORLD-FACT.

6. *The new Life of which Christ is the Source and Organic Principle, is in all respects a true* HUMAN *Life.* It is in one sense a divine life. It springs from the *Logos.* But it is not the life of the Logos separately taken. It is the life of the Word made flesh, the divinity joined in personal union with our humanity. It was not in the way of show merely that Christ put on our nature; as many of the old Gnostics believed, and as the view that multitudes still have of the Christian salvation, would seem to imply. He put it on truly and in the fullest sense. He was Man more perfectly than this could be said of Adam himself, even before he fell; humanity stood revealed in his person under its most perfect form. Not a new humanity wholly dissevered from that of Adam; but the humanity of Adam itself, only raised to a higher character, and filled with new meaning and power, by its union with the divine nature. The new creation in Christ Jesus appeared originally only in this form, and can hold in no other to the end of time.

7. *Christ's life, as now described, rests not in his separate person, but passes over to his people; thus constituting the* CHURCH, *which is his body, the fulness of Him that filleth all in all.* This is involved in the view already taken of his Person, as the principle of the new creation. The process by which the whole is accomplished, is not mechanical but organic. It takes place in the way of history, growth, regular living development. Christ goes not forth to heal the world by outward power as standing beyond himself; he gathers it rather into his own person, that is, stretches over it the law of his own life, so that it is made at last to hold in him and from him altogether, as its root. As individuals, we are inserted into him by our regeneration, which is thus the true counterpart of that first birth that makes us natural men. We are not however set over into this new order of existence wholly at once. This would be magic. We are apprehended by it, in the first place, only as it were at a single point. But this point is central. The new life lodges itself, as an efflux from Christ, in the inmost core of our personality. Here it becomes the principle or seed of our sanctification; which is simply the gradual transfusion of the same exalted spiritual quality or potence through our whole persons. The process terminates with the resurrection. All analogies borrowed from a lower sphere to illustrate this great mystery, are necessarily poor, and always more or less perilous. Perhaps the best is furnished in the action of a magnet on iron. The man in his natural state centres upon himself, and is thus spiritually dead. In his regeneration, he is touched with a divine attraction, that draws him to Christ, the true centre of life. The tendency and motion here come not of himself, grow not out of what he was before. They are in obedience simply to the magnetic stream that has

reached him from without. The old nature still continues to work. The iron is not at once made free from its *gravity*. But a new law is producing at every point an inward nisus in the opposite direction; which needs only to be filled with new force continually from the magnetic centre, to carry all at last its own way. "I, if I be lifted up, says Christ, "will draw all men unto me!"

8. *As joined to Christ, then, we are* ONE *with him in his life, and not simply in the way of a less intimate and real union.* The new birth involves a substantial change in the centre of our being. It is not the understanding, or the will simply, that is wrought upon in a natural or supernatural way. Not this or that power or function of the man is it, that may be called the seat of what is thus introduced into his person. Life is not thinking, nor feeling, nor acting; but the organic unity of all these, inseparably joined together. In this sense, we say of our union with Christ, that it is a new *life*. It is deeper than all thought, feeling, or exercise of will. Not a quality only. Not a mere relation. A relation in fact, as that of the iron to the magnet; but one that carries into the centre of the subject a form of being which was not there before. Christ communicates his own life substantially to the soul on which he acts, causing it to grow into his very nature. This is the *mystical union*; the basis of our whole salvation; the only medium by which it is possible for us to have an interest in the grace of Christ under any other view.

9. *Our relation to Christ is not simply parallel with our relation to Adam, but goes* BEYOND IT, *as being immeasurably more intimate and deep.* Adam was the first man; Christ is the archetypal man, in whom the true ideal of humanity has been brought into view. Adam stands related to the race as a simple generic head; Christ as the true Centre and universal basis of humanity itself. Our nature took its start in Adam; it finds its end and last ground only in Christ. It comes not with us to the exercise of a free, full personality, till we are consciously joined to the person of the divine *Logos* in our nature. In a deep sense thus, Christ is the universal Man. His *Person* is the root, in the presence and power of which only all other personalities can stand, in the case of his people, whether in time or eternity. They not only spring from him, as we all do from Adam, but continue to stand in him, as an all present, everywhere active personal Life.* In this way, they all have part in his divinity itself;

---

*Personality is constituted by self-consciousness. This includes, in our natural state, no reference whatever to an original progenitor. Adam forms in no sense the centre of our life, the basis of our spiritual being. But the *Christian* consciousness carries in its very nature, such a reference to the person of Jesus Christ. It consists in the active sense of this relation, as the true and proper life of its subject. The man does not connect with Christ the self-consciousness which he has under a different form, in the way of outward reference merely; but this reference is comprehended in his self-consciousness itself, so far as he has become spiritually renewed. Christ is felt to be the centre of his life; or rather this feeling though the hypostatical union, as such, remains limited of course to his own person. The whole Christ lives and works in the Church, supernaturally, gloriously, mysteriously, and yet really and truly, "always, to the end of the world." Glory be to God!

10. *The mystical union includes necessarily a participation in the entire* HUMANITY *of Christ.* Will any one pretend to say, that we are joined in *real* life-unity with the everlasting *Logos*, apart from Christ's manhood, in the way of direct personal mutual inbeing? This would be to exalt ourselves to the same level with the Son of God himself. The mystical union then would be the hypostatical union itself, repeated in the person of every believer. Such a supposition is monstrous. Those who think of it only impose upon themselves. For the conception of a *real* union, they substitute in their thoughts always one that is moral in fact. The Word became flesh in Christ, for the very purpose of reaching us in a real way. The incarnation constitutes the only medium by which, the only form under which, this divine life of the world can ever find its way over into our persons. Let us beware here of all Gnostic abstractions. Let us not fall practically into the condemnation of Nestorius. But allowing the humanity of Christ to be the indispensable medium of our participation in his person as divine, will any dream only of his human soul as comprehended in the case? Then the whole fact is again converted into a phantom. The life of Christ was *one*. To enter us at all in a real way, it must enter us in its totality. To divide the humanity of Christ, is to destroy it; to take it away, and lay it no one can tell where. What God has joined together, we have no right thus to put asunder. Christ's humanity is not his soul separately taken; just as little as it is his body separately taken. It is neither soul nor body as such, but the everlasting, indissoluble union of both.

11. *As the mystical union embraces the whole Christ, so we too are embraced by it not in a partial but* WHOLE *way.* The very nature of life is, that it lies at the ground of all that may be predicated besides of the subject in which it is found, in the way of quality, attribute, or distinction. It is the whole at once of the nature in which it resides. A new life then,

may be said to be itself his life, the form in which he exists as a self-conscious person. It is with reason, therefore, that *Schleiermacher* speaks of the communication which Christ makes of himself to believers, as moulding the *person*, since he imparts, in fact, a new higher consciousness, that forms the basis of a life that was not previously at hand, the true centre of our personality under its most perfect form. In this case the person of Christ is the ground and fountain of all proper Christian personality in the Church. It is only as he is consciously in communication with Christ as his life centre, (which can be only through an actual self-communication—*Wesensmittheilung*—of Christ's life to him for this purpose,) that the believer can be regarded as a *Christian*, or new man in Christ Jesus. So *Olshausen*: "Die Persönlichkeit des Sohnes selbst, als die umfassende, nimmt alle Persönlichkeiten der Seinigen in sich auf, und durchdringt sie wieder mit seinem Leben, gleichsam als der lebendige Mittelpunct eines Organismus, von dem das Leben ausströmt und zu dem es wiederkehrt." *Comm. John* XIV., 20.

to become truly ours, must extend to us in the totality of our nature. It must fill the understanding, and rule the will, enthrone itself in the soul and extend itself out over the entire body. Besides, the life which is to be conveyed into us in the present case, we have just seen to be in all respects a true human life before it reaches us. It is the life of the *incarnate* Son of God. But as such, how can it be supposed in passing over to us, to lodge itself exclusively in our *souls*, without regard to our bodies? Is it not a contradiction, to think of a *real* union with Christ's humanity, which extends at least only to one half of our nature? In the person of Christ himself, we hold with the ancient Church the presence of a *true body* as well as of a reasonable soul. Shall this same Christ, as formed in his people, be converted into an incorporeal, docetic, Gnostic Christ, as having no real presence except in the abstract soul? Or may his bodily nature continue to hold in this case in the soul simply, separately taken? Incredible! Either Christ's human life is not formed in us at all, or it must be formed in us as a *human* life; must be corporeal as well as incorporeal; must put on outward form, and project itself in space. And all this is only to say, in other words, that it must enter into us, and become united to us, in our bodies as truly as in our souls. In this way, the mystical union becomes real. Under any other conception, it ends in a phantasm, or falls back helplessly to the merely moral relation that is talked of by Pelagians and Rationalists.

12. *The mystery now affirmed is accomplished, not in the way of two different forms of action, but by one and the same single and undivided process.* Much of the difficulty that is felt with regard to this whole subject, arises from the inveterate prejudice, by which so commonly the idea of human life is split for the imagination into two lives, and a veritable dualism thus constituted in our nature in place of the absolute unity that belongs to it in fact. The Bible knows nothing of that abstract separation of soul and body, which has come to be so widely admitted into the religious views of the modern world. It comes from another quarter altogether; and it is as false to all true philosophy, as it is unsound in theology and pernicious for the Christian life. Soul and body, in their ground, are but one life; identical in their origin; bound together by mutual interpenetration subsequently at every point; and holding for ever in the presence and power of the self-same organic law. We have no right to think of the body as the prison of the soul, in the way of Plato; nor as its garment merely; nor as its shell or hull. We have no right to think of the soul in any way as a form of existence of and by itself into which the soul as another form of such existence is thrust in a mechanical way. Both form *one* life. The soul to be complete to develope itself at all as a soul, *must* externalize itself, throw itself out in space; and this externalization

is the body.* All is one process, the action of one and the same living organic principle, dividing itself only that its unity may become thus the more free and intensely complete. There is no room to dream then of a bodily communication with Christ on the part of believers, as something distinct from the communication they have with him in their souls. His flesh cannot enter our flesh, under an abstract form, dissevered from the rest of his life, and in no union with our souls as the medium of such translation. This would be the so called Capernaitic communion in full; not mystical, but magical; incredible and useless at the same time. The process by which Christ is formed in his people, is not thus two-fold but single. It lays hold of its subject in each case, not in the periphery of his person, but in its inmost centre, where the whole man, soul and body, is still one undivided life. As in the case of the mind it is neither the understanding, nor the will, that is apprehended by it, so in the case of the person also it is neither the soul nor the body, separately considered, that is so apprehended; it is the totality which includes all; it is the *man* in the very centre and ground of his personality. Christ's life as a *whole* is borne over into the person of the believer as a like *whole.* The communication is central, and central only; from the last ground of Christ's life to the last ground of ours; by the action of a single, invisible, self-identical, spiritual

*To some, possibly, this representation may seem to be contradicted by what the Scriptures teach of the separate existence of the soul between death and the resurrection; and it must be admitted, that we are met here with a difficulty which it is not easy, at present, to solve. Let us, however, not mistake the true state of the case. The difficulty is not to reconcile scripture with a psychological theory; but to bring it into harmony with itself. For it is certain, that the Scriptures teach such an identification of soul and body in the proper human personality, as clearly at least as they intimate a continued consciousness on the part of the soul between death and the resurrection. The doctrine of *immortality* in the Bible, is such as to include always the idea of the resurrection. it is an ἀνάστασις ἐκ τῶν νεκρῶν. The whole argument in the 15th chapter of 1st Corinthians, as well as the representation 1 Thess. IV. 13–18, proceeds on the assumption that the life of the *body*, as well as that of the soul, is indispensable to the perfect state of our nature as human. The soul then, during the intermediate state, cannot possibly constitute, in the biblical view, a complete man; and the case requires besides, that we should conceive of its relation to the body as still in force, not absolutely destroyed but only suspended. The whole condition is interimistic, and by no possibility of conception capable of being thought of as complete and final. When the resurrection body appears, it will not be as a new frame abruptly created for the occasion, and brought to the soul in the way of outward addition and supplement. It will be found to hold in strict organic continuity with the body, as it existed before death, as the action of the same law of life; which implies that this law has not been annihilated, but suspended only in the intermediate state. In this character, however, it must be regarded as resting in some way, (for where else *could* it fist,) in the separate life, as it is called, of the soul itself; the slumbering power of the resurrection, ready at the proper time, in obedience to Christ's powerful word, to clothe itself with its former actual nature, in full identity with the form it carried before death, though under a far higher order of existence. Only *then* can the salvation of the soul be considered complete. All at last is *one* life; the subject of which is the totality of the believer's person, comprehending soul and body alike from the beginning of the process to its end.

law. The power of Christ's life lodged in the soul begins to work there immediately as the principle of a new creation. In doing so, it works organically according to the law which it includes in its own constitution. That is, it works as a *human* life; and as such becomes a law of regeneration in the body as truly as in the soul.

13. *In all this of course then there is no room for the supposition of any* MATERIAL, *tactual approach of Christ's body to the persons of his people.* It is not necessary, that his flesh and blood, materially considered, should in any way pass over into our life, and become locally present in us under any form, to make us partakers of his humanity. Even in the sphere of mere nature, the continuity of organic existence, as it passes from one individual to another—mounting upwards for instance from the buried seed, and revealing itself at last, through leaves and flowers, in a thousand new seeds after its own kind—is found to hang in the end, not on the material medium as such through which the process is effected, but on the presence simply of the living force, immaterial altogether and impalpable, that imparts both form and substance to the whole. The presence of the root in the branches of the oak, is not properly speaking either a local or material presence. It is the power simply of a common life. And why then should it be held impossible, for Christ's life to reach over into the persons of his people, whole and entire, even without the intervention of any material medium whatever—belonging as it does pre-eminently to the sphere of the Spirit? Why should it seem extravagant, to believe that the *law* of this life, apart from all material contact with his person, may be so lodged in the soul of the believer by the power of the Holy Ghost, as to become there the principle of a new moral creation, that shall still hold in unbroken organic continuity with its root, and go on to take full possession of its subject, soul and body, under the same form?

14. *Such a relation of Christ to the Church involves no* UBIQUITY *or idealistic dissipation of his body and requires no* FUSION *of his proper personality with the persons of his people.* We distinguish between the simple man and the universal man, here joined in the same person. The possibility of such a distinction is clear in the case of Adam. His universality is not indeed of the same order with that of Christ. But still the case has full force, for the point now in hand. Adam was at once an individual and a whole race. All his posterity partake of his life, and grow forth from him as their root. And still his individual person has not been lost on this account. Why then should the life of Christ in the Church, be supposed to conflict with the idea of his separate, distinct personality, under a true human form? Why must we dream of a fusion of persons in the one case, more than in the other? Here is more, it is true, than our relation to Adam. We not only spring from Christ, so far as our new life is concerned, but stand in him perpetually also as our ever living and ever present root. His *Person* is always thus the actual bearer of *our* persons. And yet there is no

mixture, or flowing of one into the other, as individually viewed. Is not God the last ground of all personality? But does this imply any pantheistic dissipation of his nature, into the general consciousness of the intelligent universe? Just as little does it imply any like dissipation of Christ's personality into the general consciousness of the Church, when we affirm that it forms the ground, out of which and in the power of which only, the whole life of the Church continually subsists.* In this view Christ is personally present always in the Church. This of course, in the power of his divine nature. But his divine nature is at the same time *human*, in the fullest sense; and wherever his presence is revealed in the Church in a real way, it includes his person necessarily under the one aspect as well as under the other. With all this however, which is something very different from the conception of a proper ubiquity in the case of Christ's body, we do not relinquish the thought of his separate human individuality. We distinguish, between his universal humanity in the Church, and his humanity as a particular man, whom the heavens have received till the time of the restitution of all things. His glorified body, we doubt not, is possessed of qualities, attributes and powers, that transcend immeasurably all we know or can think of a human body here. Still it is a body; a particular body; having organized parts and outward form. As such of course, it must be defined and circumscribed by local limits, and cannot be supposed to be present in different places at the same time.

15. *The mystical union, holding in this form, is more intimate and real, than any union which is known in the world besides.* Even in nature, the most close connection is not that which holds in the way of mere local contact or outward conjunction. There may be an actual transfusion of one substance into another, with very little union in the end. A simply *mechanical* unity, one thing joined to another in space, is the lowest and poorest that can be presented to our thoughts. Higher than this is the

---

*It is not unusual to hear it objected to the view of such a comprehension of the general Christian life in the life of Christ, as is here maintained, that it leads to a sort of pantheism, in which no room is left for the idea of a separate individual consciousness on the part of the believer. But this objection, if it have any force, must hold not only against such a life union with Christ as is here advocated, but against any union with him whatever that may be considered real, and not simply moral. Then all the best old English divines, as Professor Lewis has well remarked, such as Howe, Baxter, Owen, &c.. must fall under condemnation as teaching the Bhuddist doctrine of spiritual annihilation. "Such a philosopher," he adds, "as the author of the '*Blessedness of the Righteous*,' would teach us that the soul's consciousness of being in Christ, and of having one life with him, might give a higher sense of a more glorious and blessed individuality, than could be derived from any other state or being. . . . Paul was not afraid of saying, that 'in God we live, and move, and are,' or of speaking of the Church as being 'the fulness of him that filleth all in all,' or of declaring that 'our life is hid with Christ in God.' Neither whilst there remained in him the individual consciousness of so blessed a state, was he afraid of the declaration, ζῶ δὲ, οὐκ ἔτι ἐγώ, ζῇ δὲ ἐν ἐμοὶ ΧΡΙΣΤΟΣ,—*I live, not I, but Christ liveth in me.*"

Holy Spirit-val (body included) →

chemical combination; which however is still comparatively outward. The *organic* union, as it holds for instance between the root and topmost branches of the tree, is far more inward and close. Though they do not touch each other at all, they are one notwithstanding in a sense more true, than can be affirmed, either of the different parts of a crystal, or of the elements that are married in the constitution of atmospheric air. Of vastly higher character still, is the union of head and members in the same human body. But even this is a poor image of the oneness of Christ with his people. There is nothing like this in the whole world, under any other form. It is bound by no local limitations. It goes beyond all nature, and transcends all thought.

16. *The union of Christ with believers is wrought by the power of the* HOLY GHOST. The new birth is from the Spirit. It is by the Spirit the divine life is sustained and advanced in us, at every point, from its commencement to its close. There is no other medium, by which it is possible for us to be in Christ, or to have Christ in ourselves. The new creation holds absolutely and entirely, in the powerful presence of the Holy Ghost. Hence it is said, "He that is joined to the Lord, is one *Spirit;*" and the indwelling of Christ and his Spirit in believers is spoken of as the same thing. But for this very reason, we have no right to dissolve this unity again in our thoughts, by making the presence of the Spirit a mere substitute for the presence of Christ himself. Where the one is, there the other is truly and really at the same time. The Spirit, proceeding from the Father and Son and subsisting in everlasting union with both, constitutes the form, in which and by which the new creation in Christ Jesus upholds itself, and reveals itself, in all its extent. It is not *Nature*, but *Spirit*. So in the Person of Christ himself, the root of this creation. The Spirit was never brought near to men before, as now through the incarnate Word. It dwelt in him without measure. Humanity itself was filled completely with its presence, and appears at last translucent with the glory of heaven itself by its means. Forth from the person of Christ, thus "quickened in the Spirit," the flood of life pours itself onward continually in the Church, only of course by the presence and power of the Holy Ghost; for it holds in no other form. Not however by the presence and power of the Holy Ghost, as abstracted from the presence of Christ himself; as though he were the fountain only, and not the very life-stream too, of the new creation, or could be supposed to be in it and with it by the intervention only of a presence, not involving at the same time and to the same extent his own. "The Lord is that Spirit." He reveals himself in his people, dwells in them and makes them one with himself in a real way, by his Spirit. In this view, the new life formed in them is *spiritual*; not natural or physical, as belonging simply to the first creation. But this does not imply at all, that it is limited to the soul as distinguished from the body. There is no absolute opposition here between the idea of body and the idea of Spirit.

Here is a spiritual *body*, as well as a body natural, according to the apostle. The Spirit of Christ, in his own person at least, fills the whole man, soul and body. All is spiritual, glorious, heavenly. His whole humanity has been taken up into the sphere of the Spirit, and appears transfigured into the same life. And why then should it not extend itself, in the way of strict organic continuity, as a *whole* humanity also, by the active presence of Christ's Spirit, over into the persons of his people? A spiritual life no more excludes the thought of the body in the one case, than it does in the other.

17. *Christ's life is apprehended on the part of his people only by* FAITH. The life itself comes to us wholly from Christ himself, by the power of his Spirit. The magnetic stream is poured upon us from abroad. If we move at all, it is only in obedience to the divine current thus brought to bear upon our souls. To live in this at all, however, it is necessary that we should surrender ourselves spontaneously to its power. This is faith; the most comprehensive, fundamental act of which our nature is capable. The man swings himself, in the totality of his being quite off from the centre of self, on which hitherto his consciousness has been poised, over upon Christ, now revealed to his view, as another centre altogether. The birth of a new *life*, in the strictest sense, as we have already seen. Faith, of course, is not the principle of this life. It is only the medium of its introduction into the soul, and the condition of its growth and development when present. But as such it is indispensable. The process of our sanctification is spiritual, and not mechanical or magical.*

18. *The new life of the believer includes degrees, and will become complete only in the* RESURRECTION. Only in this form could it have a true human character. All life, in the case of man, is actualized, and can be actualized, only in the way of process of gradual historical development. So in the case before us, there is the seed; and when it springs, "first the blade, then the ear; and after that, the full corn in the ear." The new life struggles with the old, like Jacob and Esau in the same womb! The Christian carries in himself two forms of existence, a "law of sin and death" on the one hand, and "the law of the spirit of life in Christ Jesus" on the other; and the power of the last is continually opposed and restrained by the power of the first. From its very start, however, the life of Christ in the believer is a whole life; and in all its subsequent progress it reveals its power continually, under the same character. From the first it includes in itself *potentially* all that it is found to become at the last. The life of the tree is only the same life, that was comprehended originally in the seed from which it has sprung. So it is with all life. All that belongs, then, to the new life of the Christian, conceived as complete at the last day, must

---

*"Living faith in Christ," says Schleiermacher, "is nothing but the self-consciousness of our union with Christ"

be allowed to be involved in it as principle and process from the beginning. In every stage of its progress it is a true human life, answerable to the nature of its organic root, and to the nature also of the subject in which it is lodged. It is always, as far as it prevails, the law of a new nature for the body as well as for the soul. The full and final triumph of the process, is the resurrection; which is reached in the case of the individual, only in connection with the consummation of the Church as a whole. The bodies of the saints in glory will be only the last result, in organic continuity, of the divine life of Christ, implanted in their souls at their regeneration. There is nothing abrupt in Christianity. It is a supernatural constitution indeed; but as such it is clothed in a natural form, and involves in itself as regular a law of historical development, as the old creation itself. The resurrection body will be simply the ultimate outburst of the life, that had been ripening for immortality under cover of the old Adamic nature before. The winged psyche has its elemental organization in the worm, and does not lose it in the tomb-like chrysalis. Let us not be told, that this is to suppose two bodies in the person of the believer at one time. Does the new life, abstracted from the body, involve the supposition of two *souls*? The cases are precisely parallel. The man is one, soul and body. But a new organic law has become lodged in the inmost centre of his personality, and is now gradually extending its force over the entire constitution of his nature as a whole. It does not lay hold of one part of his being first, and then proceed to another, in the way of outward territorial conquest; as though a hand or foot could be renovated before the head, or the understanding apart from the will, or the soul in no connection with the body. The whole man is made the subject of the new life at once. The law of revolution involved in it extends from the centre to the extreme periphery of his person. The old body becomes itself, in a mysterious way, the womb of a higher corporeity, the life-law of Christ's own glorious body; which is at last, through the process of death and the resurrection, set free from the first form of existence entirely, and made to supersede it for ever in the immortality of heaven.

SECTION III.

THE LORD'S SUPPER.

19. "*A sacrament is a holy ordinance instituted by* CHRIST; *wherein, by sensible signs,* CHRIST *and the benefits of the new covenant are represented,* SEALED *and* APPLIED *to believers.*" Thus the Westminster Shorter Catechism, echoing the voice of the whole Reformed Church, as it had sounded throughout Christendom for a century before. The *signs*, as such, make not the sacrament. They are only one part of it. The other part is found in the invisible grace, that is sacramentally or mystically joined with the signs. To be complete, that is to be at all a true sacrament, the ordinance must comprehend both. In other words the invisible grace enters as a necessary constituent element into the idea of the sacrament; and must be of course *objectively* present with it wherever it is administered under a true form. Whether it shall become available to the benefit of the participant, must depend on the presence of the conditions that are needed to give it effect. All turns here at last on the exercise of faith. But the objective presence of the grace itself, as an essential part of the sacrament, is none the less certain and sure on this account. It belongs to the ordinance in its own nature; which, in this view, is not a picture or remembrancer simply for the mind, but a true and real exhibition of that which it represents. The sign and the thing signified are, by Christ's institution, mysteriously bound together, so as to form in the sacramental transaction one and the same presence. Not as though the last were in any way included in the first, as its local or material receptacle. The conjunction is in no sense such as to change at all the nature of the sensible sign, in itself considered, or to bring it into any physical union with the grace it represents. But still the two form one presence. Along with the outward sign, is exhibited always at the same time the represented grace. The union of the one with the other is mystical, and peculiar altogether to the nature of a sacrament; but it is not for this reason *less* real, but only a great deal *more* real, than it could be possibly under any natural and local form. The invisible grace thus made present by sensible signs in the sacraments, is "Christ *and* the benefits of the new covenant." Not the *benefits* of the new covenant only; but Christ himself also, in a real way, as the only medium of a real communication with the benefits. Christ first, and *then* and *therefore* all his benefits; as inhering only in his person, and carrying with them no reality under any different view.

20. *"The Lord's Supper is a sacrament, wherein, by giving and receiving bread and wine according to Christ's appointment, his death is showed forth, and the worthy receivers are, not after a corporal and carnal manner, but by faith, made partakers of* HIS BODY AND BLOOD, *with all his benefits, to their spiritual nourishment and growth in grace."* Thus again the Westminster Shorter Catechism. Here are sensible signs, bread and wine solemnly given and received. Here also we have the invisible grace, Christ and his benefits. To make the case clearer, it is Christ's "body and blood, with all his benefits;" the first of course as the basis and medium of the last. The visible and invisible are different, and yet, in this case, they may not be disjoined. They flow together in the constitution of one and the same sacrament. Neither of the two is the sacrament, abstracted from the other. The ordinance holds in the sacramental *transaction*; which includes the presence of both, the one materially, for the senses, the other spiritually, for faith. Christ's body is not in or under the bread, locally considered. Still, the power of his life in this form is actually exhibited at the same time in the mystery of the sacrament. The one is as truly and really present in the institution, as the other. The elements are not simply significant of that which they represent, as serving to bring it to mind by the help of previous knowledge. They are the pledge of its actual presence and power. They are bound to it in mystical, sacramental union, more intimately, we may say, than they would be if they were made to include it in the way of actual local comprehension. There is far more then than the mere commemoration of Christ's death. Worthy receivers partake also of his body and blood, with all his benefits, through the power of the Holy Ghost, to their spiritual nourishment and growth in grace.

21. *The sacrament of the Lords Supper has reference directly and primarily to the* ATONEMENT *wrought out by Christ's death on the cross.* So in the words of institution, it is his body broken, and his blood *shed* for the remission of sins, that are held up to view. It is not simply of Christ but of the "body and blood" of Christ, that is of Christ as sacrificed and slain for the sins of the world, that worthy receivers are made to partake in the holy ordinance. Not as though the sacrament were itself a sacrifice, or included in its own nature any expiatory force, in the way dreamed of by the Church of Rome. It serves simply to ratify and advance the interest, which believers have already, by their union with Christ, in the new covenant established through his blood. Only under this form, can the salvation of the gospel stand us in stead. We are sinners and as such need redemption. Only through the medium of Christ's sufferings and death, can we come to have any part in his glory. He must be our righteousness, in order that he may be our life. Hence our first relation to him as believers, is that which is formed in our justification; that "act of God's free grace, wherein he pardoneth all our sins, and accepteth us as

righteous in his sight, only for the righteousness of Christ imputed to us, and received by faith alone." And so our whole subsequent Christian life, as it grows forth from this objective righteousness, may be said to involve a constant return to it, and dependence upon it, on to the end of our course. We need no new atonement; but we do need to fall back perpetually on the one sacrifice for sin, which Christ has already made upon the cross, appropriating the power of it more and more to our souls, as the only ground of our salvation. The Lord's Supper accordingly, concentrating in itself as it does, in some sense, the force and meaning of the whole Christian life, has regard to this sacrifice always as the great object of its representation. It is the sacrament of Christ's death, the communion of his body and blood.

22. *As the medium however by which we are thus made partakers of the new covenant in Christ's death, the Holy Supper involves a real communication with the* PERSON *of the Saviour, now gloriously exalted in heaven.* Our justification, as we have seen, rests on the objective merit of Christ, by whose blood alone propitiation has been made for the sins of the world. But this justification, to become ours in fact, must insert us into Christ's life. It reaches us from abroad, the "act of God's free grace;" but *as* God's act, it is necessarily more than a mere declaration or form of thought. It makes us to be in fact, what it accounts us to be, *in Christ*. The ground of our justification is a righteousness that *was* foreign to us before, but is *now* made to lodge itself in the inmost constitution of our being. A real life-union with Christ, powerfully wrought in our souls by the Holy Ghost, is the only basis, on which there can be any true imputation to us of what he has done and suffered on our behalf. And so, in the whole subsequent progress of our Christian life, our interest in his merits can be renewed and confirmed only in the same way. We must have Christ himself formed in us more and more in a real way, in order that "he may be made unto us of God, wisdom, and righteousness, and sanctification, and redemption." The eucharistic communion then, as serving to confirm our interest in the one sacrifice accomplished on the cross, must include a true participation in the life of him by whom the sacrifice was made. We can make no intelligible distinction here, between the crucified body of Christ and his body as now glorified in heaven. Both at last are one and the same life. To partake of the "broken body" and "shed blood" of the Redeemer, if it mean a real participation in his person at all, must be to communicate with him as now exalted at the right hand of God. For it is not a dead contract or a dead sacrifice we have to do with in this case; the "new covenant in Christ's blood" can hold only in the power of that indissoluble life, by which Jesus, once put to death in the flesh, is now quickened forever in the Spirit. The virtue of this covenant is not only represented, but *sealed* also and applied, to believers; which means, not merely that they have in the sacrament a general pledge that God will be

faithful to his own promises, but that the grace which it exhibits is actually made over to them, at the time, in this very transaction itself The grace however, namely the merit of Christ's sufferings and death, has a real character only as rooted in a living way in Christ's person; and it can become ours by new application, accordingly, no farther than Christ himself is made over to us at the same time. "To eat the crucified body and drink the shed blood of Christ" then, in the language of the Heidelberg Catechism, "is *not only* to embrace with a believing heart all the sufferings and death of Christ, and thereby to obtain the pardon of sin and life eternal; *but also,* BESIDES THAT, to become more and more united to his sacred body by the Holy Ghost, who dwells both in Christ and in us; so that we, though Christ is in heaven and we on earth, are notwithstanding flesh of his flesh and bone of his bone; and that we live, and are governed forever, by one Spirit, as members of the same body are by one soul."

23. *The real communication which believers have with Christ in the Holy Supper, extends to his* WHOLE *person.* To be real, and not simply moral, it *must* be thus comprehensive. We may divide Christ in our thoughts, abstracting his divinity from his humanity, or his soul from his body. But no such dualism has place in his actual person. If then he is to be received by us at all, it must be in a whole way. We partake not of certain rights and privileges only, which have been secured for us by the breaking of his body and shedding of his blood, but of the veritable substantial life of the blessed Immanuel himself, as the fountain and channel by which alone all these benefits can be conveyed into our souls. We partake not of his divinity only, nor yet of his Spirit as separate from himself, but also of his true and proper humanity. Not of his humanity in a separate form, his flesh and blood disjoined from his Spirit; but of the one life, which is the union of both, and in virtue of which the presence of the one must ever involve in the same form, and to the same extent, the presence of the other.

24. *Christ communicates himself to us, in the real way now mentioned,* UNDER THE FORM *of the sacramental mystery as such.* It is not as the object of thought simply or lively recollection, that he is made present in the ordinance. Nor is it by the activity of our faith merely, that he is brought nigh. His presence is identified objectively with the sacrament itself; and we receive him in the sacrament as the bearer of his very life itself, in the form in which it is here presented to our view. This implies no *opus operatum*, no mechanical or magical force in the use of the elements. All is by the Spirit; and for the communicant himself, all hangs upon the condition of faith. But still the grace exhibited, the action of the Spirit is here present, belongs to the sacrament in its own nature; and where the way is open for it to take effect at all, by the presence of the proper conditions on the part of the communicant, it serves in itself to

convey the life of Christ into our persons, Such is the sound *feeling* of Dr. Owen, the great Puritan divine, when he tells us: "This is the greatest mystery of all the practicals of our Christian religion, a way of receiving Christ by eating and drinking, something peculiar, that is not in the hearing of the word nor in any other part of divine worship whatsoever; a peculiar participation of Christ, a peculiar acting of faith towards Christ." The presence of which we speak is not in the bread and wine materially considered; but in the sacramental mystery as a whole. This consists of two parts, the one outward and visible, the other inward and invisible. These however are not simply joined together in time, as the sound of a bell, or the show of a light, may give warning of something with which it stands in no farther connection. They are connected by a true inward bond, so as to be different constituents only of one and the same reality. This union is not mechanical nor local, but as the old divines say, *mystical* or *sacramental*; that is peculiar to this case and altogether incomprehensible in its nature, but only all the more real and intimately close, on this very account.

25. *Christ communicates himself to us in the sacrament only in a spiritual,* CENTRAL *way.* Not his body by one process, and his Spirit by another; but his whole life, as a single undivided form of existence, by one and the same process. Not by the mechanical transplantation of some portion of his glorified body into our persons, to become there the germ of immortality in a physical view; but by the conveyance of his life in its inmost substance, by the power of the Holy Ghost, over into the very centre of our souls. The communication is in this view wholly independent of all material contact or conjunction. It holds altogether in the sphere of the Spirit. Christ reveals his presence in us centrally, as the power of the new spiritual creation, which is comprehended in his person; and which in this way is made to extend itself out organically, over the entire living man; as the life of the vine is re-produced, with all its properties and qualities, in every branch to which it extends.

26. *The Lord's Stepper is the medium of a real communication with Christ, only in the case of* BELIEVERS. The object of the institution is to confirm and advance the new life, where it has been already commenced. It has no power to convert such as are still in their sins. The grace which it exhibits, can be apprehended only by faith. Those who come to the Lord's table unworthily, as to a common meal, without being in a state to discern the Lord's body, eat and drink only judgment to themselves. They receive in no sense Christ's flesh and blood; but the bare signs only, by which they are exhibited for the benefit of those who come in a right way. Nor is it enough that the communicant be a regenerated person; he must be in the exercise of faith at the time. A gracious state, accompanied with gracious affections in the transaction itself, is the indispensable condition of a profitable approach to the Lord in the holy sacrament. And yet, as

before said, it is not our faith at all that gives the sacrament its force; nor does this consist at all in the actings of our faith, or penitence, or love, or any other gracious affection, that may be called into exercise at the time. These constitute not, and create not, the presence of Christ in the case. On the contrary, this presence forms itself the ground from which all such affections draw their activity and strength. The force of the sacrament is in the sacrament itself. Our faith is needed, only as the condition that is required to make room for it in our souls. "Thy faith hath made thee whole," said the blessed Saviour to the woman, who came behind him in the crowd, and touched the hem of his garment. But the healing virtue went forth in fact wholly from his own person; and was present there, as an ample remedy for all diseases, independently altogether of any application that might be made to him for relief. The women's faith formed the necessary condition only on her own part, for her becoming the recipient of the grace which was thus at hand. So in the case before us. The virtue of Christ's mystical presence is comprehended in the sacrament itself, and cannot be said to be put into it in any sense by our faith. This serves only to bring us into right relation to the life, that is thus placed within our reach. Faith puts not into the sacrament, what it has power instrumentally to draw from it for our use.

27. *Christ's mystical presence in the Eucharist, as now affirmed, leaves no room for the idea of* TRANSUBSTANTIATION *or* CONSUBSTANTIATION. According to the first of these errors, the bread and wine are changed into the actual substance of the Saviour's body and blood. According to the other, the proper Lutheran view, the Saviour's true body and blood are so contained and carried in the elements, that the reception of these even on the part of the impenitent and unbelieving, is supposed to involve the reception also of the other. Both these views are chargeable with the error of supposing an identification of Christ's presence in the eucharist with the elements as such. According to the Roman theory, this is permanent; the bread remains Christ's body, even when carried away afterwards to another place. By the Lutheran doctrine, the relation which binds them together holds only in the sacramental transaction itself; but while it holds, it is such that the *elements* in some way bear the divine life which they represent, so that it is received along with them in an oral, corporeal manner. This seems to imply a communication of the bodily life of Christ, not physically, of course, but supernaturally, to the body of the believer, in an immediate and direct way; in which case, the sacramental fruition as something different from the oral reception of the elements on the one hand, and the spiritual participation of Christ's body and blood on the other, becomes no better than an empty word, to which we can attach no meaning, unless it be as we think of mere blind magic. But the presence here affirmed, is not such as to identify the body of Christ in any way with the sacramental symbols, separately considered. It is not bound

to the bread and wine, but to the act of eating and drinking. In the service of the eucharist, and by its means, the believer is made to partake of Christ's body and blood. The outward transaction, where faith is at hand, involves this inward fruition, and forms the vehicle or channel by which it is accomplished. But the outward is not itself the form or mode in which the inward here takes place. The participation of Christ is wholly spiritual. He communicates himself, by the Spirit, to the soul of the believer, in a central way, according to the general law of the new creation to which this mystery belongs. No room is left here for the supposition of a mere corporeal communication, the transference of Christ's life directly into the bodies of his people, even though conceived to be in a wholly hyperphysical way. This, it is felt, would be only a mechanical and outward union in the end; the action at best of the power of the Spirit, on nature as such; by which a magical character must necessarily be imparted to the ordinance, as in the Church of Rome. It would imply, besides, a dualism in our proper life, that must overthrow its reality altogether. As the life itself is one, so it is to be renovated and sanctified through the provisions of the gospel as a single whole, from its ground or centre, and not by influences exerted in any way upon its organic volume apart from this. The new nature, to be real, must spring perpetually from the inmost being of its subject, in the form of spirit; and every fresh impulse, accordingly, which it is made to receive from its fountain in Christ, in whatever way, can be communicated to it only in this general form. So the participation of Christ's life in the sacrament, is in no sense corporeal, but altogether spiritual, as the necessary condition of its being real. It is the soul or spirit of the believer that is immediately fed with the grace, which is conveyed to it mystically in the holy ordinance. But this is in fact a fruition that belongs to the entire man; for the life made over to him under such central form, becomes at once, in virtue both of its own *human* character, and of the *human* character of the believer himself, a renovating force that reaches out into his person on all sides, and fills with its presence the undivided totality of his nature. In whatever sense the communication may be *real* at all, as distinguished from figurative, imputative or simply moral, it must be real for the whole man, and not simply for a part of the man.

SECTION IV.

FALSE THEORIES EXPOSED.

The way is now open for an appeal to the scriptures, which must be regarded, of course, as the ultimate standard of truth in this whole case. Christianity is not a philosophical theory; nor is it conveyed to us in the form of an infallible outward tradition. It exists, indeed, for itself, as a permanent supernatural constitution in the Church; but to be understood in this character, it must be measured and interpreted continually by the written word of God, which has been graciously committed to the keeping of the Church for this very purpose. The mere presumptions, then, which have been established in favour of the sacramental doctrine now stated, though of great weight certainly in themselves, are not enough to establish the doctrine itself. This can be done only by the authority of the Bible, the testimony of God's *Word* sustaining and confirming the testimony of God's *Church*.

Before we pass on to this inquiry, however, this might seem to be the proper place for noticing the inextricable difficulties and contradictions with which the whole subject of the believer's union with Christ is necessarily embarrassed, where it is not admitted to hold in the form which has now been brought into view. It is an easy thing to raise objections to the church doctrine in this case, where the objector is allowed to shift his own position at pleasure, without being required to give any properly scientific account of his faith, in its ulterior connections and relations. This is often done, through want of true theological cultivation, where all that would be needed to satisfy, or at least to silence, opposition, would be merely some general insight into the difficulties that are involved in the standpoint from which the objection proceeds. Nothing is more common than for men to deceive themselves here with conceptions, or it may be with words only, which are found on examination, to carry with them no consistency or force whatever.

The *Socinian* view, (Rationalism without disguise,) can never of course satisfy the Christian heart or understanding. It makes Christianity to be of the same order simply with other systems of religion; only under a more perfect form; as unfolding a clearer revelation of divine truth, a better system of ethical rules and precepts, and higher motives to virtue, particularly in the character and example of Christ himself. At last however it comes to no real union with God, the problem towards whose satisfaction all religion, in its very nature, may be said to struggle. In this respect, it is at best but an exalted style of Judaism, or an improvement rather on the philosophical schools of Paganism. It throws the man back always upon himself, his own separate powers and resources, the capabilities of the *flesh* as such, to perfect his nature and make himself meet for heaven. But against all this, the whole life of the Christian revolts. He knows that *such* a salvation is not what he needs; and he knows, with equal certainty, that it is not what he has found in Christ. All this too, he sees to be in full contradiction to the representations of the Bible. Christ is greater than Moses and all the prophets, and infinitely more also than Paul and the whole company of the apostles. He saves not by his doctrine and example merely, but by redemption and renovation, reaching to the inmost life of his people. If this be not the case, Christianity is shorn of all its glory, and the whole gospel turned into a dream.

The *Pelagian* affects to make more of our salvation by Christ. The miracle of the incarnation, and the great facts to which it opened the way in his history, are admitted, and allowed to have their weight in the scheme of redemption. But their power comes after all at last to this, that they serve to unfold truth under new aspects and in new relations, and to furnish new motives and helps to piety in an outward way. Here is indeed a peculiar plan or method of salvation, such as the light of nature never could have reached, and involving in fact a system of wholly supernatural arrangements for its accomplishment. Still however, the whole is something external to the subject of the salvation himself. It is an admirably contrived array of facilities, provided in God's great mercy for his use, by which he has it in his power to escape the pollutions that are in the world through sin, and lay hold of glory, honour and immortality. But he is left in the end to make use of them, in the same way precisely that he might be expected, on the Socinian hypothesis, to turn to saving account Christ's precepts and example. We are thrown back again, upon the conception of a simply moral salvation, to be constructed out of such material in the way of *life*, as the subject of it may be found to possess in his own nature, when brought under the action of this divine process of education.

But the theory may rise higher. To the force which belongs to the truth itself in its relation to the human mind, it may join the influences of God's *Spirit*, graciously interposed to clothe the truth with effect. Such agency we often hear attributed to the Spirit, by those who at the same time reject altogether the thought of any *immediate* change wrought by it in the nature of the human soul itself. God's grace in this form, they say, is brought to bear on the soul, *mediately* only, by the intervention of his word, which he uses instrumentally for the purpose, infusing into it light and power. But surely those who talk in this way, do not stop at all to consider the exact sense of their own words. What do they mean, when they speak of the Spirit, as infusing light and power into the truth? Can be do so, (apart from a direct influence on the soul itself,) in any other way than by so ordering the presentation of the truth to the mind, that it shall be placed in the most favourable position for exerting the power which belongs to it in its own nature? But what is this more than such moral suasion, as may be exercised over the spirits of men in a merely human way, by appeals addressed to the understanding and will? The order of influence at least remains the same, though it may be exhibited under a divinely exalted form. In this view, the process of salvation, in the midst of all the high sounding terms that may be employed to describe it, falls back again to the stand-point already noticed. It is a salvation by the power simply of truth, presented in the form of doctrine and precept. This truth includes the supernatural facts of the gospel, the mission, sufferings, death and resurrection of Christ, the outward apparatus in full, if we may use the expression, of the Christian redemption; and along with this we have the "moral suasion" of the Holy Ghost, which, according to the unintelligible hypothesis, invests the whole representation with a more than natural evidence and power. All turns at last however on the way in which the mind thus addressed, may be wrought upon and moved to act, in the use of such resources and capabilities as are already comprehended in its nature. It matters not whether the facts I contemplate be natural or supernatural in their character, whether the truth which challenges my regard be brought near to me by man or angel, or by God himself; if all hang at last on the relation of mere knowledge, and the stimulus thus imparted to my will, I am left under the dominion still of my own fallen life, in the sphere of the "flesh," and without any power to rise into the sphere of the "Spirit." The mediatorial work as something to be gazed upon and admired *beyond* my own person, can never reach the necessities of my case. It must be made over to me as my own in some way, or I am left to starve and perish spiritually in the midst of a merely moral and rationalistic redemption.

Here we are brought then to stand upon higher and more orthodox ground. The doctrine of *imputation* is introduced, to meet the demand now mentioned. The work of Christ is no longer thought of as a mere display for moral effect; it is something to be appropriated and made available in the person of the believing sinner himself, for the purposes of salvation. Mere doctrine will not answer. The case calls for an actual personal participation in what Christ has done and suffered, to take away sin and reconcile man to God. But how is this to be accomplished? By imputation, we are told. As the guilt and fall of Adam were reckoned to his posterity, though not theirs in fact, so the righteousness of Christ, and the benefits of his mediatorial work generally, are, in virtue of the terms of the new covenant, made over to all who believe in his name, and accounted to be theirs as truly as though all had been wrought out by them, each for himself, in truth. Their justification in this view is a mere forensic act on the part of God, which is based altogether on the work of Christ, and involves as such in their case no change of character whatever, but only a change of state. God regards them as righteous, though they are not so in fact, and makes over to them a full title to all the blessings comprehended in Christ's life. At the same time, he regenerates them by his Spirit, and puts them thus on a process of sanctification, by which in the end they become fully transformed in their own persons, into the image of their glorious Saviour.

But here the question rises, How can that be imputed or reckoned to any man on the part of God, which does not belong to him in reality? This is the old difficulty pressed against the orthodox doctrine by the Remonstrants or Arminians of Holland, (as previously also by the Church of Rome,) and constantly repeated by the Pelagianizing school from that time to the present. And it must be admitted to carry with it no small force; or rather we may say, that for the form in which this doctrine of imputation is too generally held, the objection is fairly insurmountable altogether. The judgment of God must ever be according to truth. He cannot reckon to any one an attribute or quality, which does not belong to him in fact. He cannot declare him to be in a relation or state, which is not actually his own, but the position merely of another. A simply external imputation here, the pleasure and purpose of God to place to the account of one what has been done by another, will not answer. Nor is the case helped in the least, by the hypothesis of what is called a *legal* federal union between the parties, in the case of whom such a transfer is supposed to be made; so long as the law is thought of in the same outward way, as a mere arbitrary arrangement or constitution for the accomplishment of the end in question. The law in this view would be itself a fiction only, and not the expression of a fact. But no such fiction, whether under the name of law or without it, can lie at the ground of a judgment entertained or pronounced by God. Can we conceive of any constitution, for instance, in virtue of which it could have been proper or possible for the divine mind, thus to set over to the account of mankind the apostacy of the angels which kept not their first estate, the two natures being relatively to each other what they are at this time? If all depended on the arbitrary pleasure of God, the force of a mere outward arrangement constituting one the representative of another without farther relation, we cannot see why the transfer of guilt might not take place from angels to men, as well as from Adam to his posterity. The very fact that our whole reason and feeling revolt against the thought in the first case, serves only to show that the proceeding must rest upon some *deeper* ground in the other. So as it regards our justification by Christ. A merely outward constitution, making him to be one with us in law simply, and giving us an interest in his righteousness only *as if* it were our own, while it is not our own in fact, cannot satisfy our sense of truth and right. All true Christians, whatever their theory with regard to the point may be, *feel* that their union with Christ is something far more than this, and that their property in the benefits of his death and resurrection rests upon a basis infinitely more sure and solid.

Do we then discard the doctrine of imputation, as maintained by the orthodox theology in opposition to the vain talk of the Pelagians? By no means. We seek only to *establish* the doctrine; for without it, most assuredly, the whole structure of Christianity must give way. It is only when placed on false ground, that it becomes untenable in the way now stated. To relieve it from objection, it must be made to appear under its true and proper biblical form. The Bible knows nothing of a simply outward imputation, by which something is reckoned to a man that does not belong to him in fact. The fall of Adam is adjudged to be the fall of his posterity, because it was so actually. The union in *law* here is a union in *life*. The fall itself forms a certain condition or state, which supposes life as its subject. And how then could the one be imputed without the presence of the other? May an attribute or quality be made to extend in a real way, beyond the substance to which it is attached and in which only it can have any real existence? The moral relations of Adam, and his moral character too, are made over to us at the same time. Our participation in the actual unrighteousness of his life, forms the ground of our participation in his guilt and liability to punishment.* And in no other way, we affirm, can the idea of imputation be satisfactorily sustained in the case of the second Adam. The scriptures make the two cases, in this

---

*All mankind descending from Adam by ordinary generation, according to the Westminster Catechism, "SINNED IN HIM, and *fell with him*, in his first transgression." This representation, it is well known, has called forth no small reproach and sarcasm even, at the expense of the venerable symbol in which it occurs. It has been charged with teaching physical depravity, and a transfer of personal character. Unfortunately, moreover, the friends of the Catechism, in their attempts to vindicate its doctrine at this point, have not always planted themselves on the proper ground for its defence. They have themselves rested on the conception of a merely external imputation, which could give its subjects at best, in the end, only a *quasi* interest in the real fact it represented. With *such* an idea of imputation, we may well say that the doctrine here proclaimed can never maintain its ground. But we meet the objection effectually, by simply descending to the proper depth of the doctrine itself. Here is no outward transfer to one, of something properly belonging only to another. The language of the Catechism is literally and strictly correct. We sinned *in* Adam, and fell *with* him, in his first transgression. That transgression was ours. The person in which it took place, formed the actual complex of the entire human race. The individual existence of every particular sinner, is but the historical evolution, in part, of the general *life*, that originally fell in this way. Original sin, accordingly, is carefully described by the Catechism, as consisting, not simply "in the guilt of Adam's first sin," but in his "want of original righteousness" also, and in "the corruption of his whole nature." So it is in fact. A fallen *life* in the first place, and on the ground of this only, imputed guilt and condemnation.

respect, fully parallel. We are justified freely by God, on the ground of
what Christ has done and suffered in our room and stead. His righteousness is imputed to us, set over to our account, regarded as our own. But
here again the relation in *law*, supposes and shows a corresponding
relation in *life*. The forensic declaration by which the sinner is pronounced
free from guilt, is like that word in the beginning when God said, *Let
there be light*, and light was. It not only proclaims him righteous for
Christ's sake, but sets the righteousness of Christ in him as a part of his
own life. And in doing this, it sets the very life of Christ in him, in the
same way. For righteousness, like guilt, is an attribute which supposes a
subject in which it inheres, and from which it cannot be abstracted without ceasing to exist altogether. In the case before us, this subject is the
mediatorial nature or life of the Saviour himself. Whatever there may be
of merit, virtue, efficacy, or moral value in any way, in the mediatorial
work of Christ, it is all lodged in the *life*, by the power of which alone this
work has been accomplished, and in the presence of which only it can
have either reality or stability. The imagination that the *merits* of Christ's
life may be sundered from his life itself, and conveyed over to his people
under this abstract form, on the ground of a merely outward legal
constitution, is unscriptural and contrary to all reason at the same time.
The legal union, to be of any force for the imputation that is here required,
must be a life union. In the very act of our justification, by which the
righteousness of Christ is accounted to be ours, it becomes ours in fact by
our actual insertion into Christ himself. He is joined to us mystically by
the power of the Holy Ghost, and becomes in this way the principle of a
new creation within us, which from the very start includes in itself
potentially, all that belongs to it already in his own person. The life thus
set over into the believer, by the creative fiat of his justification itself, is
the bearer of all the new relations in which he is thus brought to stand, as
well as of all the other *benefits* he is made to receive on Christ's account.

Even if we might conceive of an imputation of what is termed the
passive obedience of the Redeemer to his people, under a merely abstract
character, we must find every such conception inadmissible, at least in the
case of his *active* obedience; though in truth they cannot be disjoined in
this way. Allow the possibility of such an outward transfer of the value of
the atonement, how are we to have an interest in the new character to
which humanity has been raised in his person, or the triumphs he has
secured in its behalf? We need holiness as well as pardon; and the gospel
clearly represents Christ to be the fountain of the first, no less than he is
the author of the second. The obedience by which we are constituted
righteous in *both* forms, is found to be at last *his* obedience, and not ours,
except as we derive it from his person. But who can think of a merely
abstract, outward transfer of Christ's righteousness actively considered,
or as comprehended in the new character to which our nature has been

positively exalted in his life? Imputation here becomes something altogether unintelligible, if it be not allowed to involve in its very conception an extension of this life itself, truly and really, to those in whose favour it is supposed to hold. The active obedience of Christ, regarded as vicarious, has no meaning whatever, except on the basis of such a real life union between him and his people; and we find accordingly, that where the idea of this last becomes obscure or confused in the consciousness of the Church, the conception of the obedience now mentioned is always lost to the same extent.*

Christ then must be regarded as the source, in some way, of a new life for his people. So the scriptures teach. So the nature of the Christian salvation plainly requires. So the orthodox faith of the Church has always held. Christ is in the believer and the believer is in Christ; not by a moral relationship simply, and not by a legal connection only; but by the bond of a common life. Any thing lower than this, is felt to be no better in the end than rationalism itself. But it may be said, this common life is nothing more than the presence and influence of Christ's Spirit in the souls of his people, carrying forward the work of grace and transforming them gradually into his own image. This ground is often taken in fact by such as claim here the highest character for orthodoxy; and in this way, they persuade themselves that it is possible to meet, in the most satisfactory manner, all the demands of the Christian salvation as they have just been stated, with regard to the point now under consideration. They profess to accept the doctrine of the *mystical union*, as it is called, without qualification or reserve; and speak of it perhaps, with apparently earnest respect, as one of the most vital and precious truths of the gospel. And yet

---

*Both forms of obedience in the end, as Ernesti and others have shown, are the same —only different aspects, at most, of the one vicarious work of Christ in behalf of his people. The value of Christ's sufferings depended on the perfect holiness of his character; and his character, in the circumstances in which he stood, could not be complete except by his sufferings. The righteousness, however, as a whole, has two sides; one negative and the other positive; the first exhibited in the way of victory over sin and death, the other as the free activity of holiness itself in the form of life. Both necessarily are together in the transfer of Christ's righteousness to the believer. In the Roman Church, the doctrine of such a participation in the active obedience of the Saviour, was of course obscured by the view commonly taken of good works. With the Reformation, it came into full credit. But for the rationalistic period again it had no meaning. Knapp, and theologians of the same stamp, consider it unscriptural and absurd, to speak of a vicarious obedience of Christ in this form. It contradicts, they say, the great principle in religion, that every man's character is to be determined by his own works, and not by the works of another. This would be true, on the supposition of a mere outward imputation in the case; but it only shows the necessity of taking a deeper view of the whole subject. Not the works of Christ, as something sundered from his life, are made over to his people, but the triumphant power of his life itself, revealing itself in them and through them as the bearer of his righteousness in the same active form. Their virtue then is indeed their own, and yet the virtue of Christ working its proper fruits in them at the same time.

all comes to this at last, that the same Spirit which dwells in Christ, and which is called the "Spirit of Christ" on this account, dwells also in us, and makes us to be of the same mind with him more and more! This they take to be plainly the scriptural view of the case; for he that is joined to the Lord, it is said, "is one Spirit;" and Christians are represented everywhere as being under the influence of Christ's Spirit, and as filled and ruled by his presence.

But here we are in great danger of being put off with mere words and phrases, to which no clear sense is attached in the minds of those by whom they are used; so that it becomes necessary to insist on some more definite statement of what precisely is intended by those who make this representation. If their meaning were simply, that the presence of Christ in the Church, and his union with his people, hold through the medium of the Spirit, there would be no room for objection. This would accord with the scriptures, and satisfy at the same time the demands of the heart and understanding. As Christ is said to dwell in his people personally, so he is represented as dwelling in them only by his Spirit; which implies plainly that these two thoughts are in the end fully identical, and that the one presence is not only the pledge of the other, but the very form also in which it is made actually to have place. Nor is there any contradiction in this, but on the contrary vast relief, as it regards the apprehension of the mystery itself. For in this way, the whole fact of the mystical union is at once lifted above the sphere of mere nature, and exhibited to us as holding in a higher order of existence altogether. We know that Christ does not dwell in his people physically, in the common sense of this term, or according to the constitution of our present natural life in any way; and we must necessarily therefore refer the fact to a supernatural constitution, if it is to be retained in our faith at all. Such a supernatural constitution is presented to us in the new order of life, which is comprehended in the Spirit. This life springs from Christ, and reveals itself through the Spirit, as its medium, element, or form. As present himself then in the Church to the end of time, Christ dwells in his people only in this way. His presence is in the Spirit, and not in the flesh.

But this is *not* the meaning of those, to whom we now refer. Christ, they say, dwells in his people by his Spirit: but in the way only of representation, not in the way of strict personal inbeing on his own part. They sunder the Spirit of Christ from Christ himself, and tell us that the first only, and not the last is directly joined with believers in the mystical union. Only as the same Spirit dwells likewise in the glorified Saviour, he may be regarded as the bond of a living connection also between Christ in heaven and the Church on earth; since both parties are made thus, not directly but circuitously at least, to possess the same life. But here several difficulties come into view, which are in general overlooked by the theory before us altogether.

In the first place, we are not told explicitly whether the Spirit of Christ be supposed, in the case, to be identical with the idea of his divine nature, or not. Does the actual presence of the one involve the actual presence, to the same extent, of the other. In the form in which the subject is often presented, it might seem that the whole Christ, divine and human, was held to be in the Church, and in particular believers, *only* by his Spirit, as an entirely distinct form of existence, constituting the third person of the glorious Trinity. Here is a point of some importance, that needs to be definitely explained. In any case however, Christ's divinity as joined hypostatically with his humanity, cannot be regarded on this hypothesis as present. If the *Logos* be present at all, it is not in its character as incarnate, but only in the character which belonged to it before it became flesh. In any other view, the whole Christ must be held to be personally absent, and present only by proxy or substitution, in the separate agency of the Holy Ghost. How this is to be counted a true and actual presence of the Saviour himself, answerable to his own promise, and also to the strong terms in which the mystical union is spoken of in the New Testament, it is not easy certainly to perceive.

But again. What is there peculiar in the grace of the New Testament, under this view, as compared with the grace enjoyed by the saints under the Old? Does all turn upon the fuller revelation, the new facts, the more ample privileges and opportunities, that distinguish the dispensation of the gospel? The scriptures plainly teach, that the difference is more than this. Christ, as the angel of the covenant, was with his people under the old dispensation; and we know, that there were communications of the Spirit then also, under a certain form. But it is everywhere assumed in the New Testament, that the presence of the one, and the communications of the other, have become since the incarnation of a wholly different character. It devolves on the theory before us then, to say in what this difference consists. It *seems* certainly to make no account of it whatever. All would appear at least to be reduced to a difference in measure and quantity merely, the order of the grace being supposed to continue the same. The incarnation, it is assumed, was a fact of no force directly except for the Redeemer himself, separately considered. He is now in heaven, under human form, as he was in heaven before without this form; and as he manifested himself previously to the patriarchs and prophets, in his divine nature, or by his Spirit, so he continues now to manifest himself to his Church still, only with more large and free grace, in the same way. The Spirit of Christ, by which he is said to dwell in his people, has not become different at all in this view by the fact of his incarnation, from what the same Spirit was in relation to men before. He is not the medium of a new spiritual creation, established or constituted by the miracle of the incarnation itself—the divine life flowing forth upon the world, through the everlasting power of that fact, under its own peculiar and appropriate form; his agency has nothing to do with the incarnation whatever, except in an outward mechanical way; all at last resolves itself into the same abstract relation, which the Spirit of God is represented as holding to men, before Christ assumed our nature into union with himself at all. Is this what the theory *means*? If so, let the thought be distinctly proclaimed and the difficulties honestly faced which it necessarily draws in its train. Let the Church know that she is no nearer to God now in fact, that is in the way of actual life, than she was under the Old Testament; that the indwelling of Christ in believers, is only parallel with the divine presence as enjoyed by the Jewish saints, who all died in faith "not having received the promises" (Heb. 11: 13); that the mystical union in the case of Paul or John was nothing more intimate and vital and real, than the relation sustained to God by Abraham, or David, or Isaiah. Or if this be not intended nor admitted, let the true nature of the difference be explained.

And then once more; taking this presence of the Spirit for all it claims to be in this case, in what form of existence specifically must it be conceived to hold? Under the Old Testament at least, it was always an afflatus or influence simply, exerted on the soul of the person to whom it was extended. Is this all that we are to understand by it, in the Christian Church? So the theory would appear to mean. Christ dwells in us by his Spirit; and the Spirit dwells in us, by his operations, influences, graces. And this, we are told, is the mystical union, in virtue of which the life of Christ, and not simply, his benefits, are made over to our persons? But is it the actual *life* of Christ that is thus conveyed into us, by this process? Let the process itself be examined for the answer.

The same Spirit it is said, which works in Christ works also in us, fashioning its as we are into the same image. But *how* does he work? By supernatural *influence*, it may be said. But is not this to fall back again to the theory of a merely moral union with Christ, by the power of the truth only; which we have found already to be, under its highest form, but Pelagianism in disguise? Is Christ in us at last only by the divine *suasion* of his Spirit? It will be hard of course to acquiesce in this. The case calls for more. What then is that more? The Spirit, it may be said, *creates* new life in the believer. Very well. We are now fairly beyond the sphere of mere truth and moral suasion. But what now is this new life? Something of course that was not in the man before. Whence then does it come? Is it the proper life of the Spirit himself, the life of God, directly extended to the soul? This would be to repeat the mystery of the incarnation, in the case of every new believer; and such a thought of course is not for a moment entertained, by any who have come to make a clear distinction between the idea of life and that of mere influence. Whence then, we ask again, comes this new life by the Spirit? Is it an absolute creation out of nothing; a higher order of existence, including no organic, historical con- nection whatever with any law of life already at hand, whether in the man himself or beyond him, but originated in every instance as a new force altogether, superadded to the regular constitution of the world? Instead of one great miracle then in Christianity, the new creation in Christ Jesus, we should have miracles of the same order without number or end. Every believer would be a new creation, not in Christ Jesus, but in himself as the absolute starting point of a life that had never been known in the world before. And then, where would be after all the unity of this life, thus originated *de novo* in every new case, for the Church as a whole? And in what sense lastly, might it be denominated at all the *life of Christ*, who is the head of the body which it is thus supposed to fill? Is a life created from nothing by the Holy Ghost, acting in the name of Christ, without any regard whatever to his mediatorial nature, in any *real* sense the true and proper life of Christ himself as our Mediator! Is *this* the mystical union?

The theory destroys itself. Under every aspect, it is found to be contradictory, and unintelligible, and false. And yet this view is often exhibited, as furnishing a clear and satisfactory account of the union of Christ with believers; while the supposition of a real participation in his proper life is charged with mysticism and nonsense!

To this however it *must* come in the end, if the union in question is to be regarded as anything more than moral simply or legal. We have seen already that the imputation of Christ's merits to his people, requires that his life, the only real bearer of these merits, should pass over to them at the same time. And now we find, that the mere action of the Spirit upon the soul, whether in the way of suasion or creation, is not of itself this life in any true sense whatever. What is the conclusion then to which we are at last shut up? Plainly this. Christ does dwell in us by his Spirit; but only as his Spirit constitutes the very form and power of his own presence as the *incarnate* and everlasting Word. The Spirit, (which is thus truly the SPIRIT OF CHRIST,) does form us by a new divine creation into his glorious image; but the life thus wrought in our souls by his agency, is not a production out of nothing, but the very life of Jesus himself, organically continued in this way over into our persons. This the case demands. With nothing less than this, can the salvation of the gospel, as including the *absolute* truth of religion, in distinction from all Judaizing and Paganizing heresies, ever allow itself to be satisfied. And why should it be thought a thing incredible, for God to raise the dead to life in this way? Those at least who are willing to allow a new creation out of nothing in the case of the believer, ought not to find any difficulty surely in admitting a new creation from the actual substance of Christ's life as it exists already, or an extension of this life, in other words, into the believer's person. If the Spirit can be supposed to create *de novo* in the case, it is hard to see why it should be counted more difficult to conceive of an actual formation of Christ in us through the same divine medium. The first conception is indeed less immediately *real*; it swims, with fantastic form, in the distance. Can *this* be the reason, why it should be counted at times more *rational* than the other?

But allowing now that Christ does indeed dwell in his people by the real presence of his personal life, through the Spirit, and not simply by the presence of his Spirit as a surrogate for his own, is it necessary to include his *whole* life in this mystical union? To this question there would seem to be but one answer. It is with the mediatorial life of Christ that the Christian salvation, in the form now contemplated, is concerned. In *this* is comprehended the entire new creation revealed by the gospel; the righteousness of Christ, and all the benefits he has procured for his people. But the mediatorial life, by the communication of which only all this grace is made to pass over to men, is one and undivided. To be in real union with it at all then, we must be in union with it as a whole. The presence of Christ's divinity is not enough. The mediatorial life includes his humanity also, as a necessary part of its constitution. Just as little of course are we at liberty to divide his humanity itself, by supposing his soul only to be joined with his people, but not his body. Every abstraction of this sort must become involved at last, if scientifically pursued, in inextricable embarrassment. Body and soul are alike essential to the conception of a true human life; and if Christ's life be in us at all in a real way, it seems impossible to avoid the conclusion that it must be in us, as such a human life, in the one form of existence as truly and fully as in the other. Both forms of existence constitute in fact but the same living nature; and the extension of this nature, by the power of the Spirit, to the soul of the believer, involves necessarily the reproduction of the life as a whole in his person.

CHAPTER IV.

BIBLICAL ARGUMENT.

SECTION I.

THE INCARNATION.

"*The Word became flesh!*" In this simple, but sublime enunciation, we have the whole gospel comprehended in a word. From the glorious orb of light which is here made to burst upon our view, all that would else be dark and chaotic becomes at once irradiated with the bright majesty and everlasting harmony of truth itself. The incarnation is the key that unlocks the sense of all God's revelations.

It is the key that unlocks the sense of all God's works, and brings to light the true meaning of the universe. The world, and especially Man, who may be said to gather into his person at last all lower forms of existence, himself the summit of the vast organic pyramid, is a mystery that is solved and interpreted finally only in this fact. Nature and Revelation, the world and Christianity, as springing from the same divine Mind, are not two different systems joined together in a merely outward way. They form a single whole, harmonious with itself in all its parts. The sense of the one then is necessarily included and comprehended in the sense of the other. The mystery of the new creation, must involve in the end the mystery of the old; and the key that serves to unlock the meaning of the first, must serve to unlock at the same time the inmost secret of the last.

The incarnation forms thus the great central FACT of the world. It is a magnificent thought on which *Heinrich Steffens* bases his system of Anthropology, that Man is to be viewed, "as the end of a boundless Past, the center of a boundless Present, and the beginning of a boundless Future." In the most eminent sense may we say this, of Him who is the centre of Humanity itself, the Son of Man, as revealed in the person of Jesus Christ. All nature and previous history unite, to form one grand, universal prophecy of his presence. All becomes significant and complete at last, only in his person.

Nature, through all lower forms of existence, looks upwards continually to the idea of man. The inorganic struggles towards the organic; the plant towards the animal; and the animal nature, improving upon itself from one order of life to another, rests not till it is superseded finally by the human. Thus all converge towards the same end; each inferior nature foreshadowing that which is to follow, till the vast system becomes symmetrical and full, in a form of perfection which may be said to include at last and mirror the true sense of the whole.* Without man the entire world would be shorn of its meaning. It is by the medium of his personality only, that it becomes transparent with thought and is made to utter any intelligible sound. The world finds itself, comes to the knowledge of itself, in man. All is dark till it has made its way up to the sphere of human consciousness. There all becomes light. Man is the centre of nature; the key to all its mysteries; the idea, which binds its manifold parts into one, and makes them complete as a single organic whole.

But what man is to nature in this way, Christ may be said to be in some sense to man. Humanity itself is never complete, till it reaches his person. It includes in its very constitution a struggle towards the form in which it is here exhibited, which can never rest till this end is attained. Our nature reaches after a true and real union with the nature of God, as the necessary complement and consummation of its own life. The *idea* which it embodies can never be fully actualized, under any other form. The incarnation then is the proper completion of humanity. Christ is the true ideal Man. Here is reached ultimately the highest summit of human life, which is at the same time of course the crowning sense of the world,

*It is hardly necessary to say, that the idea here presented implies no possibility whatever of a regular development, on the part of any lower form of existence, upward to the sphere of that which stands above it. This thought, which has been exhibited with no small measure of plausibility by the author of the little volume entitled *Vestiges of Creation*, has been justly repudiated by the Christian world as contrary to all revelation and religion. It contradicts, besides, all sound philosophy. The process of growth and historical development can never, as such, evolve from any form of existence more than was actually involved in it from the beginning. But who can imagine at all, that the life of the animal is ever potentially present in the life of the plant. To say that the law of existence in the one case, is made to include at a certain point *more* than was comprehended in it before, is only to play with words; for the *more* which appears in that case must be considered in all respects a new creation, and in no intelligible sense whatever the product or birth of what existed previously. The difference between the animal and man, is just as broad at between the animal and the plant. There is an impassable gulph between the two forms of existence, which nothing short of a new creation can ever surmount in the case of the lower. But all this has nothing to do with the view presented in the text. It is affirmed here, simply, that the lower forms of existence look prophetically towards those which are above then. They cannot be said to carry these in their womb, in any sense; but they foreshadow their presence, and in this way find their own full meaning always in something beyond themselves. The evidence of this is so plain, that the fact will not be called in question by any who have even the most general acquaintance with the actual constitution of the world.

or that in which it finds its last and full signification. Here the human consciousness itself, the medium of order and light for the sphere of mere nature, is raised into a higher sphere, from which a new life is made to pour itself forth again over the whole world. Man finds himself in God, and wakes to the full sense of his own being, in being enabled thus to fall back, in a full, free way, on the absolute ground of his life. The one only medium of such inward, living communication with the divine nature, is the mystery of the incarnation as exhibited in the man Christ Jesus. This forms accordingly, without a figure, the inmost and last sense of all God's works. The world, from its extreme circumference, looks inward to this fact as its true and proper centre, and presses towards it continually, from every side, as the end of its entire constitution. All is one vast prophecy of the coming of Christ.

History too converges, from the beginning, always towards the same point. Not only here and there, have we solitary annunciations, more or less obscure, of the glorious advent of the Messiah. History, like nature, is one vast prophecy of the incarnation, from beginning to end. How could it be otherwise, if the idea of humanity, as we have seen, required from the first such a union with the divine nature, in order that it might be complete? What is history, but the process by which this idea is carried forward, according to the immanent law of its own nature, in the way of a regular development towards its appointed end? The introduction of *sin*—itself a world-fact, inseparably incorporated with this process almost from its start, and turning all violently into a false direction—only served to add a deeper emphasis to the meaning of life, in the view now noticed. The necessity of a real union with the divine nature, became a necessity at the same time of redemption, the loud cry of suffering humanity after an atonement for sin. The development of this want, might be said to form thus the great burden of history, onward from the fall. All of course, in this view, had a reference prophetically to the coming of Christ. The whole creation groaned and travailed in pain together, reaching forward, as it were, with earnest expectation, to the hour of this deliverance. Not only Judaism, but Paganism too, preached beforehand the great event. Both looked, from different sides, in the same direction and towards the same end. Both found their inmost meaning verified at last and explained in Christ.*

---

*Unus Christus Jesus dominus nester veniens per universam dispositionem, et omnia in se recapitulans. *Irenæus.*—Interesting on this point is *Dorner*, in the Introduction to his "Christologie," or History of the Doctrine of Christ's Person. Also, the Introduction to the Doctrine of the Trinity in its Historical Development, by *G. A. Meier*—a most able and excellent work, published in 1844; with which may be compared advantageously the Introduction to the large, very learned, but less orthodox work of *Baur* on the same subject.

Paganism must ever be of course essentially false, under all its forms. But all falsehood involves some truth, of which it is the caricature, but from which at the same time it draws its life. The time has been, when a superficial infidelity sought to bring the mysteries of Christianity into discredit, by comparing them with the mythological dreams and specula- tions of the heathen world. But that time, it may be trusted, has come to an end. Christianity as the absolute religion, *must* in the nature of the case, take up into itself, and exhibit in a perfect form, the fragments and rudiments of truth contained in all relative religions. It is not a doctrine, but a divine *fact*, into which all previous religious tendencies and develop- ments are ultimately gathered as their proper end. As in Nature, all lower developments of life, however defective or seemingly monstrous, find their true meaning and value, only as analogies and relative approxima- tions to the nature of man—whose perfection and dignity in this way they serve, not to disparage, but to authenticate and magnify; so do the ancient religions, both of the Orient and West, conspire to bear testimony in favour of Christ, falling down as it were before him, and presenting unto him gifts, "gold and frankincense and myrrh." Brahmanism, Buddhism, Parsism, the religion of Egypt and the religion of Greece, each in its own way, look ever in the same direction, and are heard to utter in the end the same voice. All prophesy of Christ; for all proclaim the inmost want of humanity to be a true union with God, and their character is determined simply by the form in which it is attempted in each case to bring this great life problem to its proper resolution. These attempts of course destroy themselves, and end in gross contradiction. The *Trimurti*, or pantheistic triad of India, falls immeasurably short of the Christian Trinity. The incarnation of *Vischnu* goes not beyond the character of a transient phantasm. *Mithras, Osiris,* the idea of a wrestling, suffering, redeeming god, *Apollo* among the Greeks, or *Hercules*, forcing his way to Olympus; all are found to be utterly helpless conceptions, as it regards the purpose they are brought forward to serve. The representation remains always inadequate and disproportionate, in the highest degree, to the idea it struggles to reach. All ends in an insurmountable dualism. An impassable gulph continues still to divide the nature of man from the nature of God. But the significance of all, in the view now considered, becomes thus only the more clear and full. Under all its manifestations, Paganism may be regarded as the unsuccessful effort of humanity, cast upon itself, to solve the problem, whose full solution is revealed at last only in the person of Christ. Christianity is the key that interprets its mysterious sense, and establishes thus its own divine character at the same time. All false religions prepare the way prophetically for the presence of the true, and serve to authenticate its mission when it has come.

Judaism, we all know, had respect to the coming of Christ, from the beginning. The preparation which in the case of the heathen world was negative only, assumed here a *positive* character. The religion of the Old Testament, from the time of Adam down to the time of John the Baptist, stood throughout on the ground of a supernatural revelation that might be said not only to foreshadow the great fact of the incarnation, but directly to open the way also for its manifestation. It is not simply the necessity of a union with God on the part of man, the cry for redemption and salvation, which it is felt can be reached only in this way, that is here made to reveal itself in the world's history; a real approximation to men on the part of God, in the way of a movement to meet this want, is exhibited at the same time. Heathenism might be said to run out in a helpless attempt violently to deify humanity itself; a process that must ever fall back, with new despair, to the point from which it started. In the religion of the Old Testament, God descends towards man, and holds out to his view in this way the promise of a real union of the divine nature with the human, as the end of the gracious economy thus introduced. To such a *real* union it is true, the dispensation itself never came. By a series of condescensions, that grew always more significant and full of encouragement as the dispensation advanced towards its proper end, God drew continually more and more near to men in an outward way. But to the last it continued to be only in an outward way. The wall of partition that separated the divine from the human, was never fully broken down. The tabernacle of the Most High was among men; but he dwelt notwithstanding beyond them, and out of them, between the cherubim and behind the veil. He spake by dreams, and visions, and clear words of prophecy, that became always more full and distinct; but the revelation to the end, was a revelation of God *to* man, and not a revelation of God *in* man—the only form in which it was possible for him to become truly known. Towards this ultimate point however the whole process of condescension constantly tended, as its necessary consummation. The meaning of the entire system lay in its reference to Christianity. Not only did it contain particular types and particular prophecies of the incarnation; it was all one vast type, and throughout one continuous prophecy, in this direction. We may say of the Old Testament as a whole, what is said of its last and greatest representative in particular. It was the voice of one crying in the wilderness, prepare ye the way of the Lord, make straight in the desert a highway for our God! It might be said in some sense to carry the Gospel in its womb. All the great truths which were afterwards brought to light by Christ, lay more or less undisclosed in its revelations, growing and ripening gradually for the full birth towards which they struggled, and to which they attained finally in his person. Without Christianity, Judaism would have no meaning, no proper reality. It becomes real, only by losing itself, and finding itself at the same time, in the new dispensation. The law, as such, made nothing perfect. All served only to harbinger the advent of the Messiah, and to proclaim his presence when he came. All foreshadowed and foretokened the mystery of the incarnation.

Here then, as before said, we reach the central FACT, at once ultimate and primal, in the constitution of the world. All nature and all history flow towards it, as their true and proper end, or spring from it as their principle and ground. The incarnation, by which divinity and humanity are joined together, and made one, in a real, inward and abiding way, is found to be the scope of all God's counsels and dispensations in the world. The mystery of the universe is interpreted in the person of Jesus Christ.

SECTION II.

THE NEW CREATION.

Christianity stands, as we have seen, in close connection with the order of the world as it existed before. Some of the early heresies pretended to magnify it, by denying all connection of this sort. They would have it, that the whole state of the world as it stood previously had been bad, and bad only; and that it was derogatory to the glory of the Gospel, to suppose any affinity whatever between it and any older form of life. It must be viewed as an entirely new order of existence, suddenly introduced from heaven, in broad, plump opposition, not only to nature, but also to the whole previous course of history. Even Judaism must be disowned, not simply as a lower dispensation, but as a false system unworthy of the true God as revealed by Jesus Christ, and at war with the great object of Christ's mission into the world. This was in fact to overthrow the incarnation itself, and to reduce it in the end to a mere phantasm, that involved no real union whatever between the divine nature and the human. To be *real* and true, and to solve at all in this way the great problem of life, the mystery *must* connect itself with the constitution and course of the world in its previous state. This we have seen to be the case in fact. Christianity forms no violent rupture, either with nature or history. It fulfils, and in doing so interprets, the inmost sense of both. Neither could be complete without its presence. Both flow over into it naturally, as their own true consummation and end.

But the Gnostic error just referred to, like all error, included also its truth; in this case a great truth. There was another error of the same period; one to which the Jewish mind especially always showed a strong tendency in the early Church. It saw in the person of Jesus *only* a continuation of the old creation; in the high form particularly which it was made to carry in the religion of the Old Testament. Thus, on the other side, the mystery fell to the ground. The old chasm between the divine and human was left to yawn as before. Christ sunk into a mere man. Against this Ebionitic heresy, the heresy of the Gnostic had its right; though maintained in a false way. Christ is not only the end of the old creation, its necessary complement and completion; he is the principle also of a new creation, in which the old is required to pass away.

"The Word became flesh, and dwelt among us—full of grace and truth." This is more a great deal than the simple continuation of the old order of the world, in the way of regular historical development. Here is a fact, which differs from all ordinary facts and events, not simply as transcending them in importance, but as being of another order altogether.

It stands before us, not as the result or product strictly speaking of any
powers or tendencies, that were comprehended in the constitution of the
world before its manifestation; but as the introduction of a new power
entirely, which was to form from that time onward the central force in the
progress of the world's history. This deserves to be well considered. Let
the case be compared with some other fact of true world-historical
moment; the rise, for instance, of Aristotle and his philosophy. How much
hung on the mind of that single man! It gave birth to an empire, which for
extent and duration may be said to have thrown the magnificence of all
the Caesars into the shade. But here was no new creation, in the strict
sense of the term. Aristotle was in all respects the product of previous
history. The philosophy that revealed itself through his person, was
nothing more at last than the development of powers that lay involved in
the life of the world as it stood before, and that waited only for the proper
time to show themselves in this form. Aristotle added nothing to humanity
as such; he was the medium only, by which it found itself advanced to the
position secured for it in his person. But Jesus Christ was no such product
of the past. It prophesied of his coming, and threw open the way for his
approach. To the mystery of the incarnation itself, however, it had no
power to rise. Here was a fact, for the evolution of which all its capabilities must have remained forever inadequate. Here was a fact, which even
the religion of the Old Testament itself had no sufficiency to generate, and
to which all its theophanies and miracles could furnish no proper parallel.
For the revelation of the supernatural under the Old Testament, as already
remarked, was always in an outward and comparatively unreal way. It
never came to a true inward union, between the human and the divine.
The supernatural appeared above nature and beyond nature only. It never
entered into it, and became incorporated with it, as the same life. However
it might be made to influence the process of history, the development of
humanity, in the way of instruction, or occasion, or motive, it could not
be said to bring a new element into the process itself. But in the person of
Christ, all is different. The supernatural is brought not only near to nature,
but into its very heart; not as a transient wonder, but to remain in union
with it forever. The everlasting Word, in a way wholly unknown before,
descends into the actual process of human history, and becomes within it
the principle and law of a second creation immeasurably more glorious
than the first. It is by no mere figure of speech, that Christ is represented
to be the author of a new creation. Nor may we say of this creation, that
it is moral simply, consisting in a new order of thought and character on
the part of men. It is no revolution of the old, no historical advance upon
the past merely, that is here brought into view; but the introduction,
literally and strictly, of a new element, a new divine force, into the very
organism of the world itself. The incarnation, in this view, is fully parallel
with the work, by which in the beginning "the worlds were framed by the

word of God;" and in the case of which, we are told "things which are seen were not made of things which do appear." As the formation of man on the sixth day, was necessary to perfect in a higher sphere, the organization already called into being in a lower; of which at the same time it could not be said to be, in any sense, the product or result; so in the end, to crown all with a still higher perfection, the Word itself, by which the heavens and the earth were created before, became permanently joined with humanity in the person of Jesus Christ, as the principle of a new earth and new heavens—the continuation and necessary complement of the previous organization, but in no sense again its historical product or birth.

On the ground of the general fact here affirmed, we ascribe to Christianity, as compared with the world in any other view, the character of *absolute* reality and truth. Nature itself is only relatively true and real. It finds its actual sense, as we have seen, only in the idea of humanity; and in this idea at last, only as actualized in the mystery of the incarnation. It is all a shadow and type of the real; but for this very reason, not the real itself. All flesh is grass; only the word of the Lord is enduring. The fashion of the world is ever passing away, like a scenic show; only Jesus Christ is "the same, yesterday, to-day, and forever." There is no other principle of reality or stability in God's creation. So all history becomes true at last only in Christ. This is exemplified, most instructively, in the religion of the Old Testament. It was altogether of God. To it pertained "the adoption, and the glory, and the covenants, and the giving of the law, and the service of God, and the promises." Of it were the fathers, and from it as concerning the flesh, Christ sprang, who is over all, God blessed forever. But still, we are expressly taught, that it stood related to the gospel throughout, only as a shadow to the substance it represents. And this is to be understood, not simply of its types and ceremonies as such. It holds in full force of its whole constitution, moral as well as ceremonial. Its truth was not in itself, but in a different system altogether to which it pointed. Its reality was in no respect absolute, but in all respects relative only. It made nothing perfect. It was the picture merely of good things to come. The Epistle to the Romans and the Epistle to the Hebrews, each in its own way, are full of this thought. We have no right to say, that the New Testament is a mere extension or enlargement of the Old, under the same form. "The law was given by Moses, but grace and truth came by Jesus Christ" (John I. 17). Among all the prophets of the old dispensation, there had not risen one greater than John the Baptist; and yet we are assured, (Luke VII. 28,) that the "least in the kingdom of God is greater than he." All previous revelations were but an approach to the truth, as manifested in Christ. "God who at sundry times and in divers manners spake in time past unto the fathers by the prophets, hath in these last days spoken unto us by his SON—the brightness of his glory and the express image of his person" (Heb. I. 1–3). All before was relative only; here we have God absolutely "manifest in the flesh." Christ is the only absolute *Prophet*, (Deut. XVIII. 18, 19. Acts III. 22, 23,) as he is the only absolute *Priest* (Heb. VIII. 4, 5). The relation of God to the patriarchs and saints generally of the Old Testament, was something that came short wholly of the relation in which he now stands to his people, as the God and Father of our Lord Jesus Christ. Their spiritual life, their union with God, their covenant privileges, all had an unreal, unsubstantial character, as compared with the parallel grace of the gospel, and constituted at best but an approximation to this grace, rather than the actual presence of it in any sense itself.* That which forms the full *reality* of religion, the union of the divine nature with the human, the revelation of God *in* man and not simply *to* him, was wanting to the Old Testament altogether. Of course all its doctrines and institutions, all its prerogatives and powers, had a shadowy, simply prophetic nature, to the same extent. Its sacraments were types only, not counterparts of the sacraments of the New Testament. Its salvation was in the form of promise, more than present fact. It became real ultimately, only in Christ; for before his appearance, we are told the patriarchs of the law could not be made perfect (Heb. XI. 13, 39, 40). The dispensation of the Spirit has its origin wholly in the person of Christ, (Luke I. 35, III. 22. John III. 34,) and could not reveal itself in the world till he was glorified (John VII. 39).

The great argument for the truth of Christianity, is the person of Jesus himself, as exhibited to us in the faith of the Church. The incarnation is the FACT of all facts, that may be said itself to authenticate all truth in the world besides. The first miracle, and the only miracle, we may say, of Christianity, is the new creation in which it starts. All else is but the natural product and expression of the life, thus introduced into the world. Nothing *so* natural, as the supernatural itself in the Saviour's person. Jesus Christ authenticates himself. All foreign, external credentials here, can have, in the very nature of the case, only a subordinate and secondary value. He is himself the principle and ground, the alpha and omega of all truth.

---

*"Christianity is nothing, if it be not the actualization and substantiation of a union, which was before, to a great extent, prophetical and ideal." *F. D. Maurice.*

SECTION III.

THE SECOND ADAM.

Christ is the principle of a new creation. To be so in truth, be must be incorporated, under this character, with the inmost life of humanity. For, as we have seen, the world centres in man; and out to its extreme physical circumference, all takes its form and complexion from the nature which thus constitutes its living, spiritual heart. To descend into the world at all then, so as to become united to its constitution as a principle of organic renovation, it was necessary that the Word should become *flesh*. The new creation reveals itself in man. Christ is the second ADAM.

His manhood was real. The incarnation was no mere theophany; no transient wonder; no illusion exhibited to the senses. "Christ, the Son of God, became man, by taking to himself a true body and a reasonable soul, being conceived by the power of the Holy Ghost, in the womb of the Virgin Mary, of her substance, and born of her, yet without sin." John makes it the mark of Antichrist to call this in question. (1 John IV. 1–3. 2 John 7.) The nature which he took upon him was truly and fully the nature of Adam; and it was not joined to him in the way of an outward accident or appendage merely. The union was inward and complete; two natures, but one single undivided person.

Christ, however, was not simply a descendant of Adam, and a brother thus of the human family, as standing in the same relation. To his natural birth must be joined his supernatural conception. He took our nature upon him; but, in doing so, he raised it into a higher sphere, by uniting it with the nature of God, and became thus the root of a new life for the race. His assumption of humanity was something general, and not merely particular.* The Word became flesh; not a single man only, as one among many; but *flesh*, of humanity in its universal conception. How else could he be the principle of a general life, the origin of a new order of existence for the human world as such? How else could the value of his mediatorial work be made over to us in a real way, by a true imputation, and not a legal fiction only? The entire scheme of the Christian salvation requires and assumes throughout, this view of the incarnation and no other. To

---

*"The justice of God requires that the same *human nature* which hath sinned, should likewise make satisfaction for sin. *Heidelberg Catechism, Quest.* 16. To be valid at all, the redemption must go as deep as the curse. But this last attaches to our nature as such. Men are sinners, because the general life of humanity has become corrupt. Their *nature* then must be restored, as the only ground on which it is possible for them to be saved individually. This is done in Christ.

make it a merely individual case, a fact of no wider force than the abstract person of Jesus himself, thus receiving his relationship to his people into their common relationship to Adam, is to turn all at last into an unreal theophany, and thus to overthrow the doctrine altogether.* Christ became man, not for himself, but for the race; that he might take our burden upon him as his own; that he might conquer death for us in our room and right; that he might lift thus our fallen nature, as such, into everlasting union with God. He gathered humanity into himself as a whole, and was constituted thus its head and sum, (ἀνακεφαλαιώσις τῶν πάντων,) in a more full and comprehensive sense than this could ever be said of Adam.

Paul in particular is very clear and very strong, in the representation of this federal or generic character on the part of Christ. He makes his relation to the human race parallel in full to that of its natural head. Adam is τύπος τοῦ μέλλοντος, (Rom. v. 14,) and Christ is ὁ ἔσχτος Ἀδὰμ (1 Cor. xv. 45). In Rom. v. 12–19, they are compared together at length, under this view. Adam is exhibited, on the one hand, as the head of our race in its fallen character. "By one man sin entered into the world, and death by sin, and so death passed upon all men, for that all have sinned." They were constituted sinners by that first act of disobedience itself. They sinned in Adam, and fell with him, in his first transgression. He stood in the case as their federal head, because he was their true organic head. *In Adamo*, according to the just affirmation of Augustine, *omnes tunc peccaverunt, quando in ejus natura adhuc omnes ille unus fuerunt.* In all this, the apostle tells us, he was the "figure of him that was to come." The gift of life by Christ is in certain respects, indeed, more than commensurate with the death and condemnation introduced by Adam. But the general nature of the relation in the two cases, is the same. Christ too is the federal head and representative of humanity as a whole. "As by one man's disobedience many were made sinners, even so by the righteousness of one shall many be made righteous." Not in the way of a mere outward

*"If Christ were only *a* man, as one along with and among many others, it would be indeed incomprehensible, how what he has suffered and done could be of any essential weight for mankind in general; he could only exert an influence by his doctrine and example. But he is to be viewed in fact, apart from his divine nature, as *the* man, that is, as realizing the absolute idea of humanity, and thus carrying it in himself potentially in the way of the *spirit*, as truly as Adam did in a *corporeal* way. This character of Christ's human nature is designated in divinity by the term *impersonalitas*; and we find even *Philo*, with an inward feeling of the deep truth, describing the *Logos* as τὸν κατ᾽ ἀλήθειαν ἄνθρωπον, that is the idea of man, the human ideal. In this general view, the Redeemer bears a twofold *representative* character; first, as he takes the place of sinful men, carrying *their* grief in *his* grief, as an offering for the sins of the world; and then again as fulfilling absolute righteousness and holiness in himself, so that the believer has not to produce them afterwards anew, but receives them in germ along with the Spirit of Christ. The first is the *obedientia passiva* of theology, the last the *obedientia activa*." *Olshausen Comm. in Rom.* v. 15.

imputation, of course, in the last case, more than in the first; for this would destroy the parallel; but on the ground of a real community of life. As the world fell in Adam organically, so it is made to rise in Christ in the same way, as the principle of a new spiritual life. Strange, that any who hold the Augustinian view of Adam's organic union with his posterity, as the only basis that can properly support the doctrine of original sin, should not feel the necessity of a like organic union with Christ, as the indispensable condition of an interest in his salvation. Pelagianism, which sees only an outward connection between the first man and his posterity, and recognizes in the race but an aggregation of single and separate units, mechanically brought together, may consistently join hands with Rationalism in resolving the relation of Christ to his Church, also into a mere moral connection. But in doing so, it shows itself to be just as superficial and false in the one case, as every earnest observer of life must feel it to be in the other.

The same parallel, under a somewhat different reference, is presented to us again, in 1 Cor. XV. 21, 22, 45–49. "As in Adam all die, even so in Christ shall all be made alive." The reference is immediately to natural death and the resurrection of the body; which, however, are only one aspect of the death and life contrasted in the other case. "The first man Adam was made a living soul; the last Adam a quickening spirit." By our natural birth, we are inserted into the life of the one; our spiritual birth secures us a like insertion into the life of the other. In both cases, the connection is inward and real. The root of righteousness in the one case, corresponds with the root of sin in the other. The mystery of Adam, to quote an old Rabbinic Saying, is the mystery of the Messiah.

SECTION IV.

CHRISTIANITY A LIFE.

Christ then was not the founder simply of a religious school; of vastly greater eminence, it might be, than Pythagoras, Plato, or Moses, but still a teacher of truth only in the same general sense. Christianity is not a *Doctrine*, to be taught or learned like a system of philosophy or a rule of moral conduct. Rationalism is always prone to look upon the gospel in this way. As Moses made known more of the divine will than the world had understood before, so Christ is taken to be only a greater prophet in the same form. But this is to wrong his character altogether. Judaism was indeed only an advance upon previous revelations; no more in fact, we may say, than a vast expansion of the system of truth exhibited through the medium of nature itself. The order of revelation, in both cases, was substantially the same. It went not beyond the character of a "report," to be received only by "the hearing of the ear." The revelation was always relative only, never absolute. It came not in any case to a full manifestation of the truth in its own form. But in the Church of the New Testament, all is different. A new order of revelation entirely bursts upon the world, in the person of Jesus Christ. He is the absolute truth itself, personally present among men, and incorporating itself with their life. He is the substance, where prophecy, even in its highest forms, had been only as sound or shadow.

Unitarians affect to make much of Christ's holy *Example*. He redeems us from our sins, they say, partly by his heavenly instructions, and partly by exhibiting himself to us as a pattern of piety, in his life and death. This, however, is to rob him still of his proper glory. It is to fall back at best into the sphere of Judaism. Christianity is more than a model merely of goodness and virtue, though allowed to be, in this view, of the most perfect construction, nay, the very mirror of the divine will itself.

Nor will it change the case materially to make the gospel an array of merely outward or moral power, in any other view. Many who count themselves orthodox, it is to be feared, come short of the truth here altogether. They get not beyond the old Ebionitic stand-point; but see in Christianity always an advance only on the grace of the Jewish dispensation, under the same form, and not a new order of grace entirely. Greater light, enlarged opportunities, more constraining motives, a new supply of supernatural aids and provisions; these are taken to be the peculiar distinction of the New Covenant, and constitute its supposed superiority over the Old. But is not this to resolve the Christian salvation as before, into a merely moral institute or discipline? If the whole evangelical apparatus—including Christ's priestly work, the atonement, his intercession in heaven, and the gracious influences of his Spirit—be regarded as an outward *apparatus* simply, through the force of which as lying beyond himself the sinner is to be formed to righteousness, the case is only parallel at best with the theory, that turns the work of redemption into a mere doctrine or example. We should have at most, in this view, an exaltation only of the religion of the Jew. Christ would be to us of the same order with Moses; immeasurably greater of course; but still a prophet only in the same sense.

In opposition to all this, we say of Christianity that it is a LIFE. Not a rule or mode of life simply; not something that in its own nature requires to be reduced to practice; for that is the character of all morality. But life in its very nature and constitution, and as such the actual substance of truth itself. This is its grand distinction. Here it is broadly separated from all other forms of religion, that ever have claimed, or ever can claim, the attention of the world. "The law came by Moses, but GRACE and TRUTH by Jesus Christ."

Such is the view presented to us in the beginning of his gospel, by the evangelist John. The Word, that existed eternally with the Father, that created the world, that had illuminated all the prophets—drawing always nearer to men as the fulness of time approached for this last revelation—now at length, in the person of Jesus, BECAME FLESH (John I. 1–18). He that spake to men mediately before, as from a distance, by the prophets, now spake to them immediately, and as it were face to face, by his Son, (Heb. I. 1, 2). "In him was LIFE," not relatively, but absolutely. It dwelt in him as an original and independent fountain, (John V. 26). "And the life was the light of men." In this character, it had revealed itself indirectly, in the human consciousness as such, and by means of partial and relative representations of truth from without, since the beginning of the world. The light shined, however, in darkness, (the result of sin,) and the darkness comprehended it not. All this was preparatory only for the mystery of the incarnation; pointing towards it, and showing its necessity. Here, in the end, the self-subsisting life itself enters into the sphere of humanity. The cry of ages, "O that thou wouldest rend the heavens, that thou wouldest come down, that the mountains might flow down at thy presence," is met with a full, all-satisfying response. The heavens *do* bow. The everlasting doors fly open. The tabernacle of God is with man, as never before. Humanity itself has become the Shechinah of glory, in the person of Immanuel. The Truth, in its absolute substance, stands revealed and accessible to all men, in the incarnate Word. "We have seen his glory," says the apostle, "the glory as of the Only Begotten of the Father." The revelation is real, commensurate with the nature of Truth itself. "No man hath seen God at any time; the Only Begotten Son, which is in the bosom of the Father, he hath declared him" (John I. 18). All former revelations, as relative only and remote, are here overwhelmed by the presence of that "True Light" itself, of which they were but broken and scattered rays. "He that hath seen me," says Christ himself, "hath seen the Father" (John XIV. 9). What an infinite contrast this, with the idea of a mere teacher, or prophet in the common sense. Only think of such language from the lips of Moses! "The life was manifested," says John, "and we have seen it, and bear witness, and show unto you that eternal life, which was with the Father, and was manifested unto us" (1 John I. 1, 2).

Christ does not exhibit himself accordingly as the medium only, by which the truth is brought nigh to men. He claims always to *be* himself, all that the idea of salvation claims. He does not simply point men to heaven. He does not merely profess to give right instruction. He does not present to them only the promise of life, as secure to them from God on certain conditions. But he says, "I AM the *Way*, and the *Truth*, and the *Life*; no man cometh unto the Father but by ME" (John XIV. 6). Men are brought to God, not by doctrine or example, but only by being made to participate in the divine nature itself; and this participation is made possible to us only through the person of Christ; who is therefore the very substance of our salvation, as here affirmed. "God hath given to us eternal life, and this life is IN his Son. He that HATH the Son, hath life; and he that hath not the Son of God, hath not life" (1 John V. 11, 12). "Verily, verily, I say unto you, he that heareth my word, and believeth on Him that sent me, HATH everlasting life, and shall not come into condemnation; but is passed from death unto life!" (John V. 24). Here again we have the idea of a *present* salvation, not in the way of promise and hope only, but in the form of actual possession. The believer *hath* everlasting life. Already, μεταβέβηκεν ἐκ τοῦ θανάτου εἰς τὴν ζωήν. It has been made a subject of controversy, whether the whole passage (John V. 19–30,) from which this declaration is taken, refers to the spiritual or to the bodily resurrection. Clearly, however, it refers to both; and in this way serves to bring into view the relation in which the one stands to the other. The spiritual resurrection includes in the end the resurrection of the body. It is all, we may say, but a single process, reaching from the point of the new birth onward to the full restoration of the whole man at the day of judgment. As such, it constitutes the true idea of everlasting life; which of course, then, must be lodged in the believer's person here, as an organic principle and incipient development, if it is to unfold itself in the complete glory of heaven hereafter. The ground of this life is wholly in Christ. He came not to tell men of it, but to reveal it in his own person for their use. To believe on him, is to be brought into substantial communication with what he is in this form. It is to pass from death to life. Of such an one it is said, "He shall never see death" (John VIII. 51). The new life of which he is the subject in his union with Christ, and which now forms his central being, cannot perish. It is everlasting and indestructible in its very nature. When the man dies, his true life thus rooted in Christ, surmounts the catastrophe, and in due time displays its triumph in the glories of the resurrection.

"I AM the Resurrection and the Life! He that believeth in me, though he were dead, yet shall he live. And whosoever liveth and believeth in me, shall never die" (John XI. 25, 26). The *resurrection* and *life* here named, are only different aspects of the same idea. The first is the form simply in which the last reveals itself, in its victorious struggle with death. Both reveal themselves together in Christ. It is in him personally, as the bearer of our fallen humanity, that death is swallowed up in victory, by the power of that divine life of which he was the incarnation. From him, the same life flows over to his people, in the way of real communication. He does not merely preach the resurrection. It is comprehended in his person. He hath in himself abolished death, and thus brought life and immortality to light through the gospel. (2 Tim. I. 10.) The revelation does not consist in this, that he has removed all doubt from the doctrine of a future state, and made it certain that men will live hereafter. It is not the doctrine, but the fact itself, that is brought to light. Immortality, in its true sense, has been introduced into the world only by Christ.

Christ leads the way to his people, in the triumph of the resurrection. He is the *captain* (ὁ ἀρχηγός) of the Christian salvation, (Heb. II. 10. XII. 2,) by whom God conducts many sons to glory. He is the *first-fruits* of the resurrection, (ἀπαρχὴ τῶν κεκοιμημένων, 1 Cor. XV. 21, 23); the *first-born* among many brethren, (Rom. VIII. 29,) to whose image all must be conformed; the beginning, the first-born from the dead (ὅς ἐστιν ἀρχή, πρωτότοκος ἐκ τῶν νεκρῶν, ἵνα γένηται ἐν πᾶσιν αὐτὸς πρωτεύων. Col. I. 18). Superficially considered, this representation might seem to imply, according to the old Arian hypothesis, that the relation of Christ to his people in the way of salvation is one of mere precedence in time only, constituting him at best the great pioneer and pattern simply, whom others are called to follow through death and the resurrection into eternal life. But the representation carries evidently a far deeper sense. The captain here, is the author also and finisher of the Christian faith. The first fruits are the life and power of the harvest itself, that follows in their train. In the first-born of the Church, Christ is at the same time the fountain of the entire new order of existence which it comprehends. This is very plain from the passage in Colossians. In the first place the apostle styles him εἰκὼν τοῦ θεοῦ τοῦ ἀοράτου, πρωτότοκος πάσης κτίσεως; not to place him in the same order with the creation, as the eldest product merely of God's power: but because ἐν αὐτῷ ἐκτίσθη τὰ πάντα, the whole creation sprang from him as the everlasting Word, in whom all was originally comprehended, (John I. 3; Heb. I. 2,) and by whom still all things consist (τὰ πάντα ἐν αὐτῷ συνέστηκε. Col. I. 17).* And parallel exactly with this relation to the natural creation, only in a far higher order of life, the apostle now declares his relation to be also to the supernatural constitution revealed in the Church. The creation itself becomes complete only in the Church, the life of nature in the life of the Spirit; as the principle of the first then, it was necessary that the *Logos* should be the principle also of the second, through its relation to which alone, as shadow, apparatus and prophecy, the first can be said to have any proper significance of reality. He is head over all things *to the Church* (Eph. I. 22). As the Church is the crown and complement of the whole world, so he from whom the world proceeds reveals his inmost life in the same as his proper body, the fulness of him that filleth all in all; and so he is "the beginning, the first-born from the dead," not only the point from which the new creation starts, but the principle also out of which all is derived; "that in all things he might have the pre-eminence (ἵνα γένηται ἐν πᾶσιν αὐτὸς πρωτεύων)." He is the first-born of the dead then, in a sense correspondent with that in which he is the first-born of the creation; because the resurrection, that is the entire life of the Church, flows forth from his person, and has its reality in him only, (ἐν αὐτῷ,) to the end. He is not in the creation however, as he is in the Church; it forms at best but a relative revelation of life; whereas in this last the absolute life which he has in himself (ἐν αὐτῷ ζωὴ ἦν, John I. 4. V. 26,) is made to reach forth into the world in a real way (ἡ ζωὴ ἐφανερώθη, 1 John I. 2). Thus "it pleased the Father that in him should all fulness (πᾶν τὸ πλήρωμα) dwell; and having made peace through the blood of his cross, by him to reconcile all things unto himself" (Col. I. 19, 20). The divine reconciliation (καταλλαγή) is accomplished for all in his person, (ἐν τῷ σώματι τῆς σαρκὸς αὐτοῦ διὰ τοῦ θανάτου,) by the blood of his cross; and becomes available only ἐν αὐτῷ, as the life in which it is comprehended is carried over to others, and made to include them as the power of a new creation in the Church.

Christianity then is a Life, not only as revealed at first in Christ, but as continued also in the Church. It flows over from Christ to his people, always in this form. They do not simply bear his name, and acknowledge his doctrine. They are so united with him as to have part in the substance of his life itself. Their conversion is a new *birth*; "not of blood, nor of the will of the flesh, nor of the will of man, but of God" (John I. 12, 13). That which is born of the flesh, is flesh." As such, it can never rise above its own nature. No cultivation, no outward aid, no simply moral appliances,

---

*Non ideo tantum primogenitus, quad tempore præcesserit omnes creaturas, sed quia in hoc a Patre sit genitus, ut per ipsum conderentur; sitque veluti hypostasis, aut fundamentum omnium. *Calvin in loc.* So he is the ἀρχή of the second or new creation, it is said afterwards, as the resurrection commencing in his person is *rerum omnium instauratio.*

can ever lift it into a higher sphere. This requires a new *life*. "That which is born of the Spirit, is spirit," all else necessarily comes short of the distinction. All else accordingly is something lower than Christianity (John III. 1–8).

Paul is full of the same general view. Religion is always with him, as it holds under the gospel, a divine life; not simply the ordinary moral life regulated by a divine rule, but the product truly and wholly of a new element or principle, carried over into the soul from Christ, by the power of the Holy Ghost. "If any man be in Christ, he is a new creature (καινὴ κτίσις); old things are passed away; behold all things are become new" (2 Cor. V. 17). The doctrine of free justification is vindicated from the objection of being favourable to sin, (Rom. ch. 6–8,) on the ground that it involves an organic change in the subject, the presence of a new order of existence, which carries the guaranty of holiness, so far as it prevails, in its own constitution. "How shall we that are DEAD to sin, LIVE any longer therein?" Baptism into Christ is baptism into his death, and so at the same time into his resurrection—the translation of the subject out of the sphere of the flesh into the sphere of the Spirit (Rom. VI. 1–7). Under the law, (chap. VII.) righteousness is impossible. But, thanks be to God, "there is now no condemnation to them which are in Christ Jesus." They are made "free from the law of sin and death" by the "law of the Spirit of life" revealed through his person. Thus what was impossible for the law, through the weakness of the flesh, "is accomplished by the grace that unites us with the life of Jesus." "The righteousness of the law is fulfilled in us"—not forensically merely in the way of imputation, but as the power of a new life also in our own nature—"who walk not after the flesh, but after the Spirit" (Rom. VIII. 1–4). Christians are "not in the flesh, but in the Spirit"—the new life sphere revealed in Christ. The resurrection power of Jesus dwells in them, at once the principle of a salvation, that will not rest till in their case too it shall have quickened the whole man into life and immortality (Rom. VIII. 9–11).

Christ is the substance, and not merely the source, of this salvation. So completely indeed is this view interwoven with the whole style of thinking in the New Testament, that we often fail for this very reason to notice the extent to which it is carried. But only think of the like representations being employed with regard to Moses, the great apostle of the old dispensation. Let *him* be exhibited as "the wisdom of God and the power of God" (1 Cor. I. 24); "made of God unto us wisdom, righteousness, sanctification, and redemption" (1 Cor. I. 30); the substance of truth and life, in whom all God's promises are yea and amen (2 Cor. I. 20); the counterpart of the light that "shined out of darkness in the beginning," by which the true knowledge of the glory of God is now revealed in the souls of men (2 Cor. V. 4, 6); the absolute principle of unity for the world, more deep and comprehensive than all forms of existence besides (Gal. III. 27, 28; V. 15. Eph. II. 13–22; IV. 14–16. Colos. I. 20; III. 10, 11). Let these, and other representations of parallel import, which are of such familiar character as applied to Christ, be transferred in imagination to Moses, or any other ancient man of God, and the full weight of the difference that holds between him and all other prophets, must at once make itself felt.

"I am crucified with Christ," says Paul; "nevertheless I live; yet not I, but Christ liveth in me; and the life which I now live in the flesh, I live by the faith of the Son of God, who loved me and gave himself for me" (Gal. II. 20). The process of the new creation in the believer finds its proper analogy, only in the all victorious resurrection of the Saviour himself—of which indeed it is but the organic continuation in the Church (Eph. I. 18–23; II. 1–7). We are God's workmanship, "created in Christ Jesus unto good works" (Eph. II. 10). All Christianity is comprehended in a living apprehension of Christ, in "the power of his resurrection and fellowship of his sufferings," in comparison with which every moral advantage is to be held of no account (Philip. III. 7–11). "Ye are dead," the apostle says, "and your life is hid with Christ in God. When Christ, who is our life, shall appear, then shall ye also appear with him in glory" (Col. III. 3–4).

The whole morality of the gospel is made to root itself in the presence and power of the new life, thus derived from Christ. This forms its grand characteristic distinction, as compared with the so called virtue of the common world. All duties are enforced, on the ground of what the christian has become by his heavenly birth, as the subject of the christian salvation. All relations hold *in Christ Jesus*. The motives to every virtue are drawn front the grace of the gospel itself, as already constituting the actual state of those on whom they are urged. The virtues are all *fruits* of the Spirit; which in this case serves only to express that higher order of life, (in contrast with the *flesh*,) into which believers are raised by their union with Christ. All morality is comprehended in the rule, "Walk in the Spirit, and ye shall not fulfil the lust of the flesh" (Gal. V. 16). It is as the dear children of God, already quickened into life and sealed with the Holy Spirit of promise, that believers are urged to put off the old man, which is corrupt according to the deceitful lusts, and to put on continually more and more the new man, which after God is created in righteousness and true holiness, (Eph. I. 13, 14; II. 1–6; IV. 1, 17–32; V. 1–33; VI. 1–9. Col. chap. III., IV. 1 Thess. II. 12; IV. 1–12; V. 4–23. Tit. II. 9–14. 1 Pet. I. 13–23; II. 1–3, 9–12). "Ye were sometimes darkness, but now are ye light in the Lord; walk as children of light" (Eph. V. 8). "Put on as the elect of God, holy and beloved, bowels of mercies, kindness, humbleness of mind, meekness, long-suffering" (Col. III. 12). "If ye be risen with Christ, seek those things which are above" (Col. III. 1). "Every man that hath this hope in him, purifieth himself even as he is pure" (1 John III. 3). Such is the tenor throughout of the Christian morality. Its superiority to other ethical systems does not consist, in its being simply a more full and accurate statement of the duties God requires of man, than can be found elsewhere; but in this rather, that it reveals the true ground of all moral relations in Christ, and refers every duty in this way to a principle, which it could not have in any other form, and which infuses into it accordingly a new character altogether. The whole structure of life, ethically viewed, becomes a new creation in Christ Jesus.

SECTION V.

THE MYSTICAL UNION.

Christ is the principle of the whole Christian salvation. From him it flows over, as the power of a divine life, into the persons of his people. This implies of course the most close and intimate connection. The union however which exists in this case, is more than that of simple derivation. Here the parallel of the first Adam fails to represent fully the mystery of the second. The order of existence in the one case transcends immeasurably the order of existence in the other. The first man was made εἰς ψυχὴν ζῶσαν (1 Cor. XV. 45. Gen. II. 7). His life was relative only, and as such creaturely, comprehended in some sense in the constitution of mere nature. Adam lived; but he could not be said to "have life in himself," as this is said of Christ (John V. 26). The second man in this view was made εἰς πνεῦμα ζῳοποιοῦν, "a QUICKENING SPIRIT." To the common human nature is superadded, in his case, a higher divine life; which with its all vivifying power quickens this nature into its own order of existence, (κατὰ δύναιν ζωῆς ἀκαταλύτον, Heb. VII. 16,) first in himself and then in his people. "Longe est majus," says Calvin *in loco*, "esse vitam aut vitæ causam, quam vivere." Christ has life in himself absolutely; and it is under this substantial form, it is made to reach over from him to the Church. As such, however, of course, it can never be separated from his person; like the life of Adam, carried forward by natural generation in his posterity. The stream here may never pass away from the spiritual Rock, out of which it gushes in the beginning, (1 Cor. X. 4). The new life of the believer is absolute too; as *real*, in distinction from all mere creaturely existence, as the life of Christ itself; but on this very account, it cannot be separated for a moment from its original ground. "Because I live"—and only for this reason—"ye shall live also" (John. XIV. 19). Christ lives *in* his people to the end of time, not simply as a natural organic root, but as a "quickening spirit." He is present with them, and mystically joined to them, in the form of LIFE; comprehending of course the most perfect personal consciousness, and freely imparting itself, as the absolute ground of all true personality, to the whole body of which he is the Head.

This union then is not of nature as such, but of the Spirit. We shall err however grievously, if we conceive of the Spirit in this case as something separate from the proper presence of Christ himself, or as forming a medium of communication only for the divine nature of Christ with the *soul* of the believer abstractly considered. Both of these suppositions stand in broad contradiction to the Scriptures, and serve equally at last to reduce the doctrine of the mystical union to a mere figment, by making it moral only, and not real.

We read of the Spirit of God, as present and active in the world, under a certain form, before the incarnation of Christ. But we must not confound this agency with the relation, in which he has come to stand to the Church since, in consequence of the union thus established between the divine nature and our own. It is by the incarnation properly, that the way has been opened for a true descent of the Spirit into the sphere of the human existence as such. John goes so far as to say there was no Holy Spirit (οὔπω γὰρ ἦν πνεῦμα ἅγιον*), till Jesus was glorified (John VII. 39). This does not mean of course that he did not *exist*; but it limits the proper effusion of the Spirit, as known under the New Testament, to the Christian dispensation as such. It teaches besides, that the person of Jesus, as the Word made flesh, forms the only channel or medium, by which it was possible for this effusion to take place. The Holy Ghost accordingly, as the Spirit of Christ, is, in the first place, active simply in the Saviour himself. In this view, however, he cannot be separated from the person of Christ. He constitutes rather the form, in which the higher nature of Christ reveals its force. In the end, the whole person of the Son of Man is exalted into the same order of existence. Humanity itself in this way, as joined with the everlasting Word, is made to triumph over the law of infirmity and mortality, to which it was previously subject in its own nature, and takes henceforward the character of *spirit*, in distinction from that of mere flesh. All this immediately, as now said, only in the person of Christ. But all, at the same time, in Christ as the second Adam. The full glorification of our nature as thus represented, was the constitution in fact of a new and higher order of life in the world, for humanity as a whole. With the final triumph of the Spirit in the glorified humanity of Christ, this higher order of life began to reveal itself with power on the day of Pentecost, (Acts II. 1–4); since which time, it has continued regularly active in the world by means of the Church; which is itself the product and extension in this way of the new creation, commencing in the Saviour's person.

In accordance with what has now been said, we find the person of Christ exhibited to us in the New Testament always under a two-fold aspect—though it remains of course essentially the same in its constitution throughout. He is presented to our view, first under a mortal form, and then in his resurrection state. In taking our nature upon him, he was made in all respects like as we are, only without sin. (Heb. IV. 15. V. 2, 7.) He appeared "in the likeness of sinful flesh" (Rom. VIII. 3); "made of a woman, made under the law" (Gal. IV. 4). The humanity which he assumed was fallen, subject to infirmity, and liable to death. In the end,

---

*The addition δεδομένον, is acknowledged, on all hands, to be spurious.

"he was crucified through weakness" (2 Cor. XIII. 4). Under all this low estate however, the power of a divine life was always actively present, wrestling as it were with the law of death it was called to conquer, and sure of its proper victory at the last. This victory was displayed in the resurrection. It was not possible that he should remain in the grave (Acts II. 24). "He was declared to be the Son of God with power, according to the Spirit of holiness, by the resurrection from the dead" (Rom. I. 4). The Spirit of holiness here (κατὰ πνεῦμα ἁγιωσύτης) stands contrasted with the "flesh," of common humanity, according to which (κατὰ σάρκα) he was of the seed of David (v. 3,) and as such capable of death. It denotes then his higher nature, in the power of which his whole person was, by this triumph, raised into a new undying state, and clothed with the attributes and prerogatives of a divine existence. In Rom. VIII. 11, the resurrection of Christ is inseparably joined with the third person of the ever blessed and glorious Trinity, as one and the same life. Whether as the Spirit of the Father, or as the Spirit of Christ himself, his agency, proceeding as it does from both, constitutes the form, in which the new creation in Christ Jesus is carried forward, first in his own person and subsequently with the Church. The resurrection state of the Saviour then, especially as made complete at his ascension, is itself *spirit* (πνεῦμα,) in the way of distinction from the flesh (σάρξ) or common mortal state in which he had appeared before. The two states are set in close contrast, 1 Pet. III. 18, where it is said: "Christ also hath once suffered for sins, the just for the unjust, that he might bring us to God, being put to death *in the flesh*, but quickened *by the Spirit*," or as it should read rather *in the Spirit* (θανατωθεὶς μὲν σαρκὶ, ζωοποιηθεὶς δὲ πνεύματι). "*Caro* hic pro externo homine apitur," says Calvin; "spiritus pro divina potentia, qua Christus victor a morte emersit." The victory however must be understood to extend to the whole man, external as well as internal, transforming the very flesh itself into spirit. It is the full triumph of Christ's higher life over the limitations with which it had been called to struggle in its union with our fallen humanity; by which this humanity itself is raised into the sphere of the same life, and completely transfused with its power, in the everlasting glorification of the Son of Man. So, 1 Tim. III. 16, "God was manifest in the *flesh*"—he emptied himself (ἑαυτὸν ἐκέτωσε, Phil. II. 7); took upon himself the form of a servant, was made in the likeness of men, and being found in fashion as a man humbled himself, and became obedient unto death, even the death of the cross; but it is added, he was "justified in the *Spirit*," the power of that higher nature, which wrought with supernatural force even under his humiliation itself, and came finally to its full and proper victory in his resurrection.* His true character came

---

*Spiritus nomine comprehendit quicquid in Christo divinum fuit ac supra hominem. *Calvin, in loc.*

thus fully into view, being vindicated or justified by this triumphant demonstration itself; as the result of which he was "received up into glory," and is set down at the right hand of God, "far above all principality, and power, and might, and dominion, and every name that is named, not only in this world, but also in that which is to come" (Eph. I. 20, 21. Phil. II. 9–11. Heb. XII. 2). The somewhat difficult passage, Heb. IX. 14, seems to find its key, in the same distinction of Christ's glorified state, from the mere mortal condition with which it had been preceded. The "eternal Spirit," (διὰ πνεύματος αἰωνίον,) through which he "offered himself without spot to God," must be understood of the divine order of existence, to which his whole person was exalted after his death, as contrasted with the dying form in which he had appeared before. This formed itself the complete triumph of the Spirit, in his person, over all that was contrary to its own nature in our fallen flesh; and in the power of it, he presented himself before God once for all, an offering of everlasting value, by which he hath perfected for ever them that are sanctified (Heb. IX. 11–14, 24–28. X. 10–14).*

Thus made perfect in the Spirit—his entire person raised above the power of death, and filled at every point with the immortality of heaven itself—the blessed Redeemer "became the author of eternal salvation unto all them that obey him." His glorification opened the way for the free outflowing of the Spirit, the same divine life with which he was himself filled, on the surrounding world, (John VII. 38, 39). "Having received of the Father," says Peter on the day of Pentecost, "the promise of the Holy Ghost, he hath shed forth this, which ye now see and hear" (Acts II. 33). He became for others, what he was thus shown to be within himself, πνεῦμα ζῳοποιοῦν (1 Cor. XV. 45), a quickening or life-giving spirit; from whom the power of a new creation was to be carried forward under the same form, in the world, by the Church, even as the fallen life of the first Adam had been transmitted in the course of nature to all his posterity.

From all this it is clear, in the first place, that we have no right to separate Christ from his Spirit, in such a way as to suppose the presence of the one where the other was not present at the same time. "Christum a Spiritu suo qui divellunt, eum faciunt mortuo simulachro vel cadaveri similem."† Thus, Rom. VIII. 9–11, the indwelling of the Spirit and the indwelling of Christ in believers, are exhibited as one and the same thing. And so, in his last discourse with his disciples, our Lord himself explicitly identifies with the promise of the Holy Ghost, the promise of his own

*So the passage is interpreted by *Bleek*, in his Commentary on the Epistle to the Hebrews, 1840; in point of learning and judgment, the highest authority in this form that could be produced.

†Calvin, on Rom. VIII. 9. By the Spirit here, he says, we are to understand, "modus habitationis Christi in nobis."

return. The coming of this divine Paraclete required indeed, as we have already seen, the removal of Christ from the earth, so far as his first form of existence (ἐν σαρκί) was concerned. He must be glorified to make room for the effusion of the Spirit. "If I go not away, the Comforter will not come" (John XVI. 7). This was to make room in fact however, only for his own return in a higher form of existence. "I will pray the Father, and he shall give you another Comforter, that he may abide with you for ever; even the Spirit of Truth; whom the world cannot receive, because it seeth him not, neither knoweth him: but ye know him; for he dwelleth with you, and shall be in you. I will not leave you comfortless (ὀρφανούς); I WILL COME TO YOU" (John XIV. 16–18, 22, 23). The best commentators of the present day, *Olshausen, Tholuck, Luecke,* &c., agree with *Luther* and *Calvin,* that the coming of himself to which the Saviour here refers, is to be understood neither of his resurrection simply nor of his second visible advent at the end of the world; but of his presence by the Spirit, of whose mission he had just spoken. It is all the same promise. The persons of the adorable Trinity are indeed distinct. But we must beware of sundering them into abstract subsistences, one without the other. They subsist in the way of the most perfect mutual inbeing and intercommunication. The Spirit of Christ is not his representative or surrogate simply, as some would seem to think; but Christ himself under a certain mode of subsistence; Christ triumphant over all the limitations of his moral state, (ζωοποιηθεὶς πνεύματι,) "received up into glory," and thus invested fully and for ever with his own proper order of being in the sphere of the Holy Ghost. In this form, he is present with the Church more intimately and really than he could be in any other. "Where two or three are gathered together in my name, there am I in the midst of them" (Matt. XVII. 20). "Lo I am with you always, even unto the end of the world" (Matt. XXVIII. 20).

No less clear is it, in the second place, that the higher order of existence to which Christ has been advanced *in the Spirit,* involves his humanity, in its full constitution both as body and soul, and is made to flow over in this form to his people. It was in view of his humanity alone indeed, that any such exaltation was required. The divine Logos, as such, had been in union with the Spirit from all eternity. But in becoming flesh, this higher life was sunk for the moment into the limitations of the fallen mortal nature with which it became thus incorporated; not of course for its own sake, but for the sake of the lower nature itself, that this might be raised, by the triumphant power of the Spirit, into the same order of existence. The glorification of Christ then, was the full advancement of our human nature itself to the power of a divine life; and the Spirit for whose presence it made room in the world, was not the Spirit as extra-anthropological simply, under such forms of sporadic and transient afflatus as had been known previously; but the Spirit as immanent now, through Jesus Christ in the human nature itself—the form and power, in one word, of the new supernatural creation he had introduced into the world. He shall *abide* with you, says the Saviour, forever, (John XIV. 16). The Spirit then constitutes the form of Christ's presence and activity in the Church, and the medium by which he communicates himself to his people. But as such he is the comprehension in full of the blessed Redeemer himself; and the life he reveals, is that of the entire glorified person of the Son of Man, in which humanity itself has become quickened into full correspondence with the vivific principle it has been made to enshrine.*

When Paul styles Christ a quickening or life-giving spirit, (1 Cor. XV. 45,) the reference is not at all to his nature as divine simply, or im-material, but to his proper manhood as such. It is the resurrection of the *body*, which he has immediately in view. "As in Adam all die, so in Christ shall all be made alive." How? By virtue of a new divine element, introduced into our nature by the incarnation, which has already tri-umphed over mortality in the person of the second Adam himself, and by which he is now the principle of the resurrection, (πνεῦμα ζωοποιοῦν,) for the body as well as for the soul, to all that believe on him to salvation. "There is a natural body," says the apostle, "and there is a SPIRITUAL bo-dy." The first springs from Adam, the second from Christ. As we have borne the image of the one, in our fallen mortal state, so must we also as Christians bear the image of the other. This will be fully reached in the resurrection. Then what is sown at death in corruption, dishonour, weakness, a mere natural body, (σῶμα ψυχικόν,) will be raised in incorruption, glory, and power, a spiritual body (σῶμα πνευματικόν). This corruptible shall put on incorruption; this mortal shall put on immortality; and so death shall be swallowed up in victory for ever. (1 Cor. XV. 42–54.) "He shall change our vile body, that it may be fashioned like unto his glorious body, according to the working whereby he is able even to subdue all things unto himself" (Phil. III. 21. John III. 2). Here is no exclusion of the body from the sphere of the spirit, as being in itself of a totally opposite nature, and on this account incapable of sharing in the same life; but the last triumph of the Spirit is made to consist precisely, in the full transfiguration of the body itself into its own image. Nor is this change to be regarded as something wrought upon the body in the way simply of outward or foreign power—as though a stone were transformed suddenly into a winged bird; for this would be to sink all into the sphere of blind dark nature. The glorification of the believer's body is the result

*Nota unitatem *spiritualem* quæ nobis cum Christo est, *non animæ tantum* est, sed pertinere *etiam ad corpus*, ut caro simus de carne ejus, &c. Alioqui infirma esset spes resurrectionis, nisi talis esset nostra conjunctio, hoc est, *plena* et solida. *Calvin, in* 1 *Cor.* VI., 15.

of the same process that sanctifies his soul. The order of existence in both cases is the same, *pneumatic*, and not simply natural or psychic. "Our life is now *hid* with Christ in God; but when Christ, who is our life, shall appear, then shall we also appear with him in glory" (Col. III. 4); our whole man, of course, like his, quickened in the Spirit and made meet for heaven. As the subjects of this new creation, steadily advancing towards its appointed end, Christians are described as being already in the Spirit and not in the flesh—that is, as participant in the pneumatic order of existence, of which Jesus Christ is the principle and the Holy Ghost the medium, and not under the power simply of our nature as derived with a fallen character from the first Adam. And this is no moral relation merely, but the actual presence of a higher life in the most *real* form, extending to the person, of the believer as a whole. His very body, accordingly, is constituted thus a temple of the Holy Ghost. (1 Cor. VI. 19.) "He that is joined to the Lord is one spirit" (1 Cor. VI. 17); not simply so far as his own spiritual nature, abstractly considered, is concerned but in the totality of his regenerated person as united with Christ in the element or sphere of the Spirit, and not in the sphere of mere nature only. "Ye are not in the *flesh*, but in the *Spirit*," says the apostle, "if so be that the Spirit of God dwell in you. Now if any man have not the Spirit of Christ, he is none of his. And if *Christ be in you*, the body is dead because of sin; but the Spirit is life because of righteousness. But if the Spirit of him that raised up Jesus from the dead *dwell in you*, he that raised up Christ from the dead, *shall also quicken your mortal bodies by his Spirit that dwelleth in you*" (Rom. VIII. 9–11).*

*That the whole spiritual life of the Christian, including the resurrection of his body, is thus organically connected with the mediatorial life of the Lord Jesus, might seem to be too plainly taught in the New Testament, to admit of any question; and yet we find many slow to allow the mystery, notwithstanding. A very common view appears to be, that the whole salvation of the gospel is accomplished, in a more or less outward and mechanical way, by supernatural might and power, rather than by the spirit of the Lord as the revelation of a new historical life in the person of the believer himself. So we have an outward imputation of righteousness to begin with; a process of sanctification carried forward by the help or proper spiritual machinery brought to bear on the soul; including perhaps, as its basis, the notion of an abrupt creation *de novo*, by the fiat of the Holy Ghost; and finally, to crown all, a sudden unprepared refabrication of the body, as an entirely new product of Almighty power at the moment, to be superadded to the life of the spirit already complete in its state of glory. But the Scriptures sanction no such hypothesis in the case. The new creation is indeed supernatural; but as such it is strictly conformable to the general order and constitution of life. It in a new creation *in Christ Jesus*, not by him in the way of mere outward power. The subjects of it are saved, only by being brought within the sphere of his life, as a regular, historical, divine human process, in the Church. The new nature implanted in them at their regeneration, is not a higher order of existence framed for them at the moment out of nothing by the fiat of God, but truly and strictly a continuation of Christ's life over into their persons. The growth of this life in them forms their sanctification. When they die, their bodies *sleep in Jesus*; so that at the last God brings them with him again, when the Church is made complete by his second coming, (1 Thess. IV. 14.) The resur-

Here then we see the nature of the mystical union. as it holds between Christ and his people. It falls not, in any sense, within the sphere of nature as such, and we cannot say of it in this view, that it is physical. But just as little are we at liberty to conceive of it as merely moral. Its sphere is that of the Spirit. In this sphere, however, it is in the highest measure *real*; far more real, indeed, than it could possibly be under any other conceivable form. Christ is not sundered from the Church by the intervention of his Spirit. On the contrary, he is brought nearer to it, and made one with it more intimately, beyond measure, in this way, than if he were still outwardly in the midst of it as in the days of his flesh. And this union, as we have seen, extends to the personal totality of the Saviour on the one side, and to the personal totality at the same time of the believer on the other. No conception can well be more unbiblical, than that by which the idea or spirit (πνεῦμα) in this case, is restrained to the form of mere mind, whether as divine or human, in distinction from body. The *whole* glorified Christ subsists and acts *in the Spirit*. Under this form his nature communicates itself to his people. They too, to the same extent, are made thus to live and walk *in the Spirit*, both in soul and body. Christ lives in

---

rection of the head and the ultimate resurrection of the members, form one process, as truly as the death of Adam and his posterity constitutes throughout but one and the same tremendous fact. *In Christ*, all shall be made alive. His resurrection is the pledge of theirs, even as the first fruits give token of the coming harvest (1 Cor. XV. 22, 23). He is "the beginning, the first-born from the dead," which, as we have seen, implies the force of a common law in the case of those that follow, (Col. I. 18.) It is the Spirit of Christ, *now* dwelling in believers, that shall in due time quicken their mortal bodies, in conformity with the power of his own resurrection state; thus bringing to full manifestation the hidden life of the sons of God, in that adoption, (υἱοθεσίαν—τὴν ἀπολύτρωσιν τοῦ σώματος), towards which their whole salvation here struggles, and without which it can never be regarded as complete, (Rom. VIII. 11, 19, 23.) It will not do, in view of such representations, to speak of the resurrection of believers as an abrupt miracle, holding no inward historical connection with the resurrection life of Christ, as it wrought in them mightily, by the Spirit, before their death. True it is ascribed to supernatural power, (1 Thess. IV. 16,) and we are referred sometimes to 1 Cor. XV. 52, as teaching that the change is to be instantaneous, and without preparation. But this is of no real weight. That the winding up of the mystery of Christianity should include revelations of divine power altogether transcending the present order of the Church, is only what might be expected; while it is quite possible that these may be found after all but the proper completion of the mystery itself, after it shall have been conducted to this point. As to the instantaneousness of the change, (so far as the passage referred to may be supposed to have the case of the dead in view at all,) it holds only, of course, of the revelation which is made to take place at the time. As Olshausen justly remarks (*Comm. in loc.*), this by no means excludes the supposition of a previous preparation in the life of the believer for this result. It implies, indeed, that there has been no development during death. But so far as the previous state is concerned, it amounts to nothing more than this, that the process which was before hidden, is now brought to burst into view suddenly, in its complete form. The birth of the butterfly, as it mounts in the air on wings of light, is comparatively sudden too; but this is the revelation only of a life, which had been gradually formed for this efflorescence before, under cover of the vile, unsightly larve.

them, and they live in Christ; and still, as their sanctification proceeds, this mutual indwelling becomes more intimate and complete, till, at last, in the resurrection, they appear fully transformed into the same image, "as by the Spirit of the Lord." (Cor. III. 18. Philip. III. 21.)

No more apt or beautiful illustration of this union between Christ and the Church can be imagined than that which he has himself furnished, in the allegory of the vine and its branches. (John XV. 1–8.) "I am the vine, ye are the branches; he that abideth in me, and I in him, the same bringeth forth much fruit; for without me ye can do nothing." To understand this of a mere moral union, is to degrade the whole subject. "It is not to be disputed," says Tholuck, "that a higher relation is here exhibited than that of master and disciple, nothing less in fact than a real oneness, (eine *wesentliche* Einheit,) effected through the medium of faith." It is well remarked by Lücke, that the earthly, here as elsewhere, is exhibited by Christ as the image or copy (*Abbild*) of the heavenly. Nature finds its divine archetype or *Urbild* at last, only in the sphere of the Spirit. Thus the connection which holds between the vine and its branches, is not so much a figure of the life union that has place between Christ and believers, as the very reflex of this mystery itself. He is accordingly the TRUE vine, in whom is revealed, in this case, the full reality, of which only an adumbration is present in all lower forms of life. The union between the vine and its branches is organic. They are not placed together in an outward and merely mechanical way. The vine reveals itself in the branches; and the branches have no vitality apart from the vine. All form one and the same life. The nature of the stock is reproduced continually, with all its qualities, in every shoot that springs from its growth, no matter how far removed from the root. And all this is only the symbol of Christ's relation to his people. Here, in a far higher sphere, the region of the Spirit as distinguished from that of' mere nature, it is one and the same life again that reigns in the root and all its branches. The union is organic. The parts exist not separately from the whole, but grow out of it, and stand in it continually, as their own true and proper life. Christ dwells in his people by the Holy Ghost, and is formed in them the hope of glory. They grow up into him in all things; and are transformed into the same image, from glory to glory, as by the Spirit of the Lord. The life of Christ is reproduced in them, under the same true human character that belongs to it in his own person.

The allegory of the *body*, as borrowed by Paul particularly from another sphere of life, in illustration of the same subject, is no less full of instruction. A common political corporation may indeed be represented by the same comparison, so far as the idea of mutual subserviency on the part of its members is concerned; as in the case of the apologue of Menenius Agrippa, once employed to compose a civil discord at Rome, which is brought forward sometimes as a parallel to 1 Cor. XII. 14–26. But

body & head

as Calvin well remarks, on this passage, the two cases are of a wholly different character; since the ground of unity in the Church is always represented by Paul to be of a far deeper nature than is to be found anywhere else; nothing less, in fact, than the life of Christ himself, mystically flowing through its entire constitution. "As the body is one, and hath many members, and all the members of that one body, being many, are one body; so also is Christ. For by one Spirit are we all baptized into one body, whether we be Jews or Gentiles, whether we be bond or free; and have all been made to drink into one Spirit." (1 Cor. XII. 12, 13, 27. Rom. XII. 4. 5.) "Christ is head over all things to the Church, which is his body, the fulness of him that filleth all in all" (Eph. I. 22, 23). From him, as its head, "the whole body, fitly joined together, and compacted by that which every joint supplieth, according to the effectual working in the measure of every part, maketh increase of the body unto the edifying of itself in love." (Eph. IV. 15, 16. V. 23, 30. Col. I. 18, 24. II. 19.) The relation here exhibited involves of course a real life union, of the most intimate character. The head is not in the members, nor in contact with them, locally; but all local connection falls immeasurably short of the bond that holds between it and the body. Nor is the union this simply, that the members are ruled and conducted by the will of the head. It is the presence of a common *life*—the animal spirit, as it has been called—always proceeding from the head into the limbs, and having no proper existence in a single limb under any other form. But does the spirit of life in this case, the basis of such organic unity, remain in the body as a mere abstract force? By no means. It rules the whole process of assimilation and reproduction, and thus calls into being continually the material volume and substance of every limb, as well as its vital activity. The head is in this way *in* the members, as the principle from which unceasingly all their existence is drawn. And so it is with the relation of Christ to the Church, only in a far higher order of life. It is no mechanical conjunction that makes them one. The case excludes the supposition of every thing like a magical or merely outward transfer of life from Christ to his people, such as is implied in the dogma of transubstantiation. But neither, on the other hand, is the conjunction simply spiritualistic; for this would be to resolve all at last into a merely moral character. In distinction from both these conceptions, we say of it that it is organic, in the fullest sense of this term. The new human life in Christ reaches over, as a central un-compounded force, *by the Spirit*, into the persons of Christ's people; and there reveals itself, with constantly reproductive energy, under the same form, true always to its own nature, till at length the whole man, spirit, soul and body, is transformed fully into its image.

Another very remarkable and most significant illustration, is employed (Eph. V. 22–33) with reference to the same subject. Even under the Old Testament, the marriage relation was frequently made the type or symbol of the covenant connection established between God and his people. So in the Apocalypse, the Church is styled the bride, the Lamb's wife, (Rev. XIX. 7. XXI. 2, 9). But all falls short of the representation which is here presented to our view. De Wette, and other commentators of like rationalistic stamp, resolve all of course in this case, as in every case of the same sort, into mere figure and sound. But this is to do violence to the whole spirit of the passage. Paul himself declares the subject to be a "great mystery;" and it is plain that he feels himself struggling throughout with a thought, too vast altogether for the reach and grasp of the mere understanding as such. Marriage itself is a mystery; not, indeed, a sacrament, in the proper sense, as it is held to be by the Church of Rome; but still of what may be termed sacramental significance and solemnity; a true and proper symbol in this view of the mystical union, as it holds between Christ and his Church.* "So ought men to love their wives," says the apostle, "as their own bodies; he that loveth his wife loveth himself." And thus the Lord regards and cherishes the Church. "For we are members of his body, of his flesh and of his bones." This means, according to *Pelagius*, "membra ejus eum debent imitari in omnibus!" How different the commentary of *Calvin*. "The passage," he tells us, "is classic on our mystical communication with Christ. It is not to be considered hyperbolical, in this view, but simple; and it not only signifies that Christ partakes of our nature, but is intended to express something deeper and more emphatic. For the words of Moses, Gen. II. 24, are quoted. And what now is the sense? As Eve was formed out of the substance of her husband Adam, that she might be as it were a part of himself; so we, that we may be true members of Christ, by the communication of his substance, coalesce with him into one body." (*Com. in loc.*) The Church may be styled thus, according to the beautiful allusion of Hooker to this comparison with the case of Eve, "a true native extract out of Christ's body." Clearly the apostle has in his mind here more than any merely figurative or moral incorporation with the Saviour. The stress of the quotation from Gen. II. 24, lies on the last clause, "they two shall be *one flesh*;" and this is applied directly to the case of Christ and the Church, (which he adds immediately, is a "great mystery,") in justification of the previous declaration, "We are members of his body, of his flesh, and of his bones." The whole passage is well exhibited, with most thorough and comprehensive exegesis, in the sense now given, by *Harless*

---

*Dass die Ehe, besonders das, worin ihre Eigenthümlichkeit besteht, Gen. II. 24, ein Heiligthum sei, so dass mit ihm das Heiligste, was eines Menschen Besitzthum wird, anschaulich gemacht werden darf, wird die Bestialität, der Sünde freilich nie begreifen; aber der Geist muss es erfahren und begreifen. Für jene schreibt auch nicht der Apostel; für sie giebt es im Himmel und auf Erden kein heiliges Geheimniss; sie findet überall nur den Fluch ihrer eigenen Verworfenheit. *Harless.*

whose commentary on the Epistle to the Ephesians, may be said to throw all others into the shade, and whose judgment in this case, especially when backed by the high authority of Calvin, no man of learning at least can fail to respect.

It is only on the ground of this real, inward life union between Christ and his people, that we can properly appreciate or understand much of the common phraseology of the New Testament, in speaking of Christians and their peculiar character and state. In various ways, Christ is described as dwelling and working *in* his people; and so on the other side, nothing is more common than for Christians to be spoken of as *in Christ*. All Christian relations hold only *in* the Lord. All Christian graces are to be cultivated, and all Christian works performed, *in* the Lord. Exemplifications are needless. The whole Christian life is represented under the same formula. *In Christ* is only another expression for *Christian* itself. So common and familiar indeed is this style, that the peculiarity by many is hardly noticed at all. But substitute Moses for Christ; and at once we must feel how wholly inapplicable such language is to a merely moral relation. The whole New Testament assumes that the relation of Christ to his people is more than moral; that it involves a real community of life, in virtue of which, as he dwells in their hearts by faith, so they may be said to be rooted and built up in him also unto every good word and work. (Eph. III. 16–19; Col. II. 6–10.)

Specially striking, in this view, are those passages in which Christians are represented as having already in Christ all that is comprehended in the complete idea of the Christian salvation. In the Saviour himself the victory over death and hell was consummated in his resurrection and ascension. In the Church, however, as a whole, and in every individual believer, the new life reveals itself as a process. In no sense can the Christian, viewed in himself, be said to be complete. And yet as comprehended in the life of Christ, he is often spoken of as actually possessing already all that this involves. Thus, as we have already seen, he is described as *having* eternal life now; though the full sense of his privilege in this respect, of course remains to be developed hereafter. His life is *hid* with Christ in God. So he is not only justified, but even sanctified and glorified in Christ. "Ye are complete in him, which is the head of all principality and power" (Col. II. 10). Paul seems at times almost to lose sight of the distinction between Christ and the Christian, in the overwhelming sense he has of their oneness. We are crucified, dead and buried with Christ, and have risen with him again to a new and higher life. (Rom. VI. 3–11. VII. 4. VIII. 11. Gal. II. 20. Phil. III. 9–12. Col. II. 12. III. 1–4.) This form of speaking is quite too strong and deliberate, to be resolved into mere rhetorical flourish. Nor will it meet the case fully, to say that it turns merely upon a certain sort of analogy, that may be supposed to hold between Christ's outward history and the spiritual

experience of the believer. The outward and inward do indeed flow
together in the two cases. But it is only because the one is really and truly
involved in the other.* The new life, *in the Spirit,* first in Christ and then
in his people, extends to the whole man; and being in both organically the
same, is found in the end to repeat itself, with true reproduction outward
as well as inward, to the utmost extremities of the body of which he is the
mystical head. Thus every Christian may be said to be in Christ
potentially from the beginning, all that he is destined to become actually
when his salvation shall be complete. The power that is actively at work
in his person, is the same all-conquering life (Phil. III. 21) that wrought
mightily in Christ, when he was raised from the dead and set at God's
right hand in the heavenly places, far above all principality, and power,
and might, and dominion, and every name that is named, not only in this
world, but also in that which is to come; and was thus constituted
gloriously head over all things to the Church, which is his body, the fulness of him that filleth all in all, (Eph. I. 19–23). And in view of this
relation, the apostle does not hesitate to add immediately afterwards, "He
hath quickened us together with Christ, and hath raised us up together,
and made us sit together in heavenly places in Christ Jesus" (Eph. II. 1, 5,
6). All in the past tense, not in the future.† So Rom. VIII. 30, not only the
calling of believers and their justification, but their glorification also, is
exhibited as something already complete, (οὺς δὲ ἐδικαίωσε, τούτους
καὶ ἐδόξασε).

On this last passage, Olshausen's remarks are particularly striking;
and closely related as they are to the whole topic now in hand, I may be
permitted to quote them in full. "The essential point, " he tells us, "in the
doctrine of Christ's *active obedience* is this, that his agency in our
salvation not *negative* in form simply, but full as much *positive*. Christ
does not simply take away sin in the case of men, and then leave them to

---

*"The acts of God for our redemption are all fulfilled and accomplished in Jesus
Christ. The several steps of development in Christ's life, are for this very reason so many
steps in the work of redemption, from his birth or incarnation on to his ascension. For *he*
is our redemption, not his doctrine, nor his work, nor his example; his work is not to be
sundered from his person; and his life and death are the form precisely in which it has been
accomplished. It is sheer nonsense to give up the personal and historical Christ, and still
think of retaining a firm hold upon Christianity." *Kliefoth. Theorie des Kultus,* §. 188. On
this ground, he urges the true significance and importance of the Church Festivals, as
related to Christ. They are not simply the memorial, but the bond also, of the proper vital
union that subsists between him and his people.

†Et certe quamvis salus nostra in spe sit adhuc abscondita, quantum ad nos spectat;
in Christo nihilominus beatam immortalitatem et gloriam possidemus. Ideo addit, *In
Christo*; quia nondum hæc quæ commemorat, in membris apparent, sed in solo capite;
propter arcanam tamen unitatem, ad membra certo pertinent. *Calvin, Comm. Eph.* II. 6.
—Christus ist der *reale* Typus für alle Lebensgestaltung der Heiligen bis aus Ende, so dass,
was sie leben, nur die Entwickelung des in Keim schon in ihm Gegebenen und von ihm aus
in ihr Wesen Gepflantzten ist. *Olshausen in loc.*

work out holiness for *themselves*, but he has by his holy life wrought out this also, for himself and for all his people; so that both, the destruction of the old and also the creation of the new, in the process of regeneration, are alike *Christ's* work, both completed by him too in his earthly state; so as to be in the first place imputed to individual believers, and then communicated to them in a gradual way. This is here most distinctly expressed by the words ἐδικαίωσε καὶ ἐδόξασε. Even the first term implies a real communication of the δικαιοσύνη Χριστοῦ (comp. Rom. III. 21); the other however, ἐδόξασε, represents it as a matter of actual possession even under its full form of holiness and perfection—though Paul had a little before (v. 23,) disclaimed this for himself and Christians generally. As then the whole human race, naturally considered, lay originally in *Adam*, and all history is thus but the development of what his nature included; so *Christ* also is the real bearer of the entire Church, the new creation, the sanctified humanity, as he not only by the virtue of his atonement destroys the old, but to the same extent creates the new also, and forms his own sacred image in every believing soul. Only in this view does it become clear, how faith is the one and all of the Christian life. The Christian is not called, either before or *after* his conversion, to *form an independent holiness* for himself; but only to receive continuously the stream of life that flows upon him from Christ; and this *reception* is itself faith. Just as the plant, when the germ has begun to grow, needs only to take in moisture, air and light, in order that it may unfold itself from within; whilst all the handling of an unskilful gardener, for the purpose of precipitating its growth in some different way, serves only to frustrate what it seeks to advance. And still this absolute *passivity* is at the same time the highest activity; since Christ works, not *without* the man, but *in the very inmost depths of his being*, infusing into the will itself the active force of his own life. Only, the believer always feels that the power of which he is thus possessed is not from himself, and his accordingly grows with his perfection; it is not *he* but Christ lives and works in him, (Gal. II. 20). Hence we may see, how in the passage before us it is just the *aorist* which is required for its proper sense; so that every attempt to get rid of this tense must be absolutely rejected. The *future* here is not in place; for with the word, "*It is finished!*" Our Lord made his whole Church, together with the κτίσις, negatively and positively complete, for all ages. No mortal can add any thing however little, to his work; all that unfolds itself in the individual members of his Church through distant centuries, is but the development of what was previously at hand in his person. The Church and every particular believer, along with the κτίσις which forms its necessary basis, are "God's workmanship created in Christ Jesus" (Eph. II. 10). Redemption is a new glorified creation, and all creation must remain for ever the prerogative of God alone. The connection imperatively requires this sense; for it is the *certainty* of salvation, as superior to all earthly contingency, that Paul wishes to establish. But there is no true certainty, except as it lies in a divine act. Salvation would be the most uncertain of all uncertainties, if it were made to rest, not on the objective act of God in Christ, but upon the fluctuating subjectivity of men themselves. Only under this objective view does the gospel become a true joyful message, which *nothing can overthrow*, and which infidelity itself can only reject."

SECTION VI.

JOHN vi. 51–58.

The sixth chapter of John is allowed on all hands to be of special interest and importance, in relation to the subject with which we are now employed. It has been of course very variously interpreted, both in ancient and modern times; since in the nature of the case, the light in which it has been regarded has always depended on the view taken of the relation in general to which it refers. The passage, v. 51–58, in which the representation of the whole chapter is advanced to its most startling climax, has been felt to be particularly difficult; as in addition to other sources of embarrassment, it has been entangled from a very early period with the sacramental question. A succinct history of the interpretation of the passage, in this view, is presented by Lücke, in an excursus appended to the second volume of his Comm. on John, 2nd edition. In the early Church *Origen* and *Basil* the Great, denied all reference in it to the sacrament of the Lord's Supper. *Chrysostom, Cyril, Theophylact,* held the opposite view; which became general subsequently in the Catholic Church. With the Reformation, the case was changed. Not only *Zuingli* and *Calvin,* but *Luther* also, on different grounds, agreed in the view that the passage refers only to the general reception of Christ by believers, and not to the eucharistic communion as such. Some have still insisted since on the other view. But the more important modern commentators generally allow, that there is no sufficient room to suppose any reference whatever to the Lord's Supper.

So far as the historical institution is concerned, this judgment is no doubt correct. But it is equally clear, that the *idea* which the Holy Supper embodies is the same that is here brought into view; just as in the conversation with Nicodemus, the idea involved in the sacrament of baptism is urged, (John III. 5,) although the sacrament itself in its proper sense was not yet instituted.

Throughout the chapter, Christ exhibits himself to the Jews, with whom he was in conversation at Capernaum, as the true source and support of all spiritual life. "Labour not for the meat which perisheth, but for that meat which endureth unto everlasting life, which the Son of Man shall give unto you; for him hath God the Father sealed.—The bread of God is he which cometh down from heaven, and giveth life unto the world.—I am the bread of life; he that cometh to me shall never hunger; and he that believeth on me shall never thirst.—This is the will of him that hath sent me, that every one which seeth the Son, and believeth on him, may have everlasting life; and I will raise him up at the last day.—Verily,

verily, I say unto you, he that believeth on me *hath* everlasting life. I am
that bread of life. Your fathers did eat manna in the wilderness, and are
dead. This is the bread which cometh down from heaven, that a man may
eat thereof and not die." After the view we have already taken of the
relation of Christ to his Church, we cannot be at a loss for a moment, with
regard to the general sense in which this strong language is to be understood. It is of course in one respect figurative; as in the nature of the case
all representations must be, that are borrowed from the sphere of nature
to render intelligible what belongs to the sphere of the Spirit. But shall we
say, that it refers only to Christ's *doctrine*, as the proper food of the soul.
Even de Wette will tell us, that such a supposition here is decidedly false.
The reference to his *person* is altogether too full and clear. Jesus himself
is the bread of life. He that cometh to ME shall never hunger. We come
indeed by faith. But in doing so, we go truly out of ourselves and become
joined to his very life, as the centre of a new consciousness in our own.
"Neque enim fides Christum intuetur duntaxat quasi procul remotum,"
says Calvin, "sed eum amplectitur ut noster fiat, et in nobis habitet; facit
ut coalescamus in ejus corpus, communem habeamus cum ipso vitam,
unum denique simus cum ipso." (*Comm. John* VI. 35.) The union involves
in this view everlasting life; not simply in the form of a promise, but as an
actual possession. Even the resurrection itself is potentially included in it,
as the proper necessary consummation of the new form of existence to
which it gives rise. The subject of this life may die; but says the Saviour,
I will raise him up at the last day. Here is something far deeper than mere
doctrine, or mere moral influence of any kind. Christ gives us life, only
by communicating himself to us in a real way.

It is commonly admitted, that with the 51st verse, some advance is
made on the general thought previously presented; and it is now for the
most part granted also, that this consists in a specific reference to Christ's
death, as the point in which especially his mediatorial character may be
said to have become complete. It is not easy indeed to avoid the feeling,
that the language carries in it such a reference.

"I am the living bread," says the Saviour solemnly, "which came
down from heaven; if any man eat of this bread, he shall live forever. And
the bread that I will give is my FLESH, which I will give for the life of the
world." By his flesh, to be given for the life of the world, cannot well be
understood anything else than the sacrifice which he has made of himself
for sin upon the cross. The Jews, we are told, now strove among themselves, saying, How can this man give us his flesh to eat?" "Then Jesus
said unto them, "Verily, verily, I say unto you, except ye eat the flesh of
the Son of Man, and drink his blood, ye have no life in you. Whoso eateth
my flesh and drinketh my blood, hath eternal life; and I will raise him up
at the last day. For my flesh is meat indeed, and my blood is drink indeed.
He that eateth my flesh and drinketh my blood, dwelleth in me and I in

him. As the living Father hath sent me, and I live by the Father; so he that eateth me, even he shall live by me."

All must feel the close correspondence, that holds between what is here said and the terms afterwards employed in the institution of the Lord's Supper. Here, as there, the participation of the believer in Christ, is made to stand particularly in eating his flesh and drinking his blood. The same idea evidently is exhibited in both cases; and whatever we find to be the sense and force of the representation in one case, we can hardly help allowing to it the same significance also in the other. In the eucharist, there is reference directly to Christ's death; it is his body broken and his blood shed for sin, of which we are called to partake. And so in the passage now before us, the reference is the same. The Saviour had spoken before of his person in general, as the bread of life. Here be fastens attention upon his person under a particular view. It is by his death, he is constituted the author of eternal life to all that turn towards him for this purpose. Except ye eat the *flesh* of the Son of Man, and drink his *blood*, ye have no life in you." "THIS—it is said in conclusion—is that bread which came down from heaven; not as your fathers did eat manna and are dead; he that eateth of *this* bread, shall live forever."

The passage then looks directly to the redemption wrought out by Christ upon the cross; but not to this, as something abstracted from his life, in the general view in which it had been presented before. It simply represents the form, under which specifically the life comprehended in Christ's person for the benefit of a dying world, becomes fully effective towards this end. The case required, as we have before seen, a deadly conflict with him that had the power of death (Heb. II. 14, 15). The Life, to show itself positively as immortality, must reveal itself negatively, in the first place, as the resurrection. Hence its whole force, and with it the whole power of the Christian salvation, may be regarded as concentrated in the idea of the atonement by which the power of sin and hell was broken by Christ's death upon the cross. "He was delivered for our offences, and so raised again for our justification" (Rom. IV. 25). But all this at last, is only the life of the Son of Man, brought into a real, and not simply fantastic, correspondence with our wants. He is still personally "the bread of life." Only, to be so in fact, be must be apprehended in the character in which he is here exhibited to our view. We must eat his flesh and drink his blood; participate actually and truly in his life, as it was made an offering for sin. This it is emphatically that constitutes him the bread which came down from heaven, of which if any man eat he shall live forever.

Not by the atonement then, as something made over to us separately from Christ's person, are we placed in the possession of salvation and life; but only by the atonement as comprehended in his person itself, and received through faith in this form. To eat the flesh of the Son of Man and drink his blood, is not to lay hold of the merits of his death simply in an abstract way, a thing impossible in the nature of the case; but to lay hold of them in Christ himself, who is made of God unto us all that we need for righteousness as well as life. Such clearly is the sense of the passage before us, taken in connection with the whole discourse of which it is a part. The hunger under which the world is suffering spiritually, does not consist merely in the want of religious instruction or new impulses and motives for the will. The aliment for which it calls, must come to it in the form of life. In this form accordingly it is exhibited by Jesus Christ, as it is to be found nowhere else. Here is the new birth of the Spirit (John III. 3, 5, 6), secured by a living reception of Christ himself (John I. 12, 13). Here is the water that quenches forever the deep inward thirst of the human soul, that never can be more than momentarily allayed from any other quarter; "a well of water" in them that receive it, "springing up into everlasting life" (John IV. 10–14). "If any man *thirst*," says the Saviour, "let him come unto ME and *drink!*" (John VII. 37, 38). Here again is the true bread of life, under the same form. "He that cometh to ME shall never hunger, and he that believeth on ME shall never thirst." Christ personally is this bread; because it is only in his person, that the *Life* of the ever-lasting Word, which is the true *Light* of men, has revealed itself in the sphere of our common human existence (John I. 4, 14). Only in this form, does he still the gnawing hunger of humanity, by supplying it with the very substance of life itself; a hunger which is otherwise like the grave, that never cries, It is enough. "He that believeth on me, HATH everlasting life." But how? What becomes of his sins, the curse of the broken law, the sentence of death already lodged in the inmost constitution of his nature? The life, which is in Christ, includes all that is needed to meet in full the demands of the entire case. It has triumphed over death, and him that had the power of death. By the sacrifice of HIMSELF Jesus has put away sin, and perfected forever them that are sanctified (Heb. VIII. 26; IX. 10, 14). The power of this sacrifice, is that particularly which imparts to his life its saving, renovating value, in the circumstances in which it is offered for our use. Still the sacrifice is only the life itself, in successful struggle with sin and death. It is not the doctrine in the case, but the *fact* only, that brings salvation; and this, let it be well considered, can never be separated from Christ's person. The bread of life then, in this view, is Christ as slain for the sins of the world, received into the believer and made one with him by the power of the Holy Ghost. We must eat his *flesh* and *drink* his blood; otherwise we can have no life. His flesh is meat *indeed*—his blood drink *indeed*; ἀληθῶς, in reality, not in a shadowy or relative sense merely, but absolutely and truly in the sphere of the Spirit. The participation itself involves everlasting life; not simply in the form of hope and promise, but in the way of actual present possession; and not simply as a mode of existence for the soul abstractly considered, but as embracing the whole man in the absolute totality of his nature, and reaching out to the resurrection of the body itself as its legitimate and necessary end. Christ once crucified, but now in glory, is the principle of immortality in every true believer. As the Resurrection and the Life, he will *raise him up at the last day.* "He that eateth my flesh and drinketh my blood, *dwelleth in me and I in him* (ἐν ἐμοὶ μένει κἀγὼ ἐν αὐτῷ)." Stronger still: "As the living, Father hath sent me, and I live by the Father; so he that eateth me, even he shall live by me." Could language more clearly teach, that the salvation which we have by Christ, including his whole mediatorial grace, comes to us only by the communication of his own life?

All this at the same time is accomplished in a purely spiritual way, through the activity of faith. Here is no oral communication with Christ's flesh and blood. And yet the communication is real. It is not the thought or image of Christ simply, that is apprehended in the case, but the very substance of his life itself, as it was once offered for sin and now reigns gloriously exalted in heaven. Such is the mystery of the new creation in the Spirit. The common understanding may object and cavil, in its old style, How can this man give us his flesh to eat? But still the testimony of God is clear and sure. God hath given to us eternal life; this life is in his Son, Jesus Christ; and it becomes ours only as we have the Son himself formed in us by the power of the Holy Ghost. This then is the very nature of faith as concerned with our salvation, that it brings its subject truly and really within the scope of this life, and subjects his whole being to its organific action; causing him thus to become a new man, or as the apostle has it, καινὴ κτίσις, more and more, on to the final resurrection, in Christ Jesus our Lord.

"It is the Spirit that quickeneth; the flesh profiteth nothing; the words that I speak unto you they are spirit, and they are life." This observation of the Saviour, occurring in close connection with the passage before us, and having reference directly to the offence which had been taken with it on the part of many as a "hard saying," (John VI. 63,) has been considered by some a clear intimation that all which had been spoken before was to be understood in the most common metonymical sense. They will have it that the whole of this most solemn representation, in which, over and over again, the necessity of eating Christ's flesh, and drinking his blood is urged, as that without which men can have no life—was intended only to bewilder and confound the *carnal* Jews; while the true meaning of it comes simply to this, that we must be joined to the Saviour, by a believing reception of his doctrine, or a simply mental correspondence with him at most in the power of his sufferings and death. But surely no exegesis could well be more poor and flat than this. It belongs itself emphatically to that very carnalism, to which it affects to be in its own way so vastly superior; for it sticks plainly in the self-same abstraction, which rendered it so difficult for the Jews of Capernaum to understand our Saviour, and by which the things of the Spirit so generally are made to appear foolishness to the mere understanding as such. The imagination that Christ by the words, *The flesh profiteth nothing*, intended simply to intimate that his flesh or body could do no good, and that he must be understood therefore to refer in what he had said to a purely moral communication with his person, must be pronounced well nigh as crass as the notion of an actual oral manducation of his material flesh itself. Spirit and flesh here are opposed in a quite different and far deeper sense. The one represents the sphere of mere nature as embraced in the fallen life of Adam, soul, body, and all. The other designates the higher order of existence, of which Christ himself is the principle (πνεῦμα ζωοποιοῦν), and which reaches out from him by the Spirit, as a new divine creation, over the whole range of our being. It is this that quickeneth or giveth life both to soul and body. The flesh on the other hand, whether as soul or body, profiteth nothing.

The bearing of all this on the question of the eucharist, must be at once evident to every reflecting mind. The passage before us has no direct reference to this ordinance, as it was afterwards to be instituted. It refers to the Christian life in general. But very plainly the idea here exhibited, is the same that is presented to us in the institution of the Lord's Supper under a different form. If such a view as we have now taken of the extra-sacramental life of the believer, on the ground of the representation here made by Christ himself, be admitted with any clear and full conviction, it will not be possible to resist the impression, that the sacrament itself can involve, to say the least, nothing less. Those on the other hand who deny a real communication with Christ's person in the eucharist, must in the nature of the case deny also a real extra-sacramental union with him to the same extent. This does not imply that the communion of the sacrament and the general Christian life, are at last simply the same thing. It comes to this only, that the order of life comprehended in the two cases is the same. A man *lives* by his food, in the same sense in which his life holds *as* life, and not in some different sense. So here, if the new life of the Christian be at last a moral relation only to the Saviour, the power of the sacrament must be of course of the same order. But if this new life stand in the form of a real incorporation with the person of the Redeemer, the power of the sacrament cannot hold in the form of mere good thoughts and good feelings. It must involve too a real participation, under its own form, in Christ's *life*.

This much then we reach for the right understanding of the Holy Supper, by what we have thus far learned of the nature of the mystical union in general. As the communion of Christ's body and blood, concentrating in itself the inmost sense of the great fact of Christianity, it can involve nothing less at least than it was supposed to involve in the Calvinistic theory, as originally held by the Reformed Church generally. "In the Supper," to use the language of Ursinus, "we are made partakers not only of the Spirit of Christ, and of his satisfaction, justice, virtue and operation; but also of the very substance and essence of his true body and blood, which was given for us to death on the cross, and which was shed for us, and are truly fed with the self-same unto eternal life." And yet this implies no local comprehension of the Saviour's body in the elements, no oral or corporeal contact with it in any way. The mystery holds not in the sphere of the flesh, but in the sphere of the Spirit. We feed upon the broken body and shed blood of Christ, by faith. But that which is imparted to us through our faith, by the power of the Holy Ghost, is the true divine human life of the Son of Man himself, objectively present in the sacramental transaction as such, and really carried over into our persons under this form.

SECTION VII.

THE SACRAMENT OF THE LORD'S SUPPER.

It must ever betray a most poor and narrow conception of the nature of Christianity as a whole, to suppose that the question of Christ's presence in the Eucharist may be settled by a few texts of scripture, taken in an isolated way, and without regard to the general revelation of which they form a part. It is not in this way, that the true weight of the scriptural evidence for any great truth is to be reached. The doctrine of the Trinity for instance is never exhibited under any such formal, categorical statement, as we find employed for the purpose in our modern catechisms and confessions. We may say the same thing of the doctrine of Original Sin. The Unitarian in the one case, and the Pelagian in the other have taken advantage of this circumstance to create distrust with regard to both. So *very* momentous and fundamental as these points are allowed to be, how is it to be accounted for, they have asked, that they have not been so plainly and directly affirmed, as to cut off at once and forever all room for scepticism or cavil? The objection is specious; but we need only to go deeper into the true idea of the Christian revelation, to feel its utter worthlessness. Christianity we have seen already to be a Life. Its form is the *spirit* that maketh alive, and not the *letter* that killeth. Its revelations are not theorems but facts; not facts in the form of mere tradition, but actually subsisting, always enduring facts; not disjointed, fragmentary facts, but a glorious system of facts, organically bound together and growing out of each other, as a single supernatural whole. A theology that builds all its doctrines upon mere abstract texts, may arrogate to itself the character of *biblical*, in the most eminent sense; but it can never have any good claim to be considered so in reality. It belongs to the very genius of *sect*, to magnify itself in this way. It always affects to be biblical, in the highest degree. It will stand upon the bible, and upon nothing but the bible. In the end however, its biblicity is found to resolve itself invariably into such a poor, circumscribed conception of revealed truth, as is now described. Isolated texts, viewed through the medium of some particular sect hobby, are made to exhaust the whole proof, whether for or against the position on which they are made to bear. But no use of the scriptures can well be more truly unbiblical than this. Christianity is not a skeleton, nor yet a corpse for the use of the dissecting room. The bible is not to be understood, by fragments, and as seen from any and every point of view where the beholder may happen to stand. All turns on the position of the beholder himself, and his power of observing and comprehending the revelation as a whole. He must stand in the truth, have sympathy with it, feel the authority that belongs to it in fact, in order that he may have power to do justice at all to its presence. What could such a spirit as that of Voltaire, be expected to understand of the apostle Paul? Who would trust the rationalism of Priestley, or the abstract spiritualism of the Quaker, in any exegetical judgment, hearing on the question of our Lord's divinity in the first case, or on the true idea of the Church in the second? All turns on the stand-point of the interpreter, and the comprehensive catholicity of his view. He must be consciously within the horizon, and underneath the broad canopy, of the new supernatural creation, he is called to contemplate; and then each part of it must be studied and expounded, in full view of its relations to every other part, and to the glorious structure in which all are comprehended as a whole. This is the true conception of biblical theology. Only under this form, can bible proof, as it is called, in favour of or against any doctrine, be entitled to the least respect.

So in the case before us, the sacramental question can never be settled by the formula of institution, *This is my body, This is my blood*, separately considered; nor by any other single text under the same abstract view. The interpretation of every such text, depends invariably and necessarily on the theological position, from which its bearings and relations are observed. Hence it means one thing to the Romanist, another thing to the Lutheran, and something different altogether to the rationalistic Socinian. The idea of settling the sense of the eucharist by the words of institution separately taken, is perfectly quixotic.

It has been said indeed, that this ambiguousness constitutes itself a strong presumption *against* the idea of any special mystery in the ordinance; since more care must have been employed, on this supposition, to guard the institution from being misunderstood. But every such judgment, proceeds on a wrong theory of the Christian revelation itself, as we have already attempted to show. Why is not the doctrine of the Trinity categorically asserted? Why have we not the constitution of Christ's person, succinctly described as in the Westminster Catechism? Why is it not taught in so many words that infants are proper subjects for baptism, and that the first day of the week was to be substituted for the seventh, as the Christian sabbath? Simply, we answer, because the Christian revelation is constructed on a wholly different plan, infinitely more worthy of its author, and infinitely better adapted for the accomplishment of its own glorious end.

The Lord's Supper can never be understood, except as viewed in its relations to the whole system of truth, which has been brought to light by the bible. The view we have already taken then, of the new creation in Christ Jesus, and his mystical relation to the Church, has all served only to open the way for placing the ordinance in its true and proper light.

The great difficulty here is, in rising to a full, abiding sense of the truth and reality of Christianity itself, as a supernatural constitution permanently established *under this character* in the world. We are too prone, to restrict the idea of supernatural interposition in this case, to the single historical person of Jesus Christ himself; an error that tends directly to throw a certain magical, docetic character, over the whole fact of the incarnation, and to sink Christianity at the same time to the form of a mere abstract spiritualism in the sphere of the flesh. For it is one thing to be spiritualistic in the flesh, and quite another thing to be divinely real in the Spirit. We must not sunder the supernatural in Christ, from the life of his body which is the Church. Christianity is strictly and truly a new creation in Christ Jesus; a supernatural order of life, revealed and made constant and abiding, in the midst of the course of nature as it stood before. As such, it includes resources, powers, divine realities, not only peculiar to itself, but altogether transcending the common natural constitution of human life. All this, at the same time, under a true historical form. The supernatural has become itself natural; not in the way however of putting off its own distinction, as compared with what nature had been before, and still is under any other view; but by falling into the regular process of the world's history, so as to form to the end of time indeed its true central stream. To question the presence of such supernatural resources and powers in Christianity, when we look at it properly, is to question in fact the revelation of the supernatural in Christ himself. Either we must fall back at best to the old Ebionitic stand-point of Christian Judaism; or we must allow that the power of a truly divine life, the constitution of the Spirit as distinguished from the constitution of mere nature, is in the Church, not transiently and sporadically as under the old Testament, but with real immanent constancy, as forming the inmost character of the Church itself.

The supernatural, as thus made permanent and historical in the Church, must, in the nature of the case, correspond with the form of the supernatural, as it appeared originally in Christ himself. For it is all one and the same life or constitution. The Church must have a true theanthropic character throughout. The union of the divine and human in her constitution, must be inward and real, a continuous revelation of God in the flesh, exalting this last continuously into the sphere of the Spirit.

Let all this be properly apprehended and felt, and it cannot fail at once to exert a powerful influence over our judgment with regard to the Lord's Supper. For it is plain, that this ordinance holds a central place in the general system of Christian worship. The solemn circumstances under which it was originally instituted, the light in which it has always been regarded in the Church, and the very instinct, we may say, of our religious nature itself, which no rationalism can effectually suppress, all conspire to show, that it forms in truth the inmost sanctuary of religion, and the most direct and close approach we are ever called to make into the divine presence. The mystery of Christianity is here concentrated into a single visible transaction, by which it is made as it were transparent to the senses, and caused to pass before us in immediate living representation. No matter how poor may be the general view entertained of the gospel, even for the lowest rationalistic spiritualism itself, the Lord's Supper, (if it be not discarded entirely, as with the unhappy Quaker,) constitutes the most significant and impressive exhibition of the grace of the New Testament; the most graphic *picture*, at least, if nothing more, of the salvation which has been procured for us by the Saviour's sufferings and death. All that is wanted, then, to make it a true sacrament to our view—the *seal* as well as the *sign* of the invisible grace it represents—is that we should have a true and full persuasion of the supernatural character of Christianity itself, as a permanent and not simply transient fact in the history of the world. Low views of the sacrament betray invariably a low view of the mystery of the incarnation itself, and a low view of the Church also, as that new and higher order of life in which the power of this mystery continues to reveal itself through all ages. Those who entertain such views may claim the credit of more than common spirituality; it may be their object professedly to exalt the character of Christ, by sinking the thought of all that is outward and material, in order to make more room, as they dream, for his being honoured in a higher form. So indeed it has ever been. The enemies of the sacraments have always affected to be more spiritual than others. And who were such sticklers for the highest order of spirituality in the early Church, as the Gnostics, who at the same time turned the whole fact of the incarnation itself into a mere docetic abstraction. Such spiritualism, as it begins in the flesh in fact, and never gets beyond it, even in its highest flights, is sure to end in it also palpably at the last. On the other hand, let the great fact of the incarnation be apprehended with full faith, as a world fact—the centre of all history—the fountain of a new creation, which is still present and progressive, not fantastically, but in the way of actual human, historical development, in the Church; let it be felt that the Church is, in very deed, the depository and continuation of the Saviour's theanthropic life itself, and as such a truly supernatural constitution, in which powers and resources wholly transcending the common order of the world are constantly at hand, involving a real intercommunion and interpenetration of the human and the divine; let all this, I say, be *felt*, and it is easy to understand how naturally and necessarily, at the same time, we must be led to see the mystery of the Holy Eucharist, epitome as it is of the mystery of the Christian salvation itself, in a corresponding light.

And is not this, it may be asked, the only true and right position for coming to any just judgment in the case? Is not Christianity in fact such a supernatural constitution, under a true historical form in the world? And may the man be trusted to interpret the sense of its mysteries, who does not feel this? Shall I go to the spiritualistic Gnostic, or Anabaptist, or Quaker, to learn the manner of Christ's presence in the Church? Shall I ask the rationalist Ammon, or Wegscheider, or Paulus, or some rationalizing Grotius or Macknight, to explain to me the words of institution, in the sacrament of Christ's body and blood? Just as reasonably might I study Paul at the feet of Voltaire. The very first and most indispensable condition to a safe and sound judgment here, is that we should stand in the full sense of what is comprehended in the idea of Christianity itself, as a true and real revelation of the supernatural in the flesh. This is of more account in the case, than all exegetical helps besides. This was emphatically the position of the primitive Church; and it was this right standpoint in relation to divine truth no doubt, more than any thing else, which served in the case of the first Christians, to set both the doctrines and institutions of Christianity in proper view, if not at once for the understanding, at least for the heart and the inward life. They saw in Christ a new order of life, divine and yet most perfectly human at the same time, really active in the flesh by the Church, and destined to triumph, (in a very little while, as they supposed,) in the form of a true earthly millennium, over the entire state of the world as it stood before. They felt that in the sphere of this new creation, they were mystically joined to the Saviour himself, by the power of the Holy Ghost, so as to participate in his very nature and life. And how then was it possible, that they should look upon the communion of his body and blood in the Lord's Supper as a mere sign or token, in the common acceptation of these terms? In the nature of the case, they could see in it nothing less than a real communication of the Saviour's life itself; and they understood, of course, and interpreted, the words of institution accordingly, as conveying the assurance of this supernatural grace, to be perpetuated in the ordinance to the end of time.

As Christianity finds a general adumbration in the religion of the Old Testament, so its sacraments in particular are specifically prefigured in the types of Circumcision and the Passover. In the case of the Lord's Supper, a still more remote analogy is presented to our view by Paganism itself, in those sacred feasts which it has been customary in all ages to hold in connection with sacrifices. Under all systems of worship, religion has ever been made to centre in the altar and the offering of sacrifice; while, by partaking of what was thus offered, the worshipper was supposed to come into the nearest communion with the object of his worship.* The sacrifice, to serve its purpose in full, must be eaten, and thus united in the most intimate and living way with the person of him, who sought to propitiate

---

*Scheibel. Das Abendmahl des Herrn, chap. 1.

the favour of heaven by its means. Whatever of value or merit it comprehended, became available through in actual participation of the sacrifice itself, in communion with the altar. The same idea, variously modified, may be said to run through the entire sacrificial system of the Old Testament. It is most strikingly exhibited, however, in the institution of the Passover.

The Passover was instituted (Ex. XII. 1–27) in connection with the memorable deliverance of the children of Israel, on the night when the Lord smote the first-born of the land of Egypt; and was ordained to be observed afterwards perpetually in commemoration of this event. The offering in the case was required to be a lamb *without blemish*. The victim must be *slain*, as an offering for sin, and its blood sprinkled on the door posts; where it became an atonement or satisfaction, in view of which the plague was not permitted to enter the dwelling thus protected. "The blood shall be to you for a token upon the houses where ye are; and when I see the blood, I will pass over you, and the plague shall not be upon you to destroy you, when I smite the land of Egypt." But it was not enough that this outward exhibition of the blood should take place, the ordinance made it necessary also that the sacrifice should *be eaten*. In this case at least, more was intended by this than an act of general communion with God. It represented the necessity of a true, living conjunction with the sacrifice itself. The lamb whose life was poured out as an offering for sin, must be itself incorporated as it were with the life of the worshipper, to give him a fair and full claim on the value of its vicarious death. It became to him an atonement, by entering really into his person. It lay in the very nature of the economy itself, that all this should be in a merely outward way. The atonement itself was only a type or shadow; and the union with the victim now mentioned was but relative and imperfect in like manner. All formed in adumbration simply of the glorious mystery of redemption, as it was afterwards to be revealed in Christ.

For it is allowed on all hands, that the Passover, as it continued to be observed afterwards, was more than a mere commemoration of the deliverance in Egypt. This event was itself a grand type of the spiritual deliverance, which has since been accomplished for the world by the death of Christ; and the paschal celebration accordingly, in calling it continually to mind, involved a prophetical reference continually by its means to the coming of this great salvation. It involved an acknowledgment of spiritual need with a profession of faith in God's covenanted grace, as it was to be revealed in due time for the removal of sin; and for the true Israelite, it carried in it a sure pledge at the same time that the atoning grace it represented would avail to preserve him personally from the power of the destroying angel. All this however on the ground of an actual union with the sacrifice itself, in the way which has been already noticed. In the end, the shadow found its full sense in the presence of the substance. The death of Jesus formed the proper end of all the sacrifices, and of the paschal offering in particular. "Behold," said the Baptist, when he pointed him out to his disciples, "the Lamb of God, that taketh away the sin of the world!" So Paul calls him expressly our Passover, who has been sacrificed for us (1 Cor. V. 7). This is still more expressively signified however by the Saviour himself, in the institution of the Holy Supper. By his own appointment, the one sacrament was formally substituted for the other. Thus was it distinctly signified, that the Passover had looked forward from the first to the sacrifice of Christ as the true atonement for sin; and that it ceased accordingly to have any meaning, when this sacrifice was offered. The sacrament of the Passover was at once abolished and fulfilled, in the sacrament of Christ's body and blood.

The two institutions then are to be considered of parallel character, and as having in some sense the same significance and force. Both look directly to the broken body and shed blood of the Redeemer, as the great and only true propitiation for the sins of the world. Their relation to each other however, is like that of the two Testaments in general. The one is relatively only, what the other is absolutely. The sacraments of the Old Testament are no proper measure, by which to graduate directly the force that belongs to the sacraments of the New. We have seen already, that the Old Testament made nothing perfect. Its ordinances and ministrations were all more or less shadowy and incomplete. The substance of their sense is revealed only in Christ. To make Baptism no more than Circumcision or the Lord's Supper no more than the Passover, is to wrong the new dispensation as really, as we should do by attributing to the levitical priesthood what is to be found only in him who is a priest forever after the order of Melchizedek. The Passover was at best but an unreal adumbration of the grace that is exhibited to us in the Lord's Supper. It was a picture or sign only of what it was intended to represent; not a sacrament at all indeed, in the full New Testament sense, but a sacrament simply in prefiguration and type. Still, as such a type, it is well adapted to illustrate the true force of the higher institution, in which ultimately it came to its end.

The Lord's Supper was instituted under circumstances, which show clearly that it was intended to take up into itself, (as the comprehension of the whole idea of Christianity,) the full typical import of the Old Testament, which might be said to find its central representation in the Passover. Through this sacrament in particular all looked forward to the great sacrifice of Calvary, as the end in which its shadows were to become real. That sacrifice was now ready to be offered. On the night in which he was betrayed—at the close of the paschal feast—with his sufferings in full view, and the full consciousness it the same time of the relation in which he stood to the old dispensation now ready to pass away in his person —our Saviour solemnly took bread, blessed and brake it, and gave it to his disciples, and said, Take, eat; *this is my body*, which is given for you:—and then again the cup, saying, This cup is the *new testament in my blood* which is shed for you, drink ye all of it (Matt. XXVI. 26–29, Luke XXII. 15–20). Thus was instituted the sacrament of the Lord's Supper, in the room of the Jewish Passover, for the use of the Church in all following time. Now it is only necessary to have some actual sense of the immensurable solemnity of the occasion it itself, to feel how perfectly frigid and rationalistic every view must be that can find nothing more in the words of institution, than that this ceremony was to be a simple conventional memorial to all ages of the Redeemer's sufferings and death. We may not indeed take the words in their strictly literal sense, as is done by the Church of Rome; but we have just as little right on the other hand, to resolve them into the merest common-place in the way of pretended figure. The occasion is too solemn, the phraseology too strikingly pregnant, for that. Let due regard be had to all the circumstances of the transaction, and it will be impossible to avoid the feeling that it requires to be understood ill a higher sense.*

What the Passover signified prophetically, and in the way of shadow, is here exhibited under the character of a real and actually present

---

*To estimate at all the force of our Saviour's words, in the case of this solemn institution, it is above all things necessary, of course, that we should have present to our minds, in a lively way, the circumstances under which all took place. That most wretched rationalist, *Paulus* of Heidelberg, resolves the whole transaction into the poorest common-place; by supposing that Jesus, his thoughts full of the violence he expected to suffer shortly after, whilst handing round to his disciples the broken bread, took occasion to say, mournfully, of the suggestive symbol, *It is my body*. The affecting words made an indelible impression on the minds of all present; and so it came to pass "very psychologically," we are told, that as long as they lived, when they afterwards broke bread together, the simple association served powerfully to recall him to their thoughts, &c. *Comm. in Matt.* XXVI. 26. And yet Paulus affects to be graphic, too, in painting the scene as it was, in order to show us how *natural* the symbolical and hyperbolical must be considered in the case! At such exegesis, we may well shudder. But may we not fear that there is oftentimes an approximation towards the same rationalistic stand-point, where the ordinance is spoken of in much more respectful terms, while at the same time its whole significance is tried by the measure of common or merely human relations? No occasion could well be more solemn, than that which gave birth to the holy institution. Let the circumstances be felt. Let the truths of overwhelming interest, presented by our Lord in his last discourse with his disciples, be present to the soul. Let the calm, divine self-possession of the Son of Man, the past and the future all in clear vision before him, be distinctly apprehended. Let it be felt, that a new creation was in fact comprehended in his person; and that the shadows of all past time were now to be made actual in the reality they foretokened. Let it be remembered that the idea of the *atonement*, the great central truth of Christianity, had never yet been distinctly enunciated by Christ himself; but here first proclaimed, just before the sacrifice was to take place, under a form intended to lodge it in the heart of the Christian worship to the end of time. Let all this be considered and *felt*, and then how poor and jejune does the interpretation become, which can find nothing beyond a cold logical figure in the actions and words of Christ, as presented to us in this perpetual sacrament of his body and blood!

salvation. For the paschal lamb, Christ solemnly substitutes himself. The Old Testament sacrament is made to give way to the power and glory of the actual grace, it was employed to foreshadow. Participation in the promise, is to become now participation in the fact itself. "This is the Lord's Passover," said Moses to the Jews at the time of its institution; and so as it was observed, from year to year in subsequent time, this word was still repeated, "It is the sacrifice of the Lord's Passover who passed over the houses of the children of Israel in Egypt, when he smote the Egyptians and delivered our houses!" (Ex. XII. 11, 27). This did not mean of course, that the paschal elements were themselves this ancient deliverance. But it *did* mean, that they were something more than a mere Fourth of July commemoration in the case. They were, in pledge and seal, the very covenant itself, such as it was, which that occasion served to ratify, as the shadow of blessings to come. In contrast with all this, and in fulfilment of its trite meaning at the same time, Christ, with direct reference to his own expiatory death now immediately at hand, makes himself over to his disciples in the sacrament of the Supper. "*This* is *my* body, broken for you—this cup is the *new covenant* in *my* blood, shed for many, for the remission of sins." Did he mean that the elements themselves were his body and his blood, literally taken? Of course not. Did he mean then only, that they were a figure of a certain truth, comprehended in his sufferings and death, which the mind was to be assisted in contemplating and embracing in this way? More, undoubtedly, than this. Under the elements here exhibited, was offered truly and really the substance itself of which the Passover was only a type—that is, the *new* covenant in Christ's death, as that in which was verified and fulfilled all that lay included as promise merely in the old. *This* is the Lord's Passover in its last and most true sense—not the sacrifice of a typical lamb simply, but *my* body, *my* blood—not the pledge and seal of blessings to come, but the new covenant itself, the pledge and seal of blessings already come, and now comprehended in this sacramental transaction, as ordained for the use of the Church, to the end of time. All of course however in the way of a living connection with the sacrifice itself. The bread and wine are not Christ's flesh, and blood as such; they are only, (but this in a real objective way,) the new covenant in his death, made actual by pledge and seal under this outward form; still a participation in the covenant, requires and implies, in the nature of the case, a participation in the very life, by which alone the expiatory value of the covenant can have any reality or force. The paschal lamb must be *eaten*, physically incorporated with the life of the worshipper, to give him part in the covenant of which it was the seal. A fleshly shadow of the true life union, on the ground of which, and by the power of which alone, we can ever have part in the blessings of the new covenant in Christ's blood. Communion with the covenant, involves of necessity communion with the sacrifice. All fleshly conceptions are to be of course excluded. The case calls for something higher than popish transubstantiation, or the kindred doctrine of the old Lutheran Church. "It is the Spirit that quickeneth; the flesh profiteth nothing." But the idea of a true participation in Christ's life, as the necessary condition of an interest in his sufferings and death, runs clearly through the whole transaction. The bread is given to be *eaten*; the wine must be *drunk*. To quote the words of another: "The breaking of the bread serves to bring into view Christ's death; the eating of the broken bread is a symbol that this death is appropriated in the way of a living union with the Saviour himself. As however Christ, in giving the bread to eat and the wine to drink, declares them to be the pledge of the new covenant itself in his blood, it follows that the bread and wine are not simply *symbols*, but that they serve to place him who eats and drinks, in real communion with the atonement through his death. And since such communion with Christ's death can have no place without a life-communion (Lebensgemeinschaft) with Christ himself, or since in other words the *new covenant* holds in the form of a real inward and living fellowship only, it follows again that the Lord's Supper involves for the worthy participant a true, personal, central communication and union with Christ's actual life."* We have in it the same fact that is presented to us in those memorable words spoken at Capernaum, to which we have already attended, and which connect themselves irresistibly with the institution of the wonderful ordinance: Except ye eat the flesh of the Son of Man, and drink his blood, ye have no life in you!

"The cup of blessing which we bless," says the apostle, "is it not the communion of the blood of Christ? the bread which we break is it not the communion of the body of Christ?" (1 Cor. x. 16). He does not mean to explain the nature of the Lord's Supper, in these words, but makes his appeal in the case simply to the view generally entertained of the institution among Christians at the time. The representation is general, and gives no new light on the mode of our communication with the body and blood of Christ in the sacrament. But this much it does most certainly imply, that the communion is something more than figurative or moral. It is the communion of Christ's *body* and *blood*—a real participation in his true human life, as the one only and all-sufficient sacrifice for the sins of the world. "Figurative language, I confess," says Calvin, "only let not the truth of the figure be put out of the way—that is, let the thing itself also be present, to be apprehended by the soul as really as the outward elements are by the mouth."

The passage, Eph. v. 22–32, has been already noticed, in connection with the general subject of the mystical union. It is proper to add here,

*Ebrard. Das Dogma von heil. Abendmahl. vol. i., p. 119.

Eph 5:22-32 - ref. to the Supper?

however, that as it includes a distinct reference to the sacrament of Baptism (v. 26, 27), as it is allowed also by the best commentators to regard in the close (v. 30–32), not merely the general communion of Christ with believers, but particularly at the same time his special communion with them in the sacrament of the Holy Supper. Such is the view of *Theodoret, Calvin, Beza, Calovius, Grotius*, fully approved and endorsed in our own time by such men as *Holzhausen, Harless*, and *Olshausen*. Calvin remarks; "Paul describes here that union we have with Christ, of which the symbol and pledge is given us in the Holy Supper. Some indeed complain that the application of the passage to the Supper is forced, since there is no mention here of the Supper, but only of marriage; in this however they are altogether mistaken. For whereas they allow only a commemoration of Christ's death in the Supper, and will not admit an actual communication, such as we assert from his own words, we urge against them this testimony: Paul declares that we are members of Christ's body, of his flesh and of his bones. Need we wonder then that he gives us his body to partake of in the Supper, that it may be to us the aliment of eternal life? Thus we show, that we teach no other representation in the Supper, than that whose truth and power are proclaimed by Paul." Harless, one of the coolest and most circumspect of commentators, holds the reference to the Lord's supper, in the passage to be beyond doubt; not so much on the ground of any particular expressions separately taken, as in view of the concinnity which is thus imparted to the whole thought from v. 23 to 32, in full harmony at the same time with the proper interpretation of the passage in its details. The general thought is the close, constant communion in which Christ, as the Redeemer, stands with his Church. Reference is made first to Baptism, under this view, as the pledge and seal of the intimate relation. From this there is then an advance, (for that is evidently the character of the representation,) to the other sacrament, in which the same mystery is still more strikingly exhibited and confirmed. "If we have come to understand the nature of the Lord's Supper," says Harless, "as unfolded in the Scriptures and held by the Protestant Church, we shall be forced to allow that the image itself, which is employed by the apostles, carries us irresistibly to this institution as its proper object."

The whole subject the apostle pronounces, in this connection, "a great mystery." This itself is sufficient to overthrow the rationalistic view, by which it is attempted to resolve the whole representation into a common figure, denoting nothing more than the close correspondence in which Christ stands with the *souls* of his people. If ever there was a clear case in exegeries, we might seem to have it here. The union of the believer with Christ, by which the two are said to be constituted one flesh, (as they are elsewhere denominated one *Spirit*,) and which the apostle *in this view*, with such deliberate reflection—pausing as it were to weigh the import of all he had said—proclaims a great mystery; this union, I say, *must* be real in the form in which it is here presented, involving an actual community of life with the glorified Son of Man in his whole person. "They are preposterous," says Calvin, "who allow in this matter nothing more, than they have been able to reach with the measure of their understanding. When they deny that the flesh and blood of Christ are exhibited to us in the Holy Supper, *Define the mode*, they say, *or you will not convince us.* But as for myself, I am filled with amazement at the greatness of the mystery. Nor am I ashamed, with Paul, to confess in admiration my own ignorance. For how much better is that, than to extenuate with my carnal sense what the apostle pronounces a high mystery!"